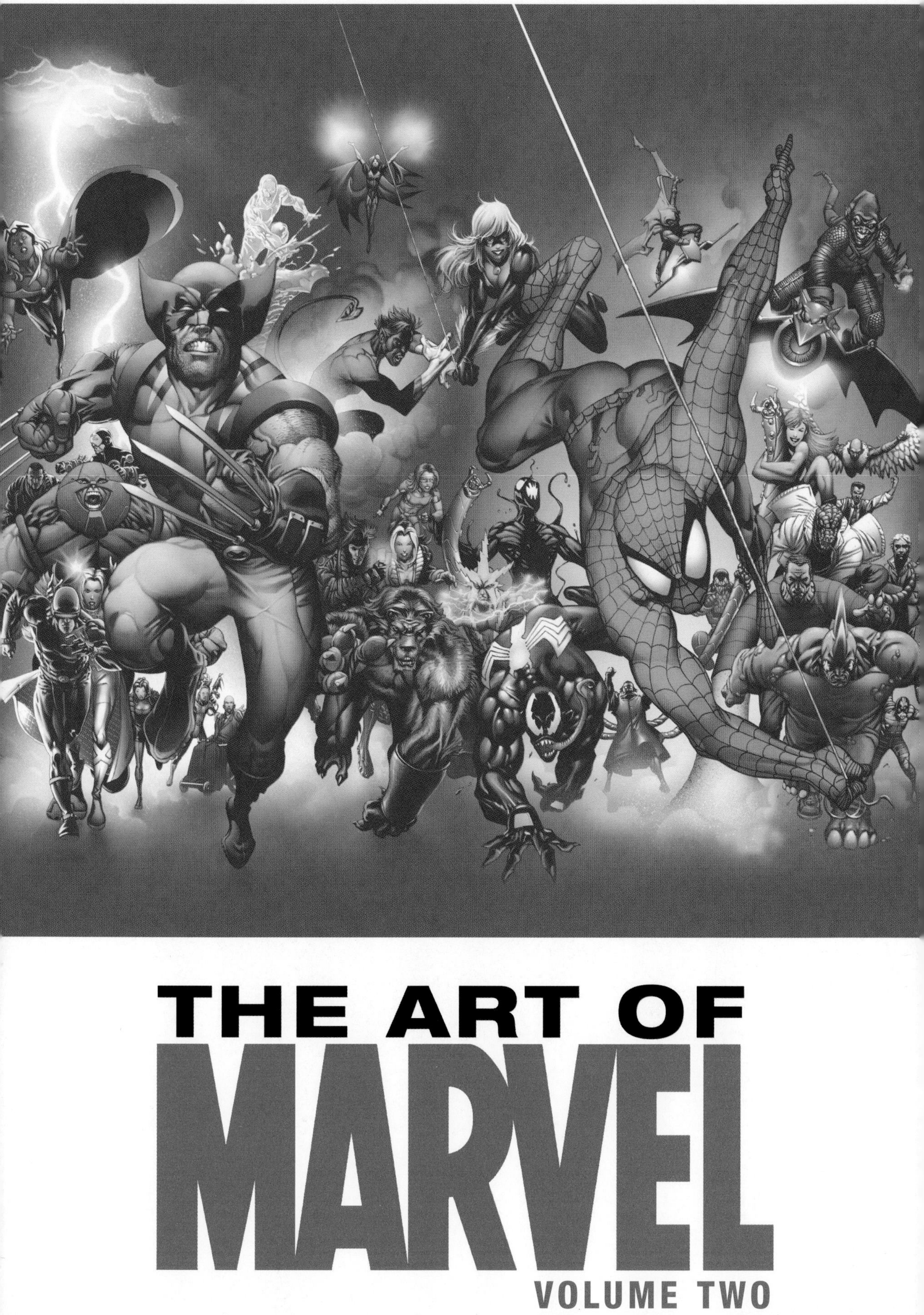

# THE ART OF MARVEL

# VOLUME TWO

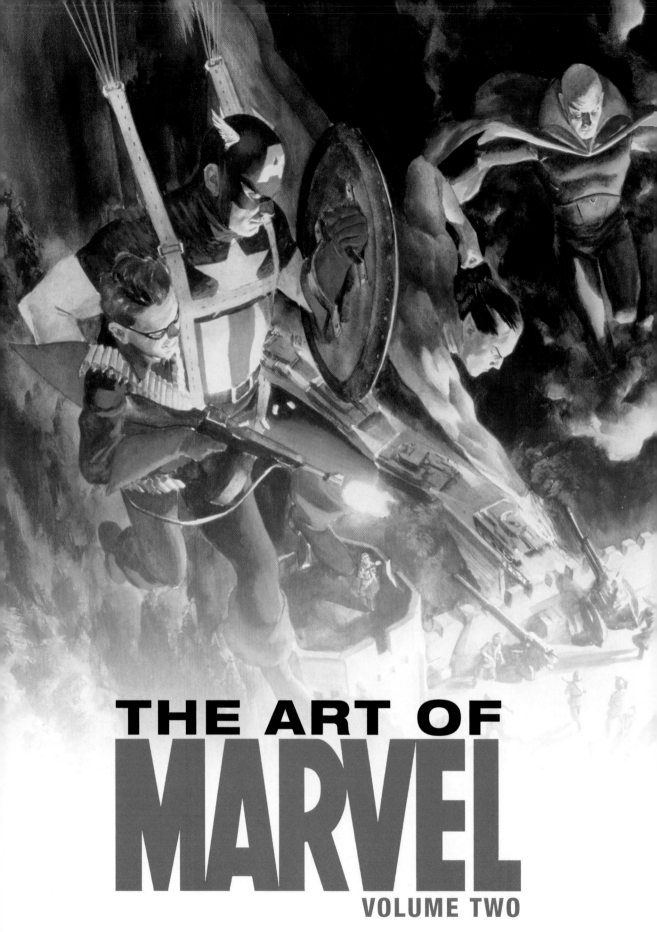

# THE ART OF MARVEL

## VOLUME TWO

**ART OF MARVEL VOL. 2.** First printing 2004. ISBN# 0-7851-1361-4. Published by MARVEL COMICS, a division of MARVEL ENTERTAINMENT GROUP, INC. OFFICE OF PUBLICATION: 10 East 40th Street, New York, NY 10016. Copyright © 2004 Marvel Characters, Inc. All rights reserved. $29.99 per copy in the U.S. and $48.00 in Canada (GST #R127032852); Canadian Agreement #40668537. All characters featured in this issue and the distinctive names and likenesses thereof, and all related indicia are trademarks of Marvel Characters, Inc. No similarity between any of the names, characters, persons, and/or institutions in this magazine with those of any living or dead person or institution is intended, and any such similarity which may exist is purely coincidental. **Printed in the U.S.A.** ALLEN LIPSON, Chief Executive Officer; AVI ARAD, Chief Creative Officer; ALAN FINE, President & CEO of Toy Biz and Marvel Publishing; DAVID BOGART, Managing Editor; STAN LEE, Chairman Emeritus. For information regarding advertising in Marvel Comics or on Marvel.com, please contact Joe Maimone, Advertising Director, at jmaimone@marvel.com or 212-576-8534.

10 9 8 7 6 5 4 3 2 1

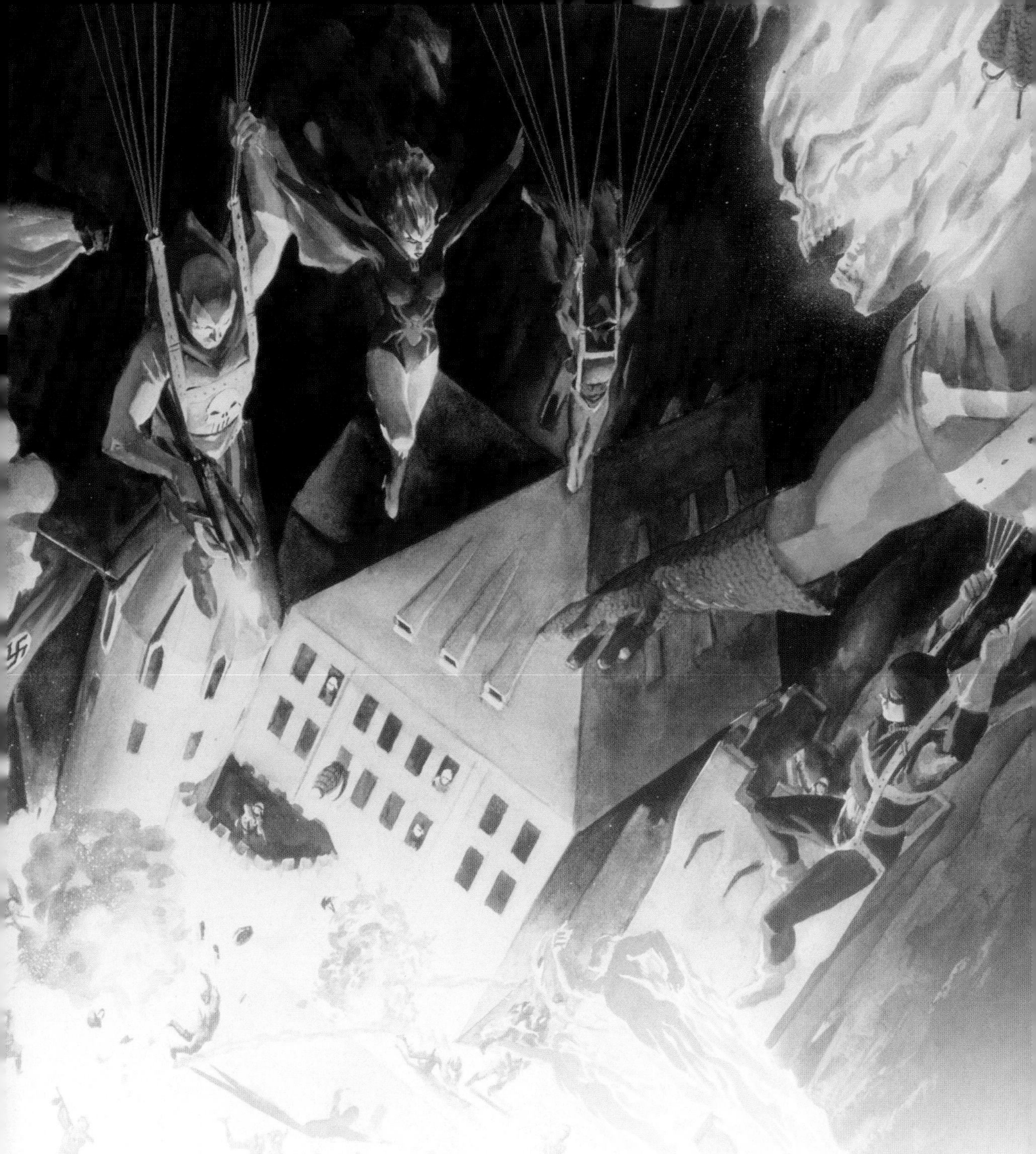

*Cover*
**SALVADOR LARROCA**
**with RICHARD ISANOVE**

*Creative Director*
**TOM MARVELLI**
*Book Designer*
**MEGHAN KERNS**

*Writer*
**IRVING FORBUSH**

*Editor*
**JEFF YOUNGQUIST**
*Assistant Managing Editor*
**MARK D. BEAZLEY**
*Assistant Editor*
**JENNIFER GRÜNWALD**

*Special thanks to*
**DAVID GABRIEL,**
**TOM BREVOORT and JEOF VITA**

*Editor in Chief*
**JOE QUESADA**
*Publisher*
**DAN BUCKLEY**

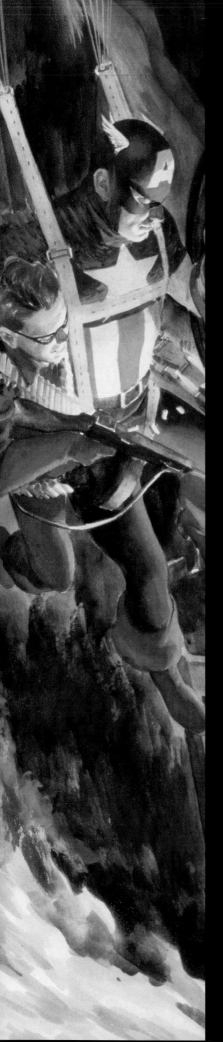

# GOLDEN AGE

The early 1940s was a frightening time for the average American citizen. After conquering most of Europe, the forces of Nazi Germany now threatened to take Great Britain. Imperial Japan's control stretched over the Pacific Rim, with Japanese fighters sending most of Pearl Harbor's U.S. Navy ships to the sea bottom. With the specter of worldwide war looming on the horizon, people turned to an entertaining escape from the newspapers' horrifying realities: the comic book. Within these four-color pages, inspiring heroes could make short work of America's foes, giving readers of all ages hope for victory against the real-life enemies that faced the United States.

At the forefront of this new medium was Timely Comics, a young company staffed by such legendary talents as Jack Kirby, Joe Simon, Bill Everett, Carl Burgos and Stan Lee. These skilled writers and artists created a memorable lineup of wartime characters — including Captain America and Bucky, Namor the Sub-Mariner, and the Human Torch. Rather than super-villains, these super heroes battled adversaries ripped right from the news headlines: Hitler, Tojo and Mussolini.

Art by Alex Ross. Opposite: *Marvel Comics #1* cover by Frank R. Paul.

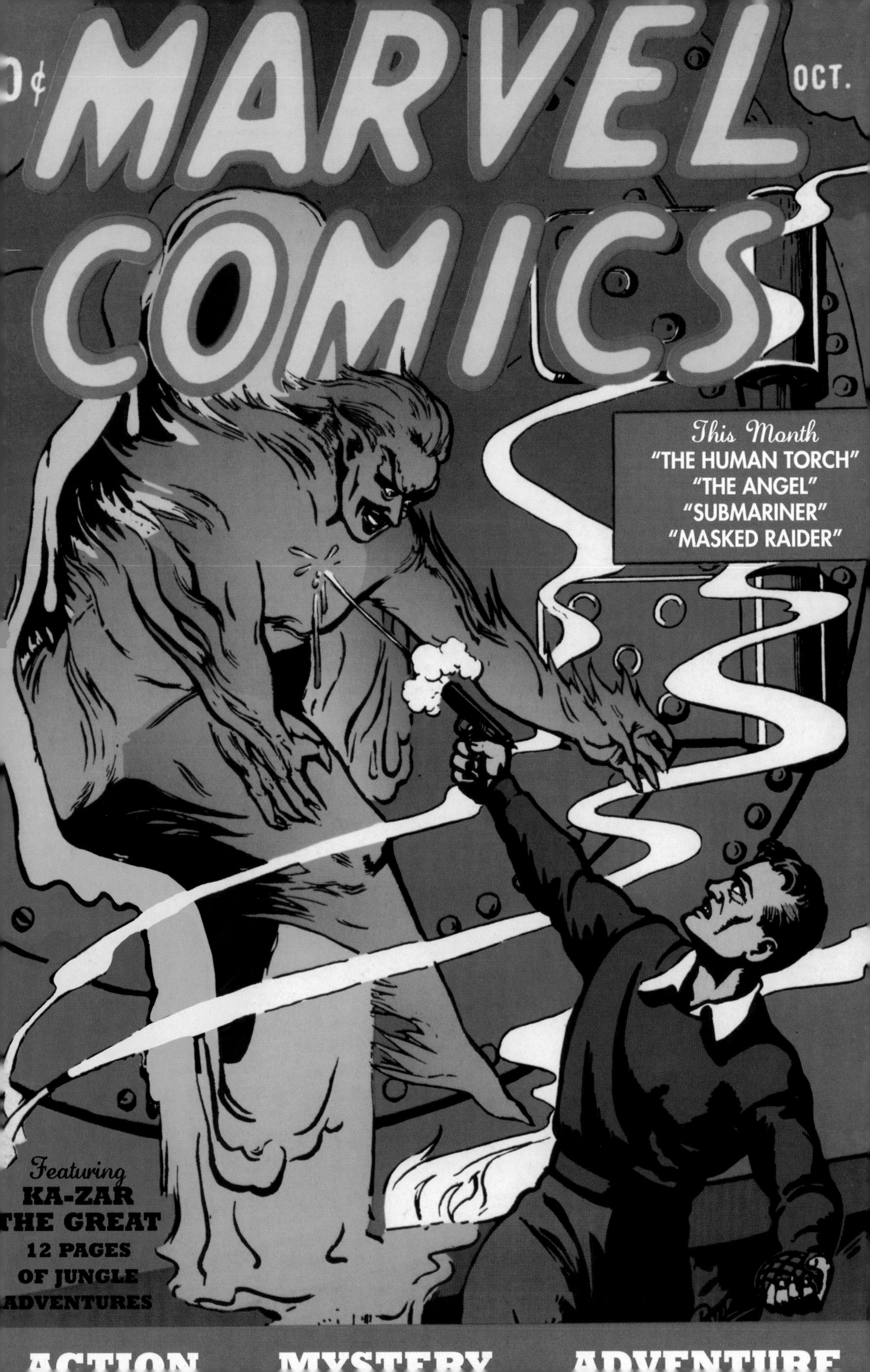
0¢
MARVEL COMICS
OCT.
This Month
"THE HUMAN TORCH"
"THE ANGEL"
"SUBMARINER"
"MASKED RAIDER"
Featuring
KA-ZAR THE GREAT
12 PAGES OF JUNGLE ADVENTURES
ACTION MYSTERY ADVENTURE

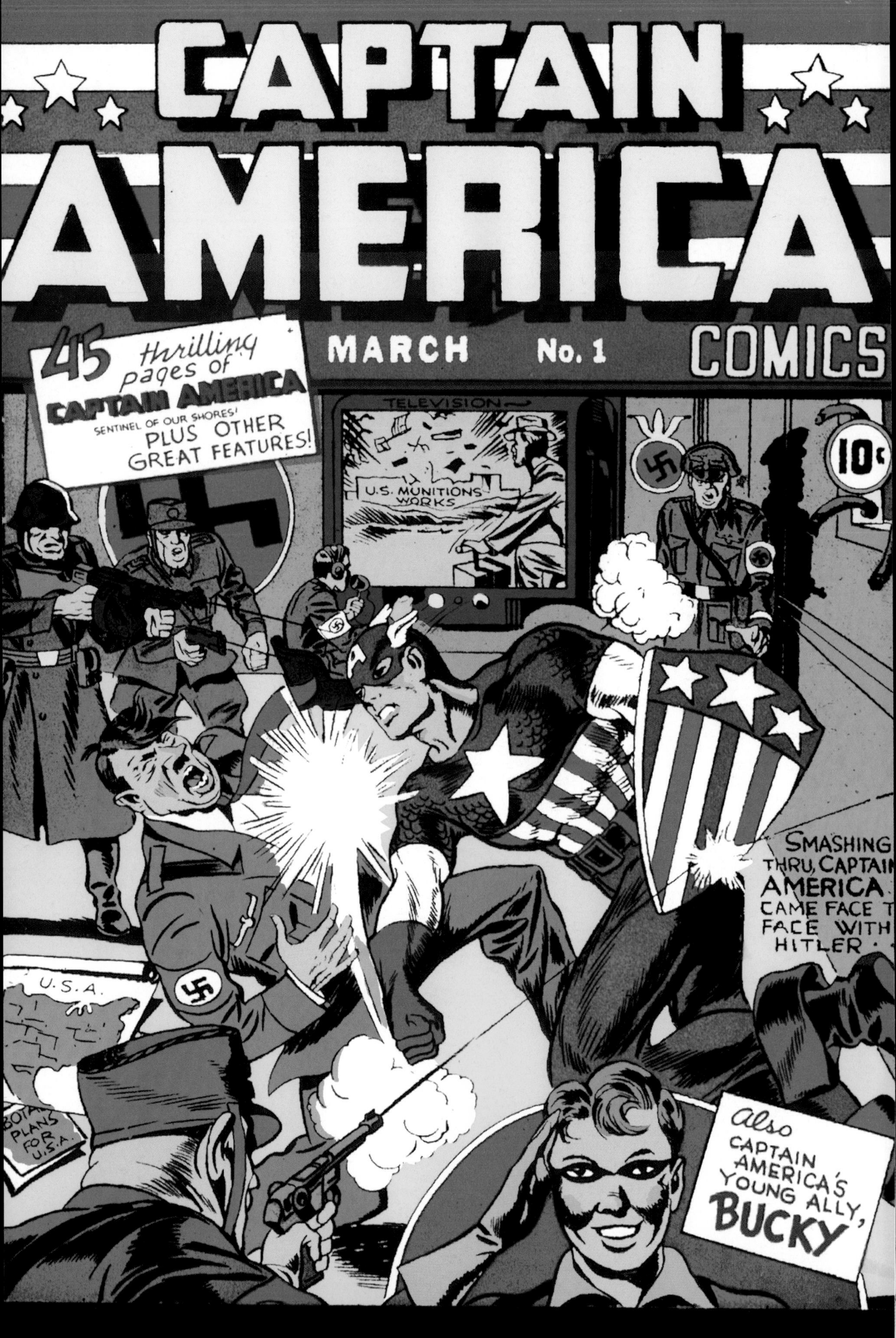
CAPTAIN AMERICA
COMICS
MARCH
No. 1
45 thrilling pages of CAPTAIN AMERICA
SENTINEL OF OUR SHORES!
PLUS OTHER GREAT FEATURES!
TELEVISION
U.S. MUNITIONS WORKS
10¢
SMASHING THRU, CAPTAIN AMERICA CAME FACE T FACE WITH HITLER
U.S.A.
PLANS FOR U.S.A.
Also CAPTAIN AMERICA'S YOUNG ALLY, BUCKY

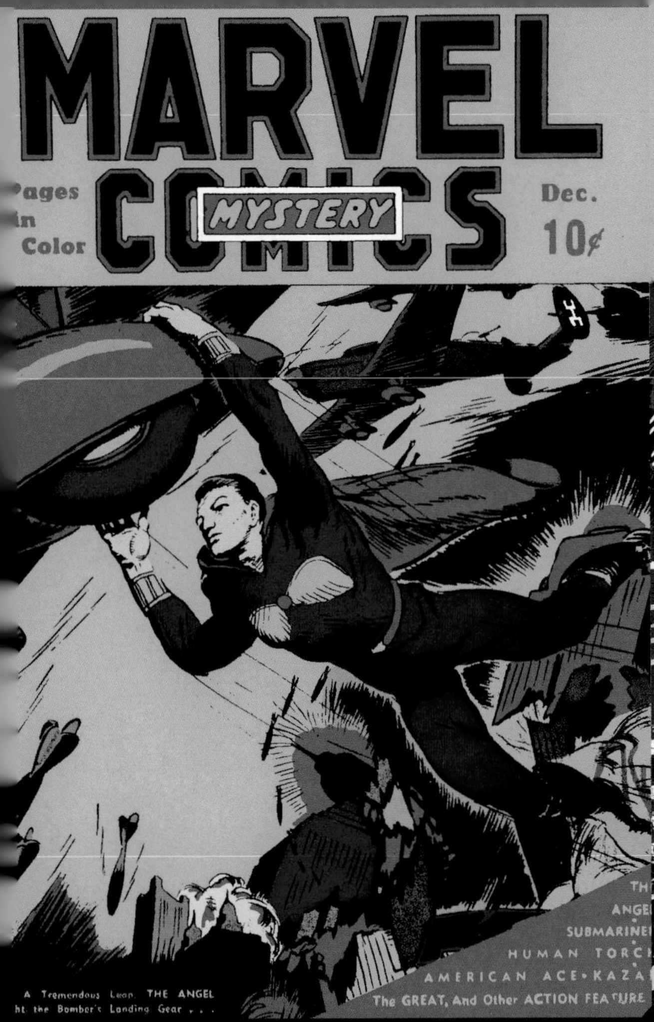
MARVEL
MYSTERY
COMICS
Pages in Color
Dec.
10¢
A Tremendous Leap, THE ANGEL
the Bomber's Landing Gear . . .
SUBMARINER
HUMAN TORCH
AMERICAN ACE
The GREAT, And Other ACTION FEATURE

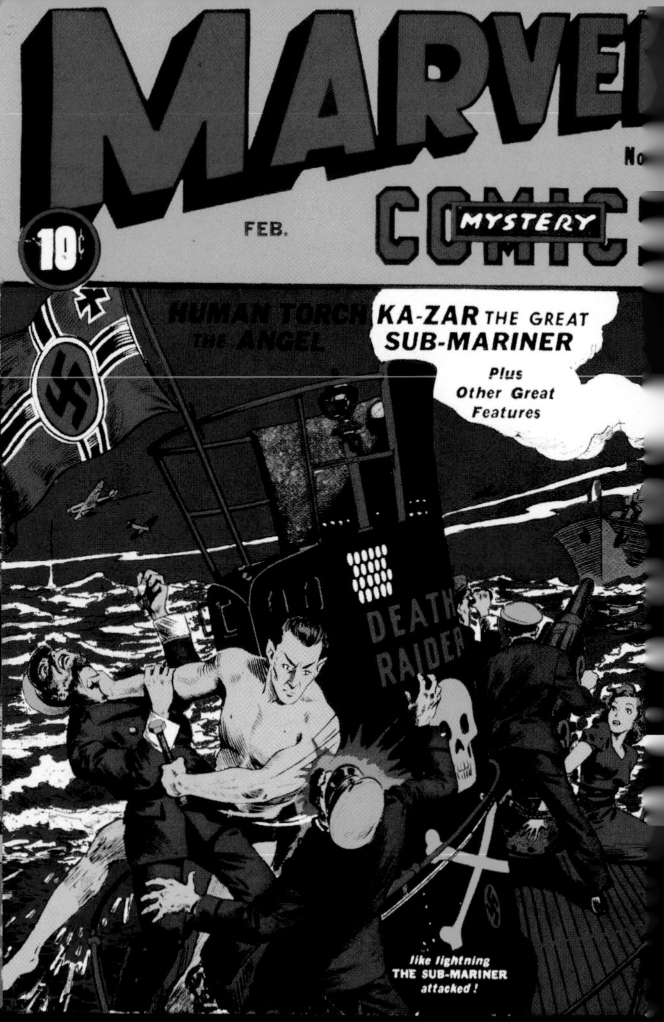
10¢
FEB.
MYSTERY
HUMAN TORCH
THE ANGEL
KA-ZAR THE GREAT
SUB-MARINER
Plus Other Great Features
DEATH RAIDER
like lightning THE SUB-MARINER attacked!

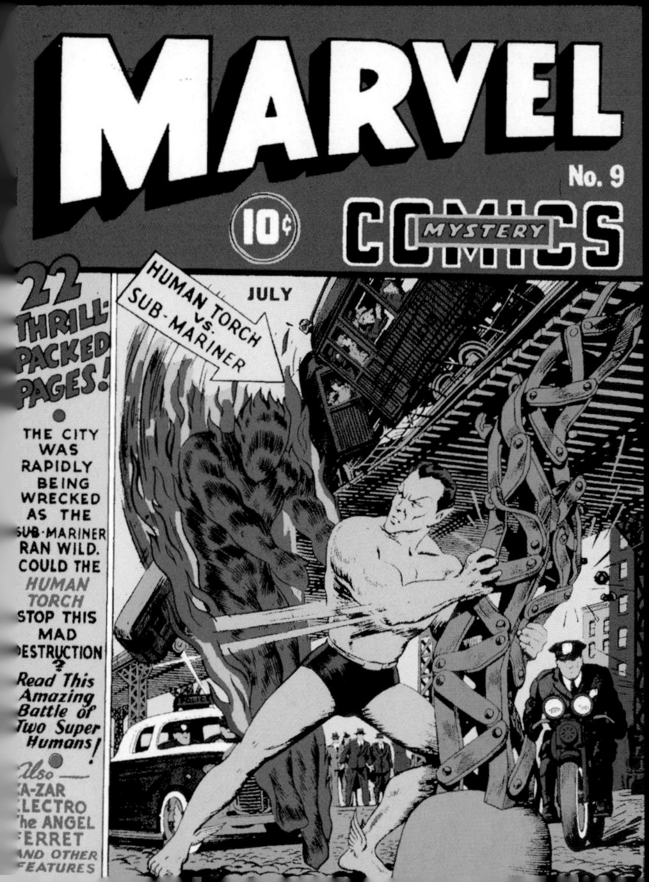
MARVEL
No. 9
10¢
MYSTERY
COMICS
22 THRILL-PACKED PAGES!
HUMAN TORCH vs. SUB-MARINER
JULY
THE CITY WAS RAPIDLY BEING WRECKED AS THE SUB-MARINER RAN WILD. COULD THE HUMAN TORCH STOP THIS MAD DESTRUCTION?
Read This Amazing Battle of Two Super Humans!
Also —
KA-ZAR
ELECTRO
The ANGEL
FERRET
AND OTHER FEATURES

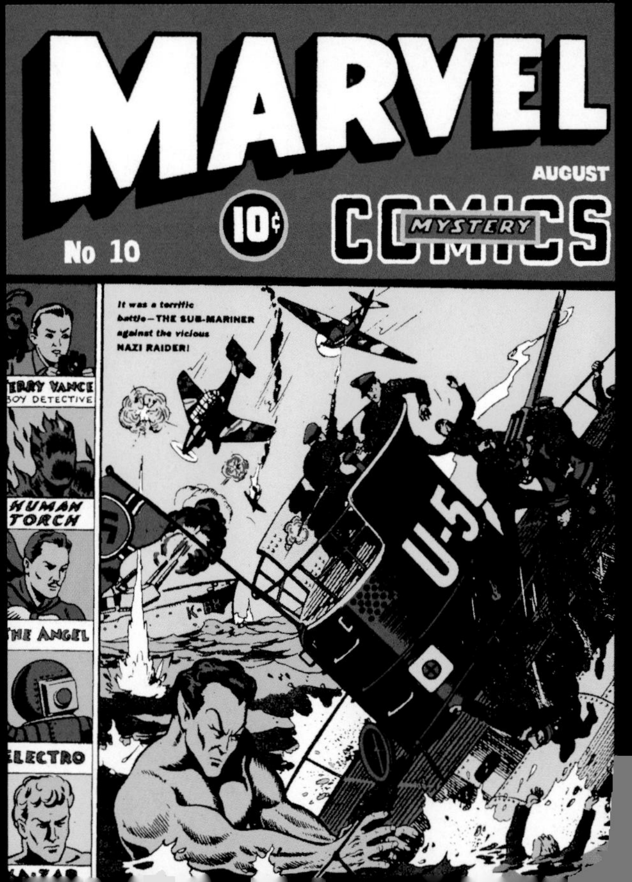
MARVEL
AUGUST
10¢
MYSTERY
COMICS
No 10
It was a terrific battle—THE SUB-MARINER against the vicious NAZI RAIDER!
TERRY VANCE BOY DETECTIVE
HUMAN TORCH
THE ANGEL
ELECTRO
U-5

# 1960s

It was August 1961, and change was in the air. Throughout the nation, a new comic book filled the stands, heralding an era of creativity soon to be dubbed the Marvel Age of Comics. *Fantastic Four #1* did not feature the squeaky-clean heroes of yesteryear, clad in gaudy primary colors and hiding behind secret identities. These were real characters placed in extraordinary circumstances. They lived together, they fought among themselves — and sometimes, they even lost to the bad guys. This was more than a change in attitude: It was the beginning of something entirely different. And readers couldn't get enough.

Thanks to the fertile imaginations of Stan Lee, Jack Kirby, Steve Ditko and others, the runaway train called Marvel showed no signs of slowing down. An unending list of heroes followed the FF with ever-increasing acclaim and popularity: the Amazing Spider-Man, the Mighty Thor, the Incredible Hulk, Daredevil, Iron Man and the X-Men, to name but a few. These were the Marvel heroes, born of conflict and a continuous struggle to balance human lives with superhuman responsibilities.

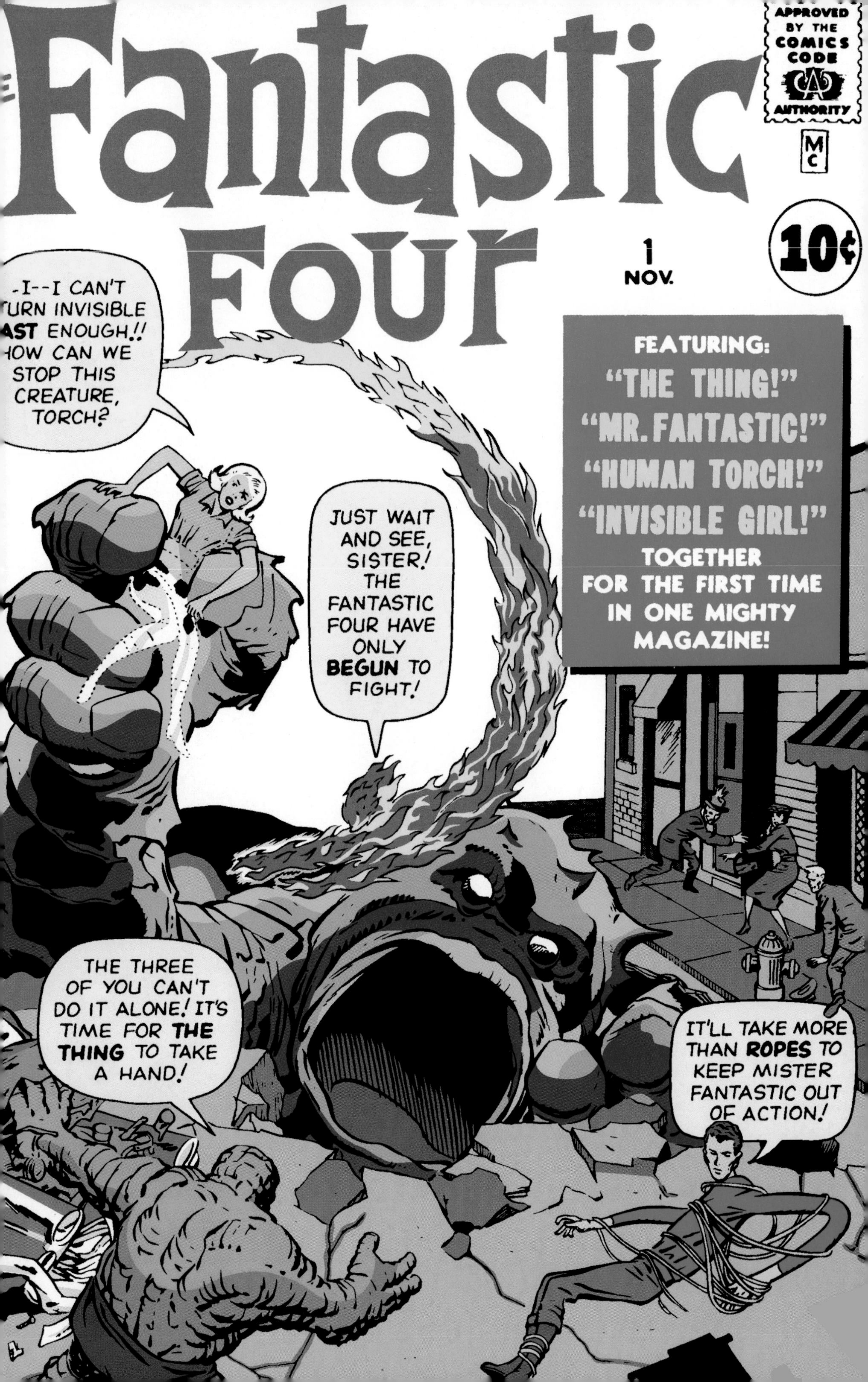
APPROVED BY THE COMICS CODE AUTHORITY
MC
Fantastic Four
1 NOV.
10¢
-I--I CAN'T TURN INVISIBLE FAST ENOUGH!! HOW CAN WE STOP THIS CREATURE, TORCH?
FEATURING: "THE THING!" "MR. FANTASTIC!" "HUMAN TORCH!" "INVISIBLE GIRL!" TOGETHER FOR THE FIRST TIME IN ONE MIGHTY MAGAZINE!
JUST WAIT AND SEE, SISTER! THE FANTASTIC FOUR HAVE ONLY BEGUN TO FIGHT!
THE THREE OF YOU CAN'T DO IT ALONE! IT'S TIME FOR THE THING TO TAKE A HAND!
IT'LL TAKE MORE THAN ROPES TO KEEP MISTER FANTASTIC OUT OF ACTION!

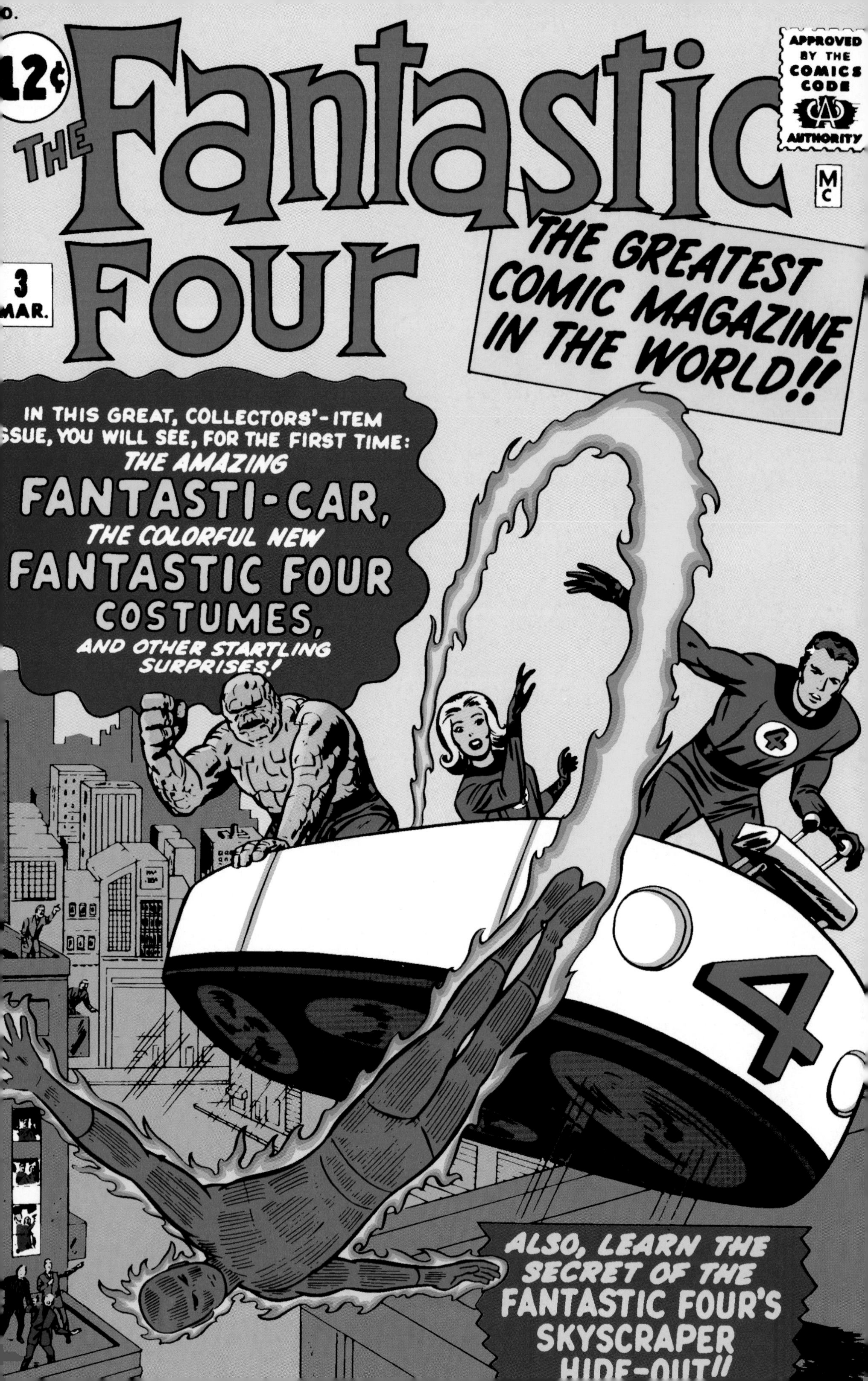

12¢
THE Fantastic Four
3
MAR.
APPROVED BY THE COMICS CODE AUTHORITY
MC
THE GREATEST COMIC MAGAZINE IN THE WORLD!!
IN THIS GREAT, COLLECTORS'-ITEM
SSUE, YOU WILL SEE, FOR THE FIRST TIME:
THE AMAZING
FANTASTI-CAR,
THE COLORFUL NEW
FANTASTIC FOUR
COSTUMES,
AND OTHER STARTLING
SURPRISES!
4
ALSO, LEARN THE
SECRET OF THE
FANTASTIC FOUR'S
SKYSCRAPER
HIDE-OUT!!

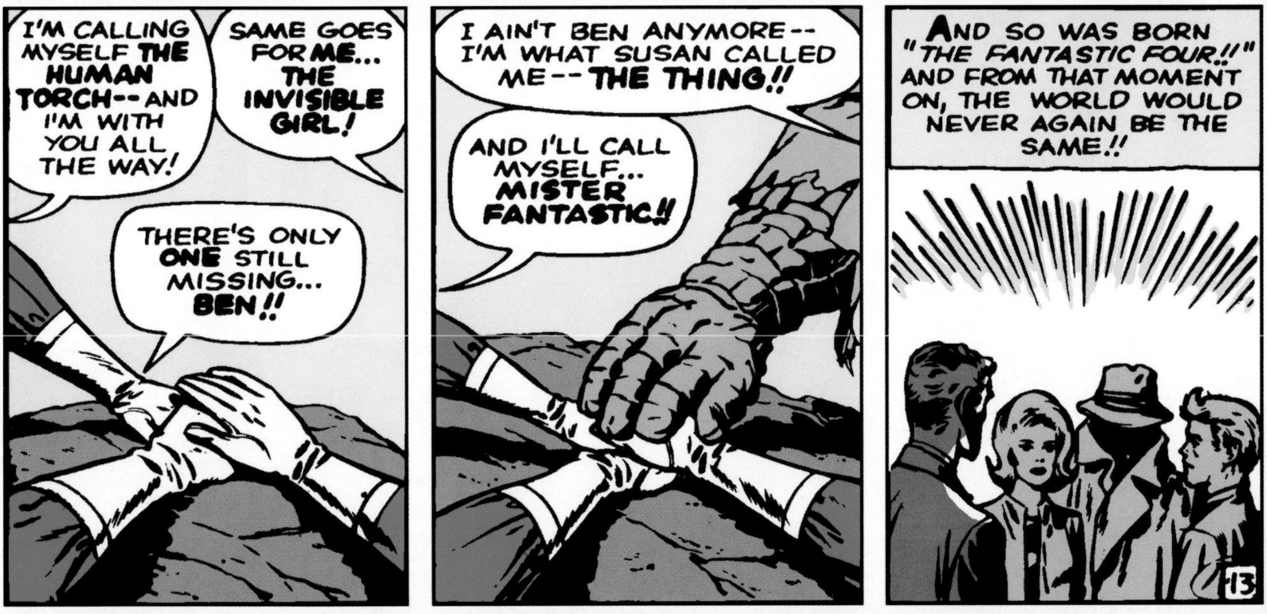
I'M CALLING MYSELF THE HUMAN TORCH--AND I'M WITH YOU ALL THE WAY!
SAME GOES FOR ME... THE INVISIBLE GIRL!
THERE'S ONLY ONE STILL MISSING... BEN!!
I AIN'T BEN ANYMORE-- I'M WHAT SUSAN CALLED ME-- THE THING!!
AND I'LL CALL MYSELF... MISTER FANTASTIC!!
AND SO WAS BORN "THE FANTASTIC FOUR!!" AND FROM THAT MOMENT ON, THE WORLD WOULD NEVER AGAIN BE THE SAME!!
13

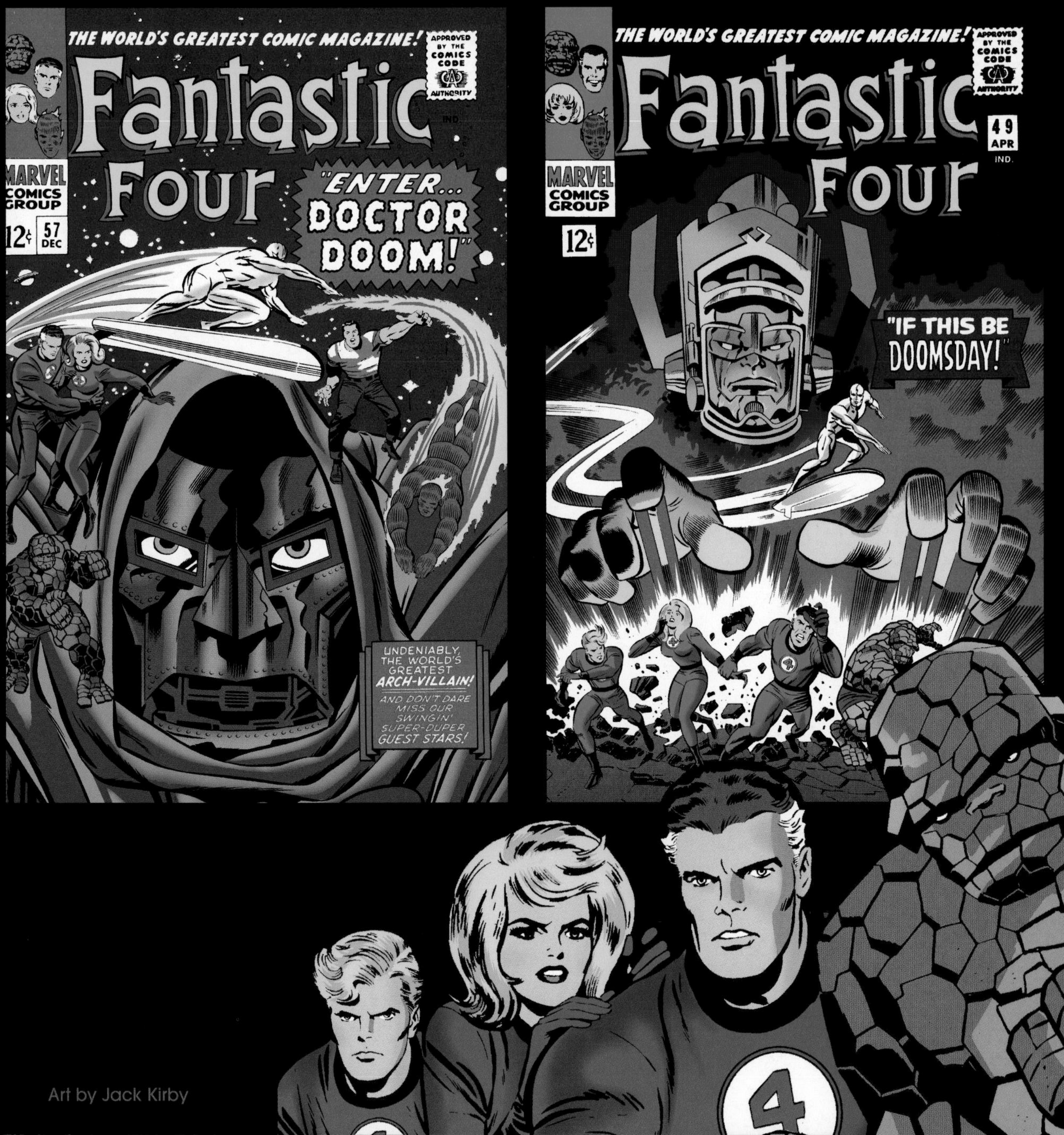
THE WORLD'S GREATEST COMIC MAGAZINE!
APPROVED BY THE COMICS CODE AUTHORITY
Fantastic Four
IND.
MARVEL COMICS GROUP
12¢ 57 DEC
"ENTER... DOCTOR DOOM!"
UNDENIABLY, THE WORLD'S GREATEST ARCH-VILLAIN!
AND DON'T DARE MISS OUR SWINGIN' SUPER-DUPER GUEST STARS!
THE WORLD'S GREATEST COMIC MAGAZINE!
APPROVED BY THE COMICS CODE AUTHORITY
Fantastic Four
49 APR
IND.
MARVEL COMICS GROUP
12¢
"IF THIS BE DOOMSDAY!"
4

Art by Jack Kirby

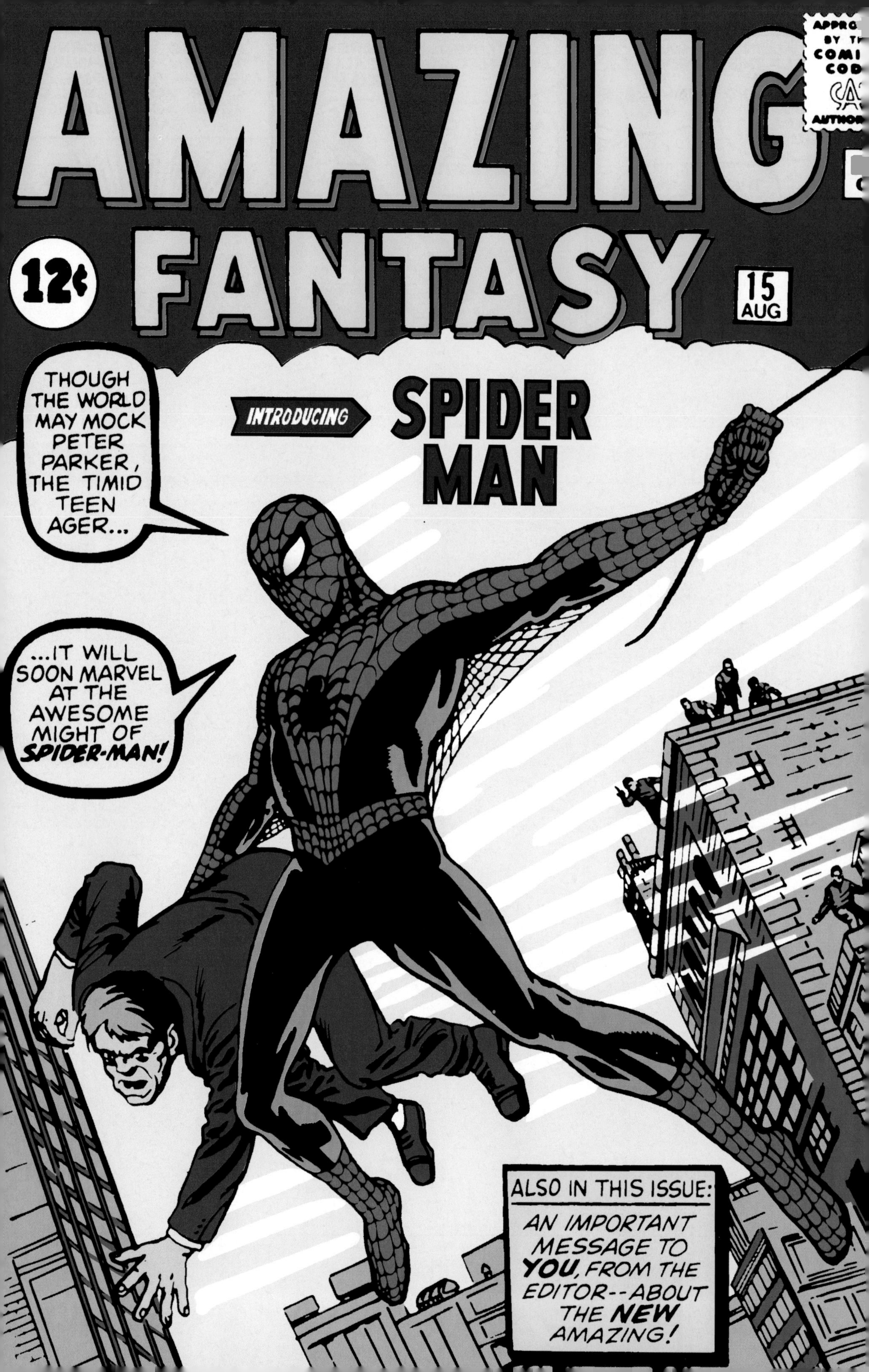
AMAZING FANTASY
12¢
15 AUG
APPROVED BY THE COMICS CODE AUTHORITY
THOUGH THE WORLD MAY MOCK PETER PARKER, THE TIMID TEEN AGER...
INTRODUCING SPIDER MAN
...IT WILL SOON MARVEL AT THE AWESOME MIGHT OF SPIDER-MAN!
ALSO IN THIS ISSUE:
AN IMPORTANT MESSAGE TO YOU, FROM THE EDITOR--ABOUT THE NEW AMAZING!

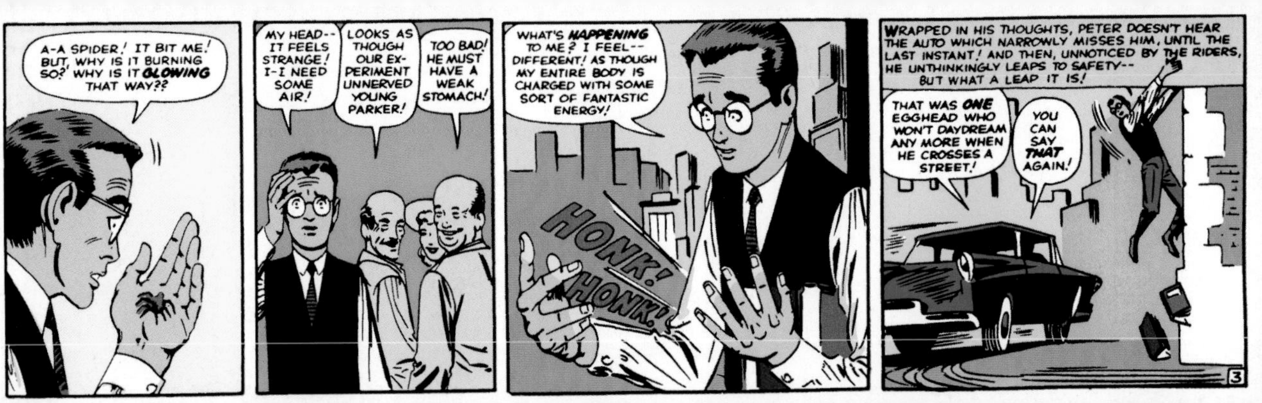
A-A SPIDER! IT BIT ME! BUT, WHY IS IT BURNING SO? WHY IS IT GLOWING THAT WAY??
MY HEAD-- IT FEELS STRANGE! I-I NEED SOME AIR!
LOOKS AS THOUGH OUR EX-PERIMENT UNNERVED YOUNG PARKER!
TOO BAD! HE MUST HAVE A WEAK STOMACH!
WHAT'S HAPPENING TO ME? I FEEL-- DIFFERENT! AS THOUGH MY ENTIRE BODY IS CHARGED WITH SOME SORT OF FANTASTIC ENERGY!
HONK! HONK!
WRAPPED IN HIS THOUGHTS, PETER DOESN'T HEAR THE AUTO WHICH NARROWLY MISSES HIM, UNTIL THE LAST INSTANT! AND THEN, UNNOTICED BY THE RIDERS, HE UNTHINKINGLY LEAPS TO SAFETY-- BUT WHAT A LEAP IT IS!
THAT WAS ONE EGGHEAD WHO WON'T DAYDREAM ANY MORE WHEN HE CROSSES A STREET!
YOU CAN SAY THAT AGAIN!
3

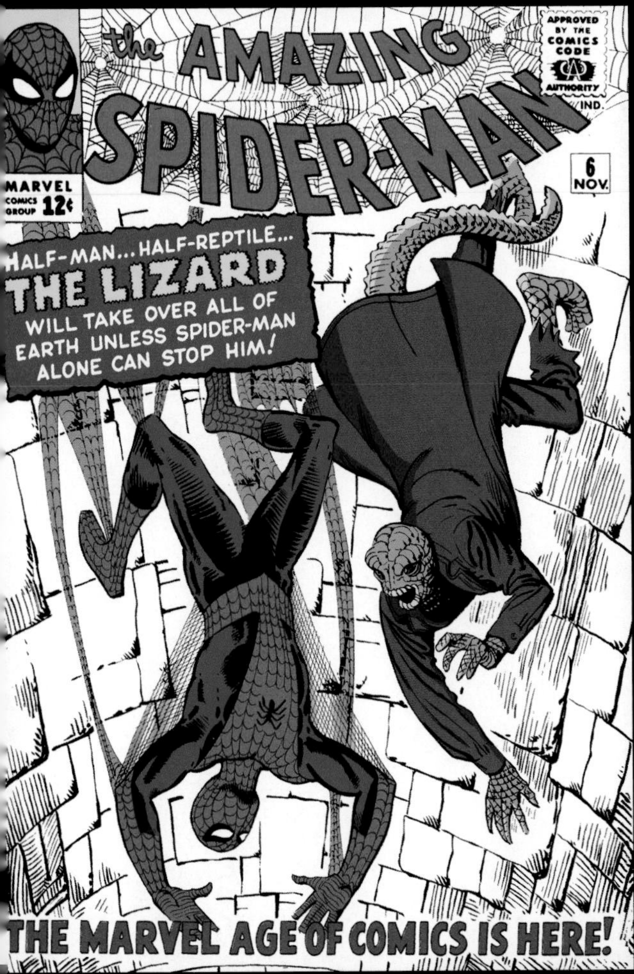
APPROVED BY THE COMICS CODE AUTHORITY
the AMAZING SPIDER-MAN
IND.
MARVEL COMICS GROUP 12¢
6 NOV.
HALF-MAN...HALF-REPTILE... THE LIZARD WILL TAKE OVER ALL OF EARTH UNLESS SPIDER-MAN ALONE CAN STOP HIM!
THE MARVEL AGE OF COMICS IS HERE!

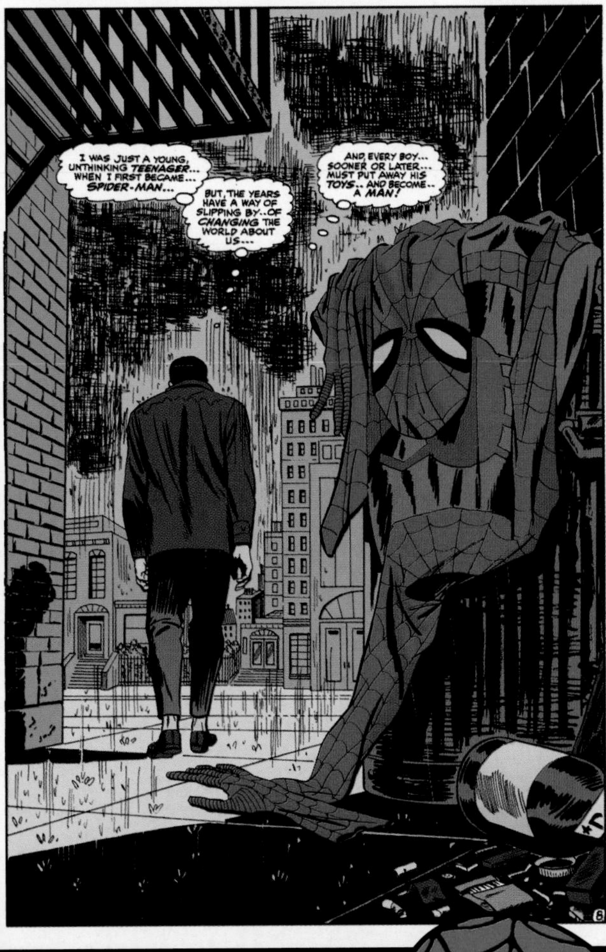
I WAS JUST A YOUNG, UNTHINKING TEENAGER... WHEN I FIRST BECAME... SPIDER-MAN...
BUT, THE YEARS HAVE A WAY OF SLIPPING BY..OF CHANGING THE WORLD ABOUT US...
AND, EVERY BOY... SOONER OR LATER... MUST PUT AWAY HIS TOYS... AND BECOME... A MAN!
8

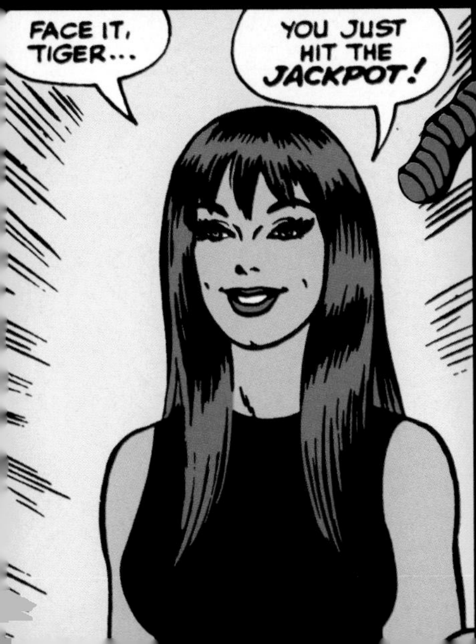
FACE IT, TIGER...
YOU JUST HIT THE JACKPOT!

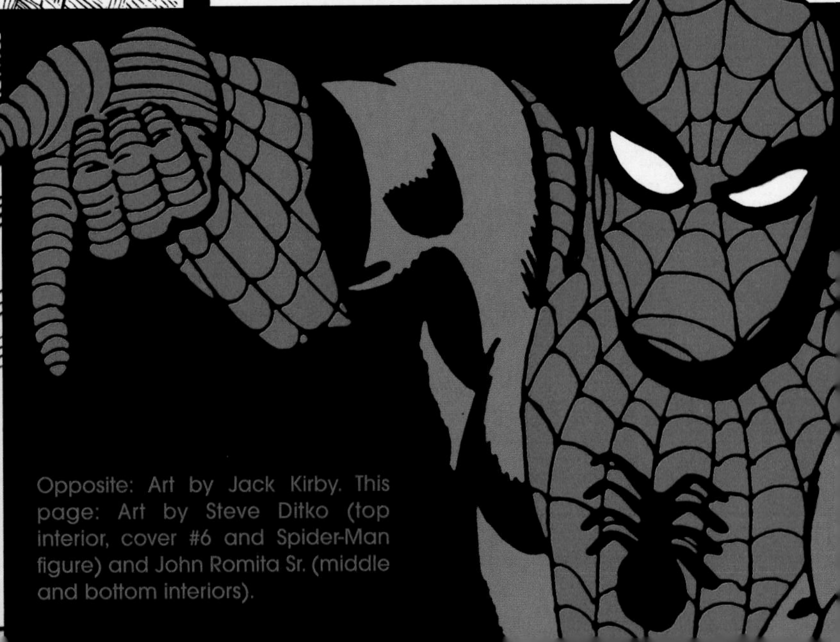

Opposite: Art by Jack Kirby. This page: Art by Steve Ditko (top interior, cover #6 and Spider-Man figure) and John Romita Sr. (middle and bottom interiors).

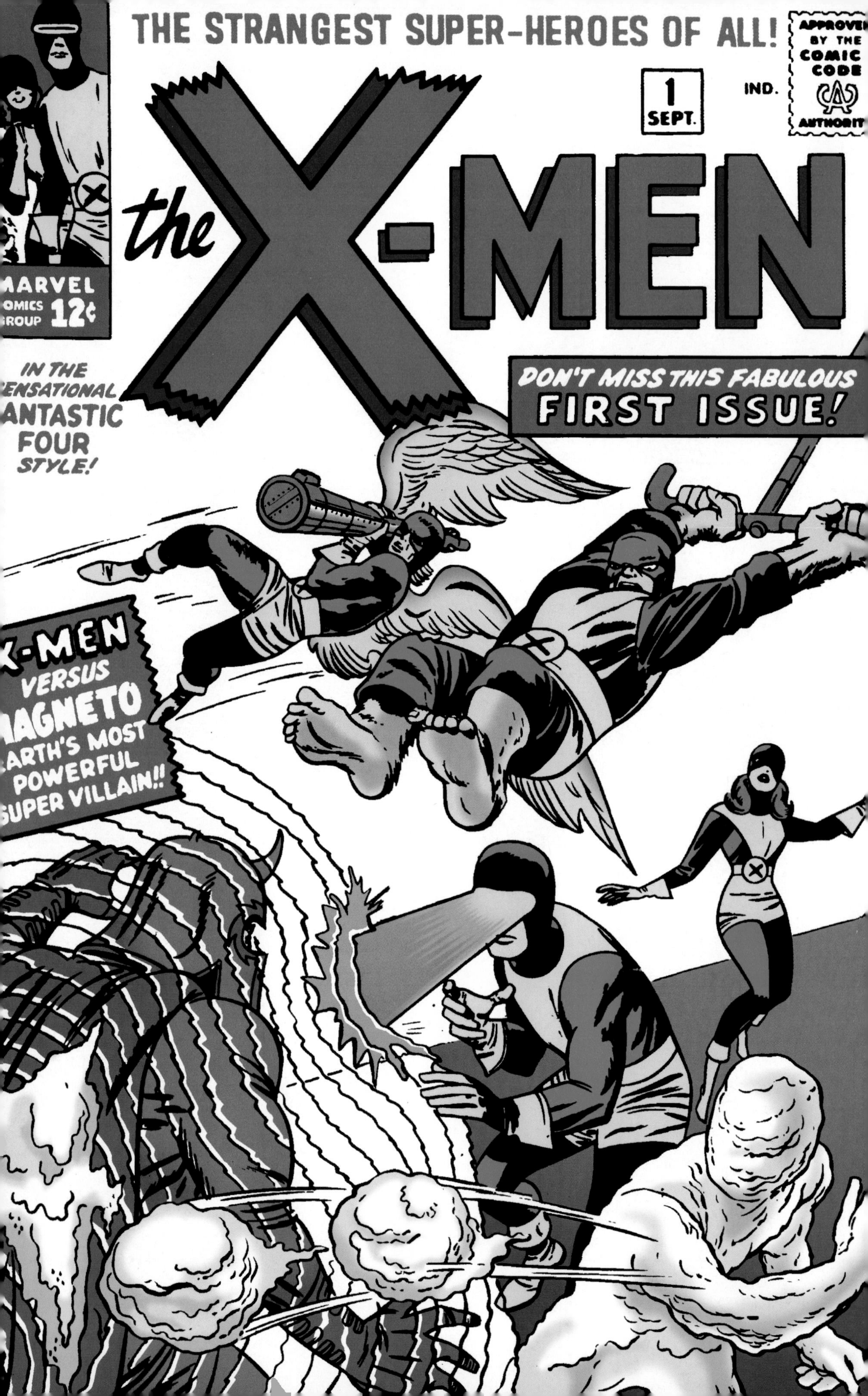
THE STRANGEST SUPER-HEROES OF ALL!
APPROVED BY THE COMIC CODE AUTHORITY
1 SEPT.
IND.
the X-MEN
MARVEL COMICS GROUP 12¢
IN THE SENSATIONAL FANTASTIC FOUR STYLE!
DON'T MISS THIS FABULOUS FIRST ISSUE!
X-MEN VERSUS MAGNETO EARTH'S MOST POWERFUL SUPER VILLAIN!!

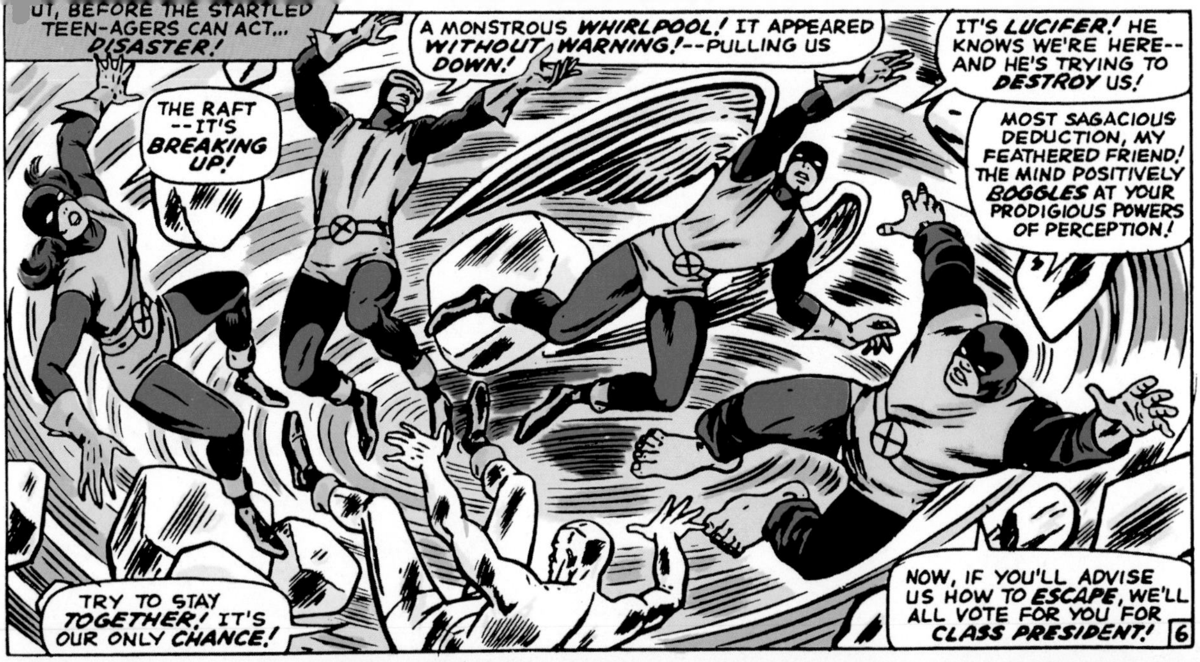
UT, BEFORE THE STARTLED TEEN-AGERS CAN ACT... DISASTER!
A MONSTROUS WHIRLPOOL! IT APPEARED WITHOUT WARNING!--PULLING US DOWN!
IT'S LUCIFER! HE KNOWS WE'RE HERE-- AND HE'S TRYING TO DESTROY US!
THE RAFT --IT'S BREAKING UP!
MOST SAGACIOUS DEDUCTION, MY FEATHERED FRIEND! THE MIND POSITIVELY BOGGLES AT YOUR PRODIGIOUS POWERS OF PERCEPTION!
TRY TO STAY TOGETHER! IT'S OUR ONLY CHANCE!
NOW, IF YOU'LL ADVISE US HOW TO ESCAPE, WE'LL ALL VOTE FOR YOU FOR CLASS PRESIDENT!
6

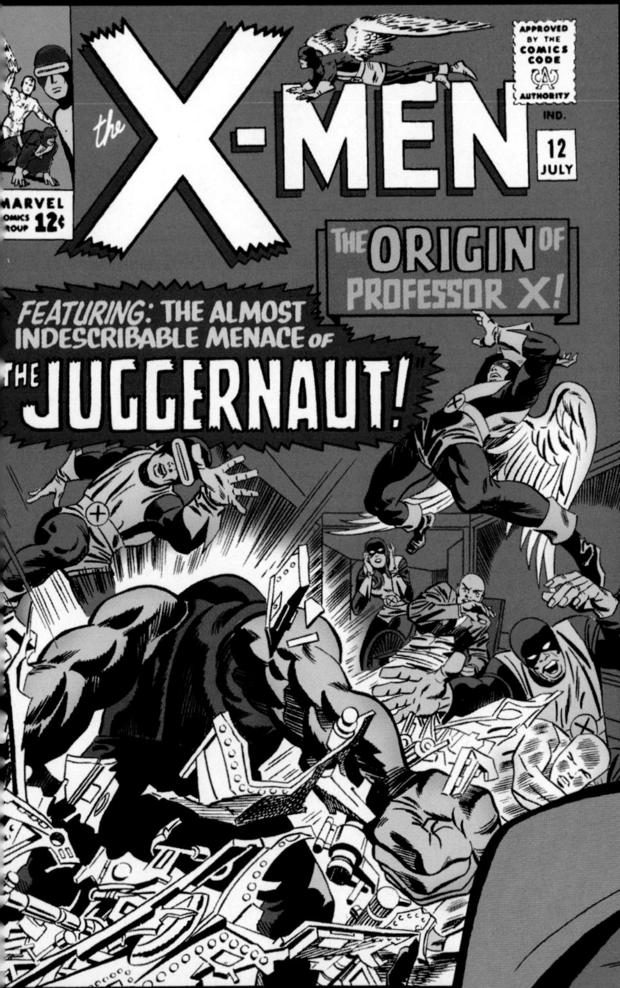
APPROVED BY THE COMICS CODE AUTHORITY
the X-MEN
IND.
12 JULY
MARVEL COMICS GROUP 12¢
THE ORIGIN OF PROFESSOR X!
FEATURING: THE ALMOST INDESCRIBABLE MENACE OF THE JUGGERNAUT!

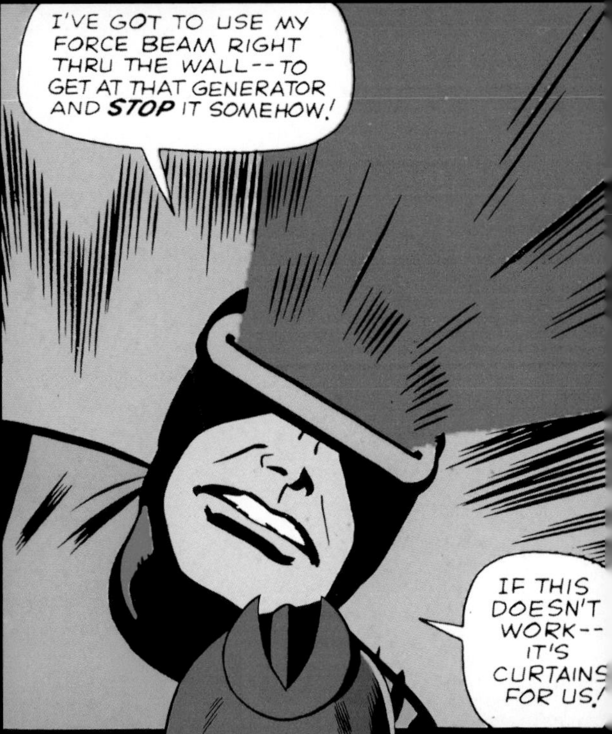
I'VE GOT TO USE MY FORCE BEAM RIGHT THRU THE WALL--TO GET AT THAT GENERATOR AND STOP IT SOMEHOW!
IF THIS DOESN'T WORK-- IT'S CURTAINS FOR US!

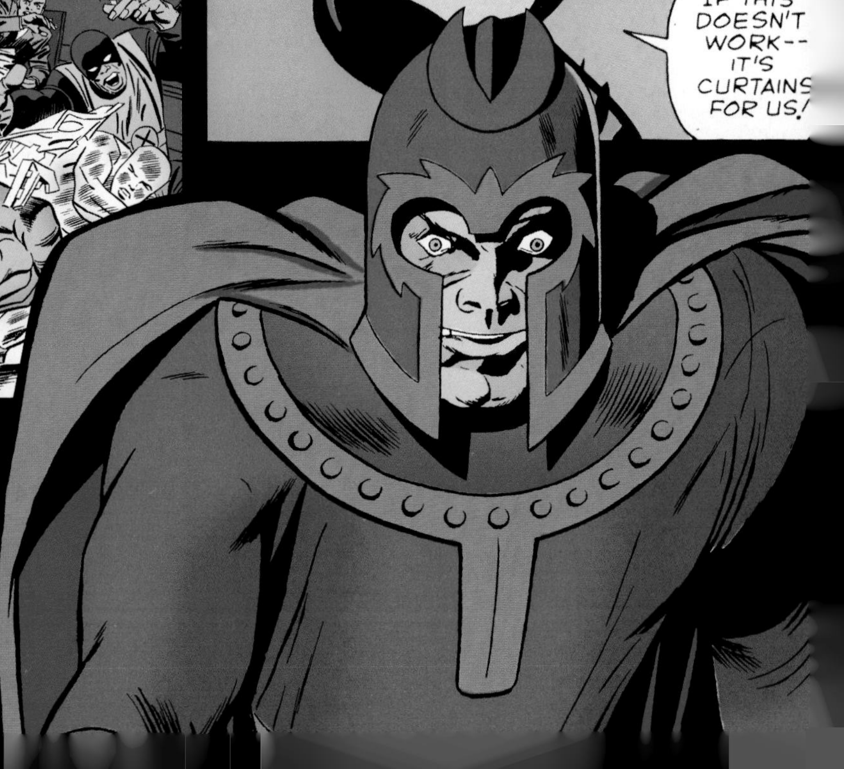

Opposite: Art by Jack Kirby. This page: Art by Werner Roth (top interior) and Kirby (cover #12, middle interior and Magneto figure).

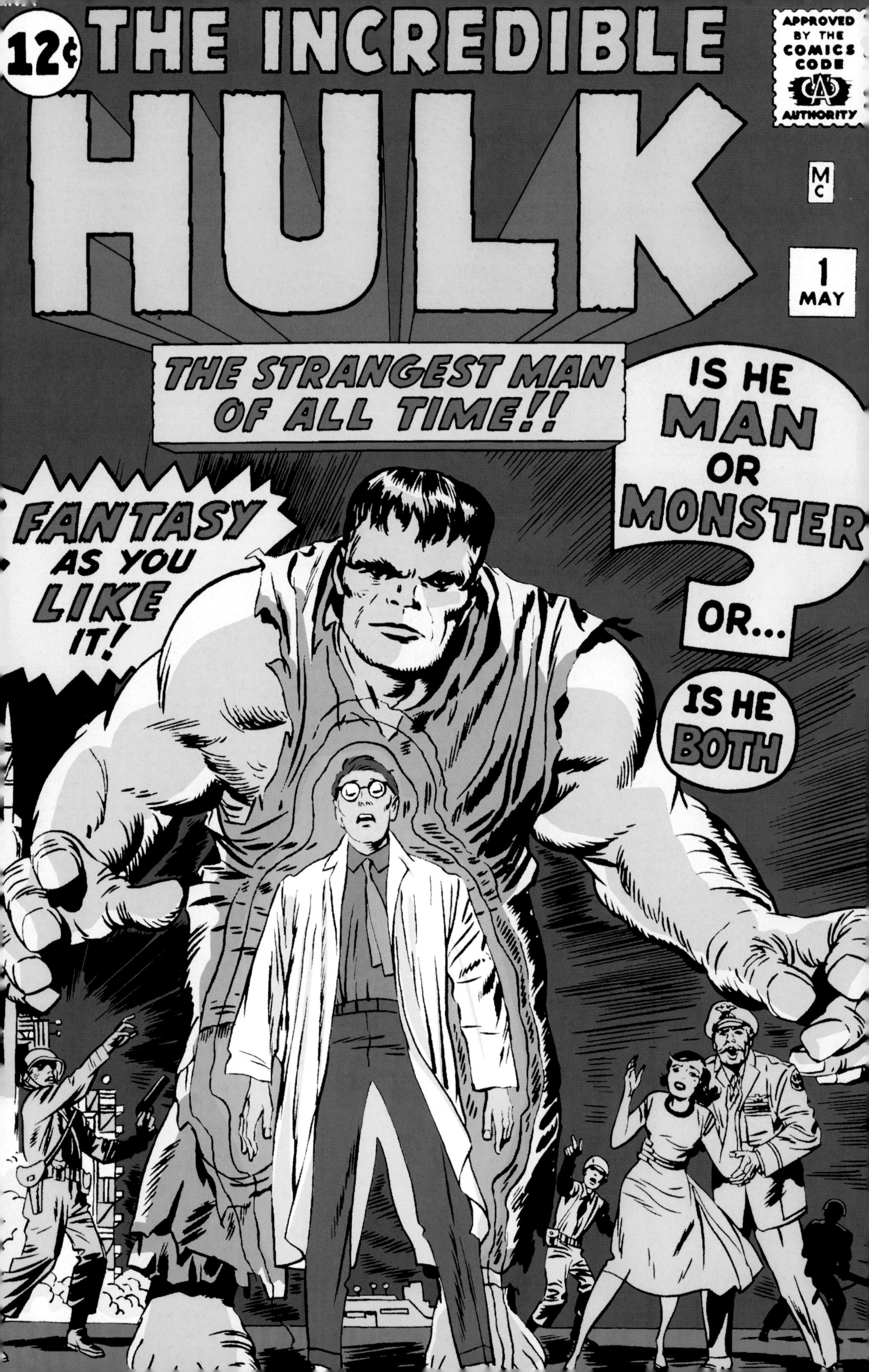
12¢
THE INCREDIBLE
HULK
APPROVED BY THE COMICS CODE AUTHORITY
MC
1
MAY
THE STRANGEST MAN OF ALL TIME!!
IS HE MAN OR MONSTER ? OR...
IS HE BOTH
FANTASY AS YOU LIKE IT!

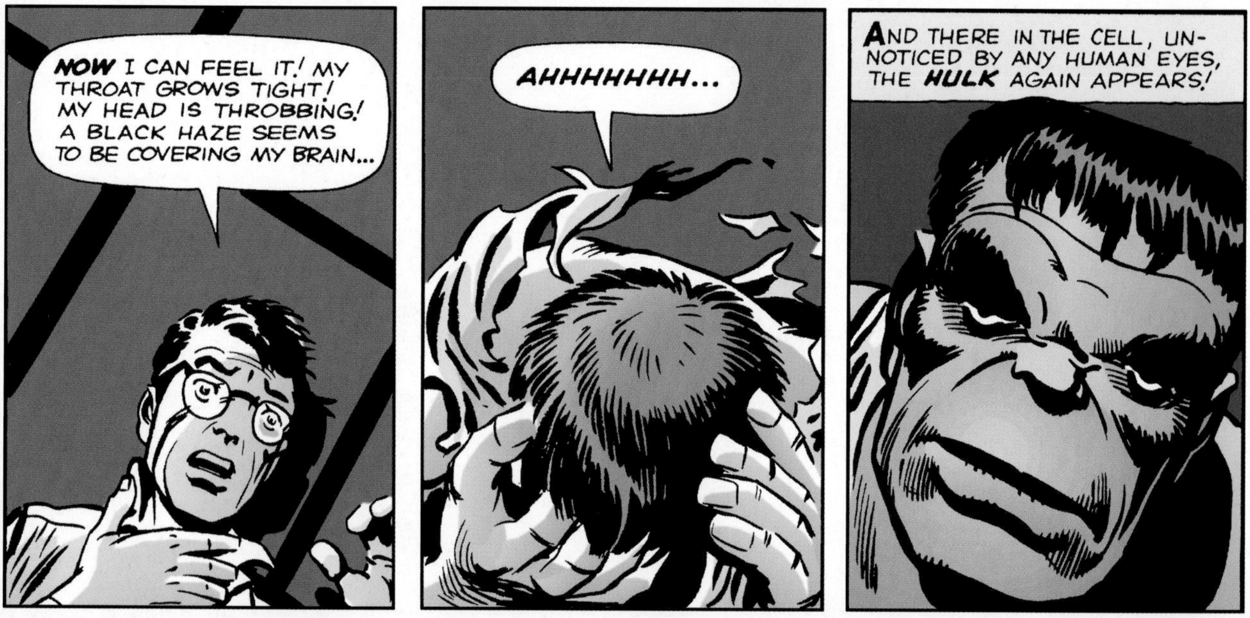
NOW I CAN FEEL IT! MY THROAT GROWS TIGHT! MY HEAD IS THROBBING! A BLACK HAZE SEEMS TO BE COVERING MY BRAIN...
AHHHHHHH...
AND THERE IN THE CELL, UNNOTICED BY ANY HUMAN EYES, THE HULK AGAIN APPEARS!

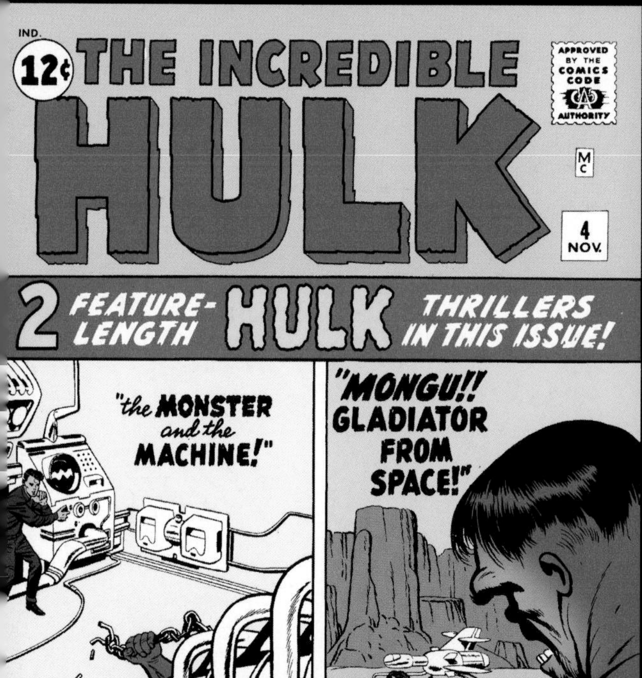
IND.
12¢
THE INCREDIBLE
HULK
APPROVED BY THE COMICS CODE AUTHORITY
MC
4
NOV.
2 FEATURE-LENGTH HULK THRILLERS IN THIS ISSUE!
"the MONSTER and the MACHINE!"
"MONGU!! GLADIATOR FROM SPACE!"
FANTASY AS YOU LIKE IT!

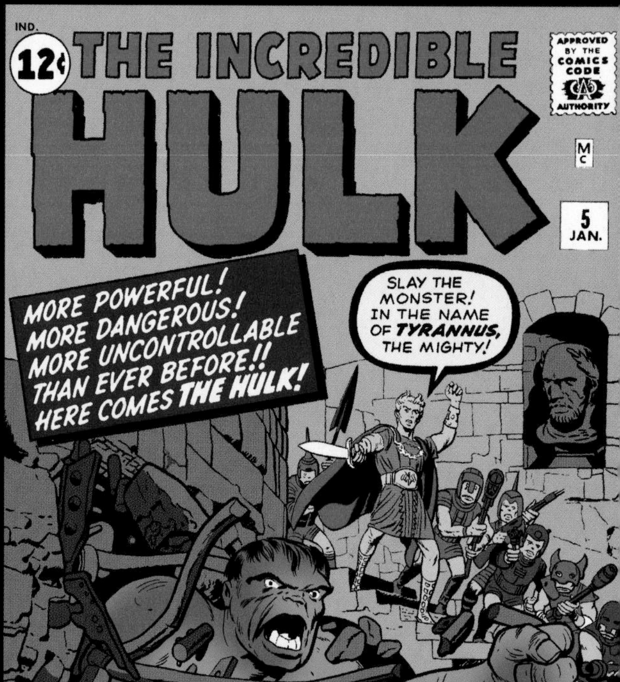
IND.
12¢
THE INCREDIBLE
HULK
APPROVED BY THE COMICS CODE AUTHORITY
MC
5
JAN.
MORE POWERFUL! MORE DANGEROUS! MORE UNCONTROLLABLE THAN EVER BEFORE!! HERE COMES THE HULK!
SLAY THE MONSTER! IN THE NAME OF TYRANNUS, THE MIGHTY!

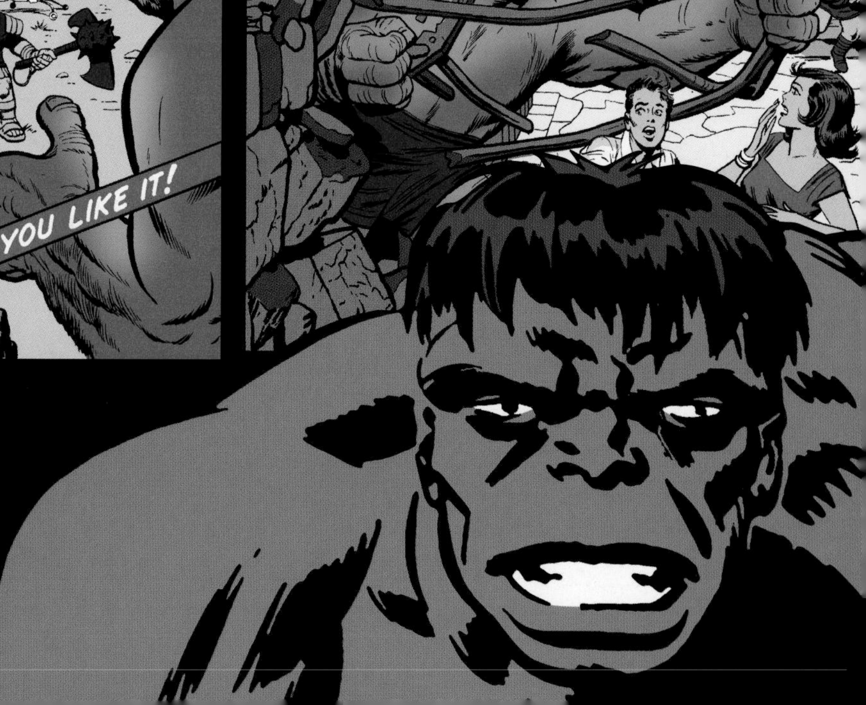

Art by Jack Kirby

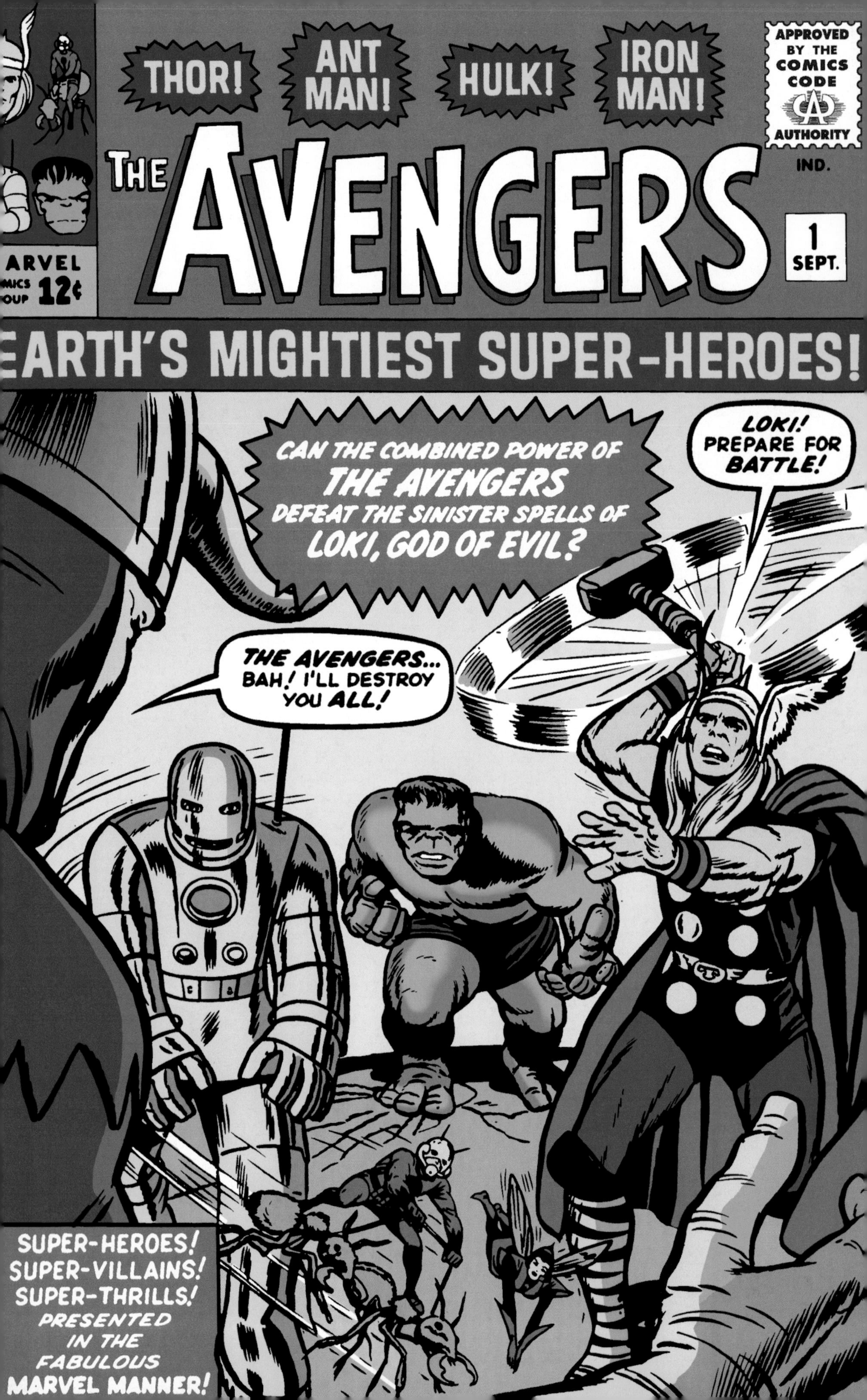
THOR!
ANT MAN!
HULK!
IRON MAN!
APPROVED BY THE COMICS CODE AUTHORITY
IND.
THE AVENGERS
1 SEPT.
ARVEL
MICS
OUP 12¢
EARTH'S MIGHTIEST SUPER-HEROES!
CAN THE COMBINED POWER OF THE AVENGERS DEFEAT THE SINISTER SPELLS OF LOKI, GOD OF EVIL?
LOKI! PREPARE FOR BATTLE!
THE AVENGERS... BAH! I'LL DESTROY YOU ALL!
SUPER-HEROES! SUPER-VILLAINS! SUPER-THRILLS! PRESENTED IN THE FABULOUS MARVEL MANNER!

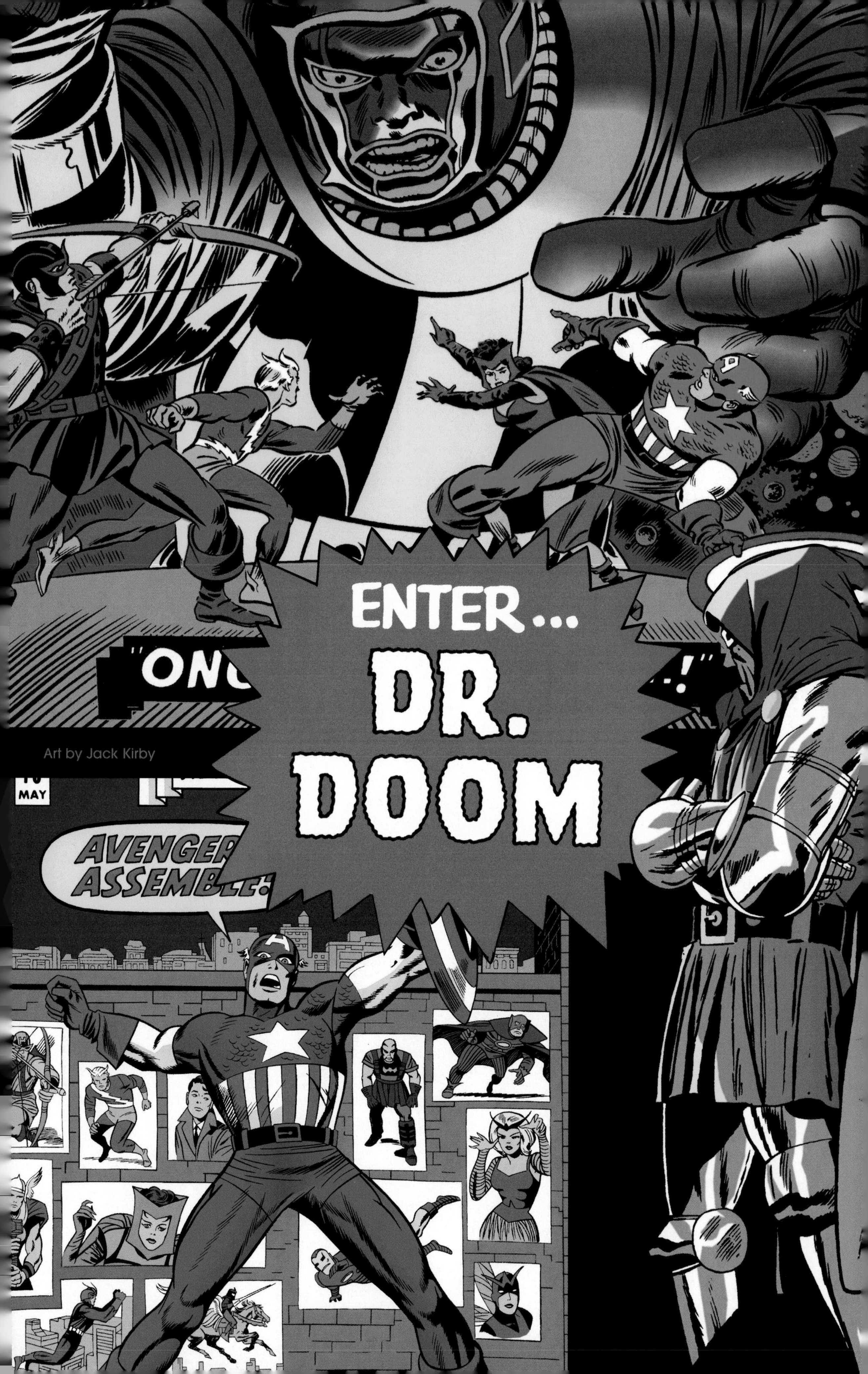
ENTER...
DR. DOOM
"ONC
..!"
MAY
AVENGERS ASSEMBLE!
Art by Jack Kirby

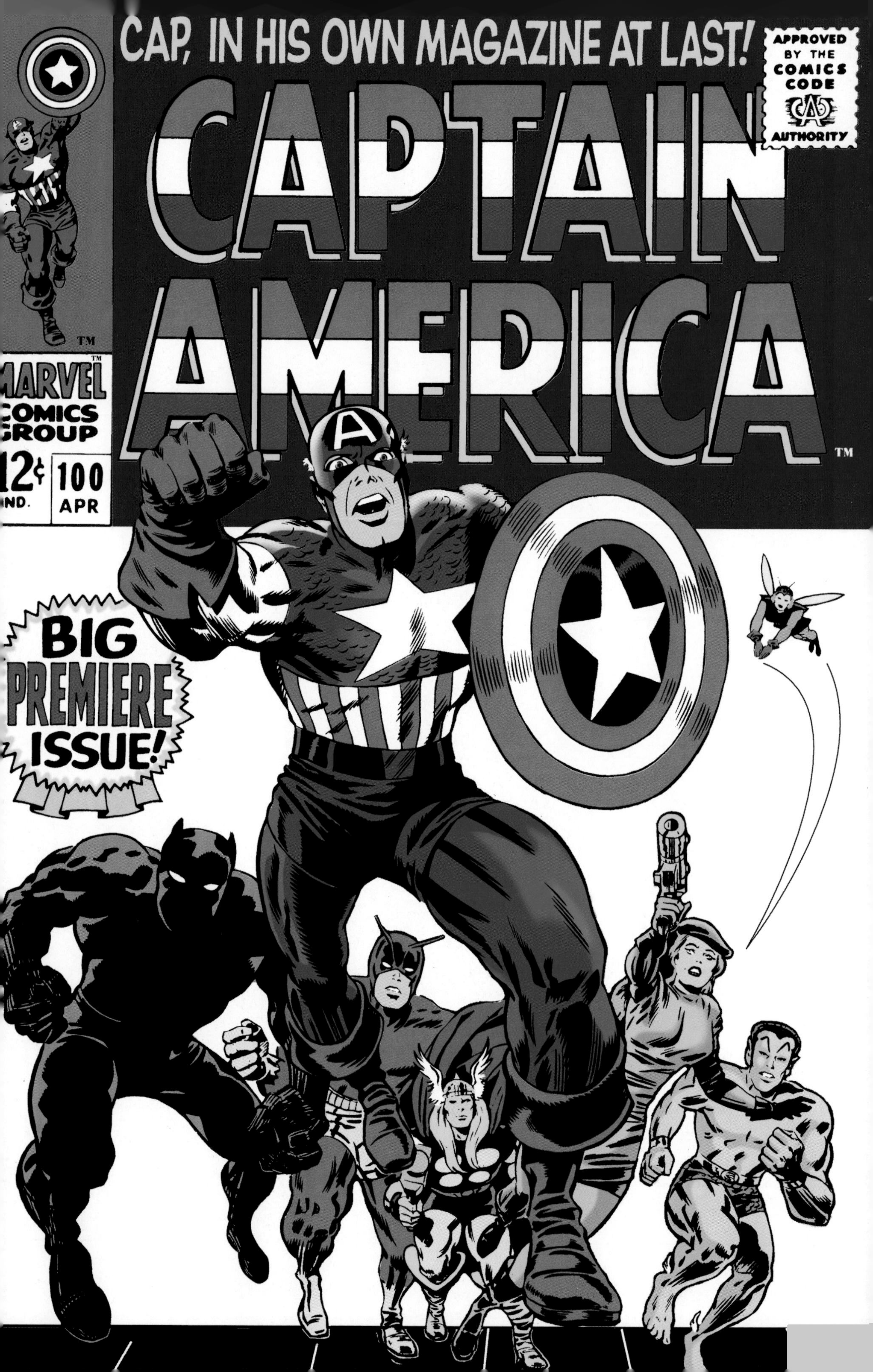
CAP, IN HIS OWN MAGAZINE AT LAST!
APPROVED BY THE COMICS CODE AUTHORITY
CAPTAIN AMERICA™
MARVEL™ COMICS GROUP
12¢ IND.
100 APR
BIG PREMIERE ISSUE!

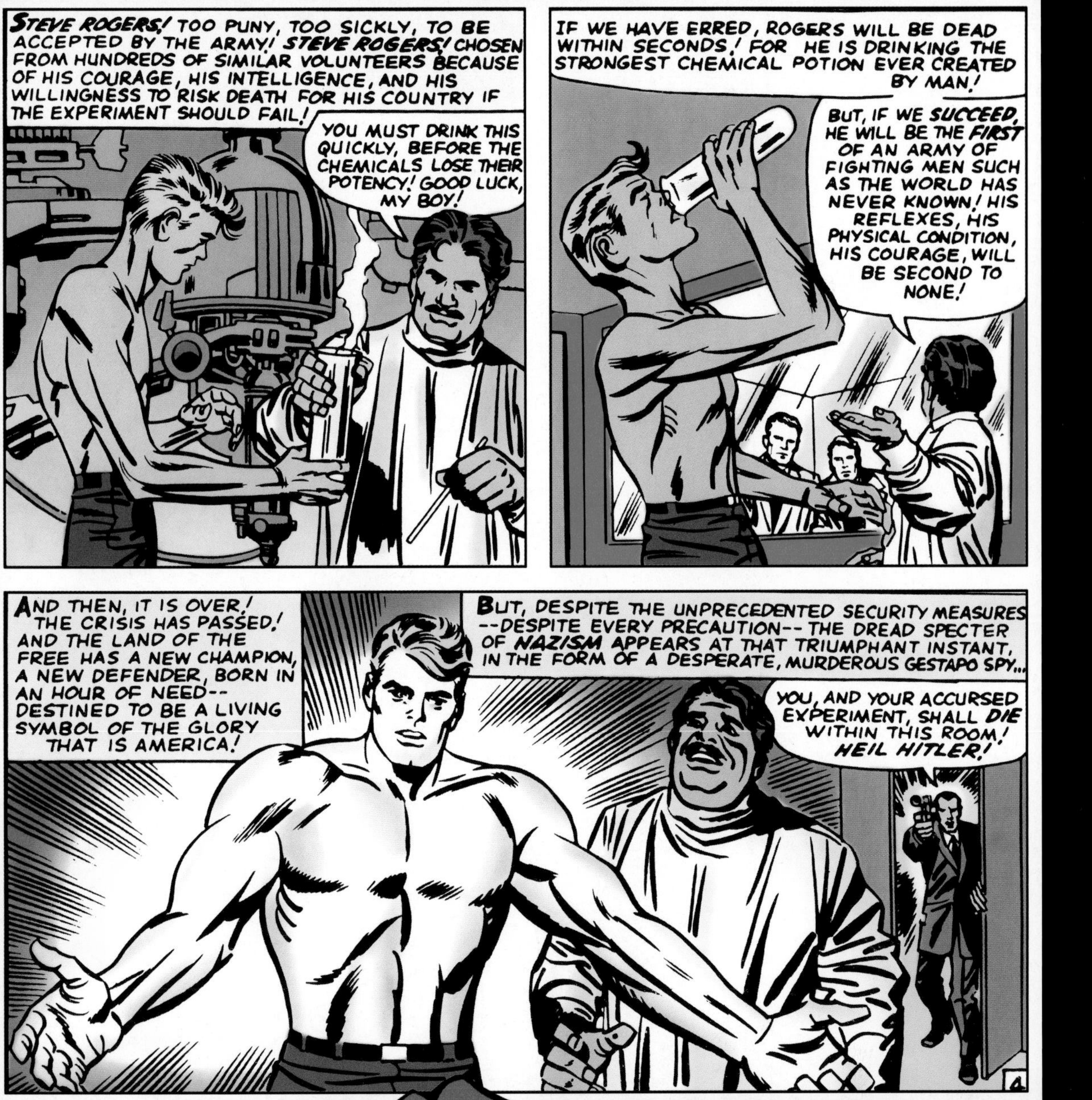
STEVE ROGERS! TOO PUNY, TOO SICKLY, TO BE ACCEPTED BY THE ARMY! STEVE ROGERS! CHOSEN FROM HUNDREDS OF SIMILAR VOLUNTEERS BECAUSE OF HIS COURAGE, HIS INTELLIGENCE, AND HIS WILLINGNESS TO RISK DEATH FOR HIS COUNTRY IF THE EXPERIMENT SHOULD FAIL!
YOU MUST DRINK THIS QUICKLY, BEFORE THE CHEMICALS LOSE THEIR POTENCY! GOOD LUCK, MY BOY!
IF WE HAVE ERRED, ROGERS WILL BE DEAD WITHIN SECONDS! FOR HE IS DRINKING THE STRONGEST CHEMICAL POTION EVER CREATED BY MAN!
BUT, IF WE SUCCEED, HE WILL BE THE FIRST OF AN ARMY OF FIGHTING MEN SUCH AS THE WORLD HAS NEVER KNOWN! HIS REFLEXES, HIS PHYSICAL CONDITION, HIS COURAGE, WILL BE SECOND TO NONE!
AND THEN, IT IS OVER! THE CRISIS HAS PASSED! AND THE LAND OF THE FREE HAS A NEW CHAMPION, A NEW DEFENDER, BORN IN AN HOUR OF NEED-- DESTINED TO BE A LIVING SYMBOL OF THE GLORY THAT IS AMERICA!
BUT, DESPITE THE UNPRECEDENTED SECURITY MEASURES --DESPITE EVERY PRECAUTION-- THE DREAD SPECTER OF NAZISM APPEARS AT THAT TRIUMPHANT INSTANT, IN THE FORM OF A DESPERATE, MURDEROUS GESTAPO SPY...
YOU, AND YOUR ACCURSED EXPERIMENT, SHALL DIE WITHIN THIS ROOM! HEIL HITLER!
4

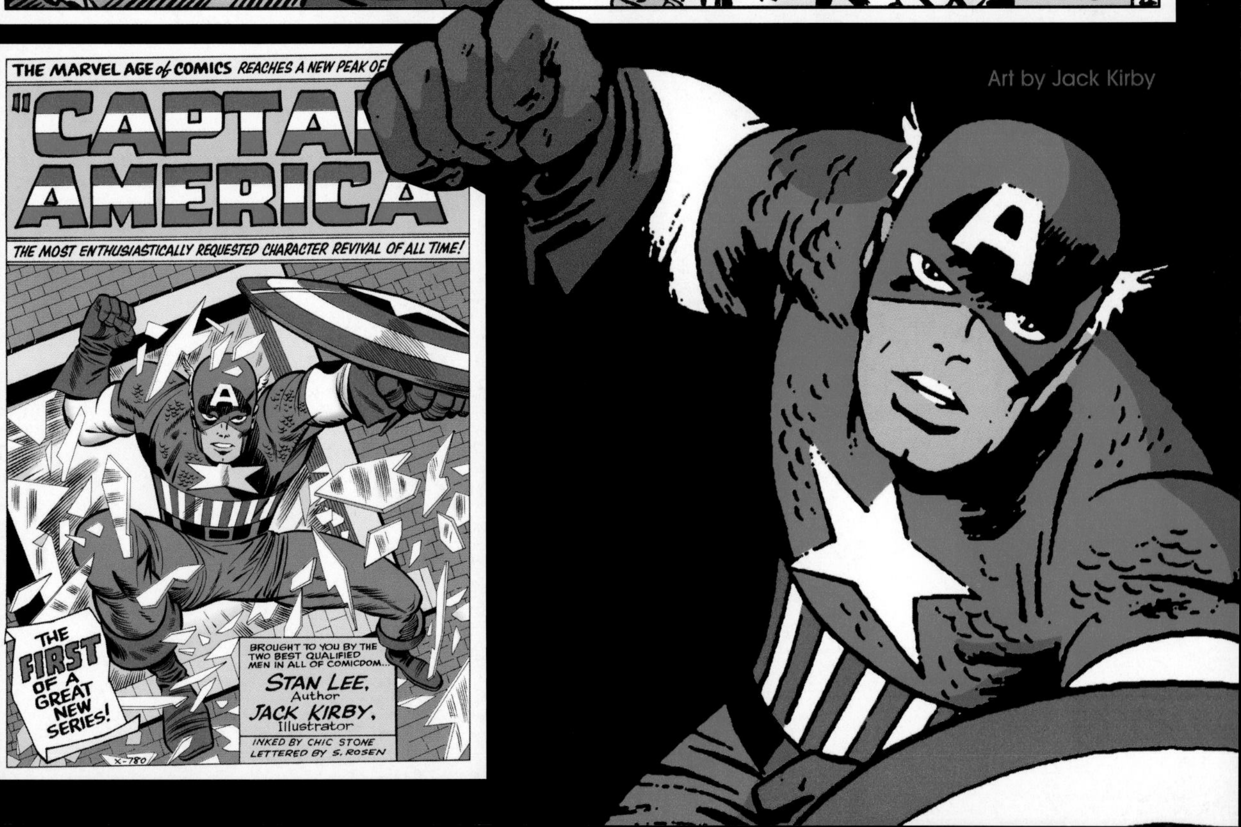
THE MARVEL AGE of COMICS REACHES A NEW PEAK OF
"CAPTA
AMERICA
THE MOST ENTHUSIASTICALLY REQUESTED CHARACTER REVIVAL OF ALL TIME!
THE FIRST OF A GREAT NEW SERIES!
BROUGHT TO YOU BY THE TWO BEST QUALIFIED MEN IN ALL OF COMICDOM...
STAN LEE, Author
JACK KIRBY, Illustrator
INKED BY CHIC STONE
LETTERED BY S. ROSEN
X-780

Art by Jack Kirby

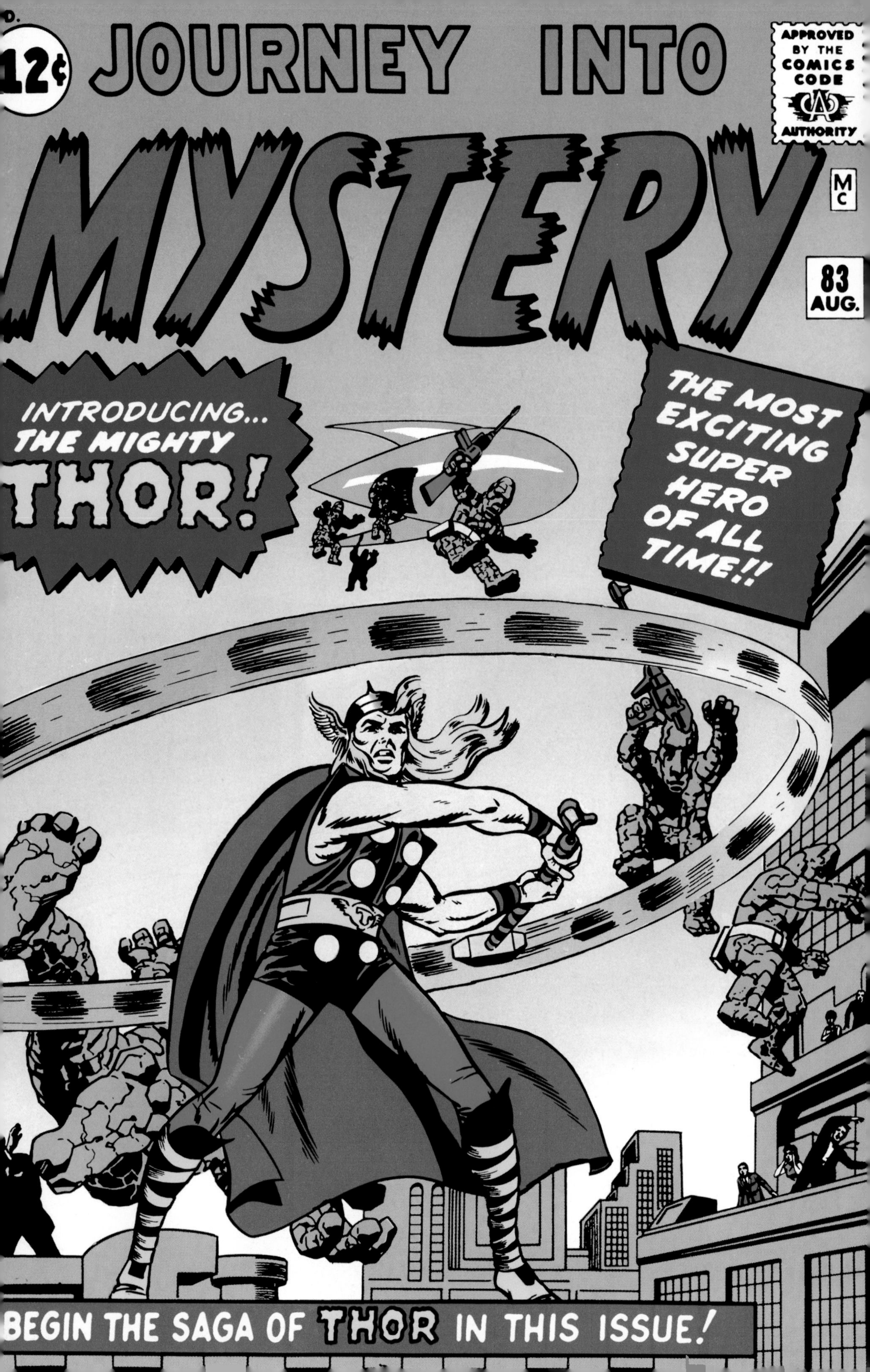
12¢
JOURNEY INTO
MYSTERY
APPROVED BY THE COMICS CODE AUTHORITY
MC
83
AUG.
INTRODUCING... THE MIGHTY THOR!
THE MOST EXCITING SUPER HERO OF ALL TIME!!
BEGIN THE SAGA OF THOR IN THIS ISSUE!

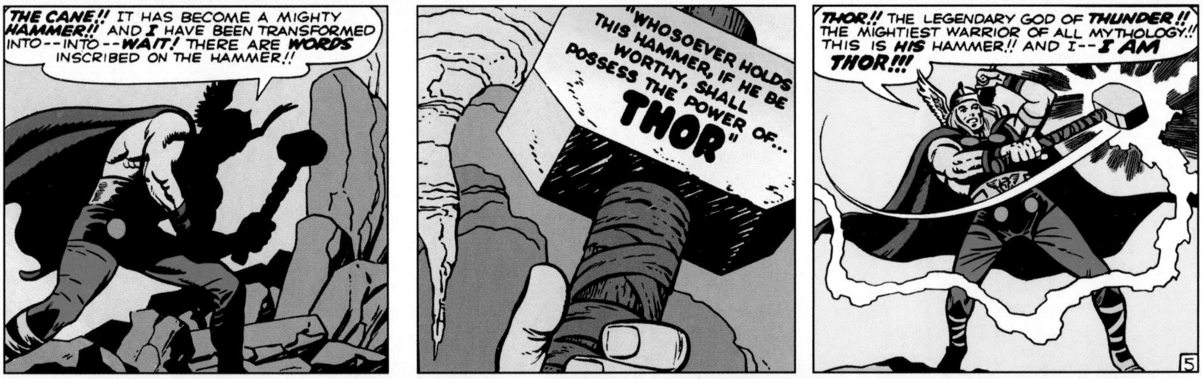
THE CANE!! IT HAS BECOME A MIGHTY HAMMER!! AND I HAVE BEEN TRANSFORMED INTO--INTO--WAIT! THERE ARE WORDS INSCRIBED ON THE HAMMER!!
"WHOSOEVER HOLDS THIS HAMMER, IF HE BE WORTHY, SHALL POSSESS THE POWER OF... THOR"
THOR!! THE LEGENDARY GOD OF THUNDER!! THE MIGHTIEST WARRIOR OF ALL MYTHOLOGY!! THIS IS HIS HAMMER!! AND I--I AM THOR!!!
5

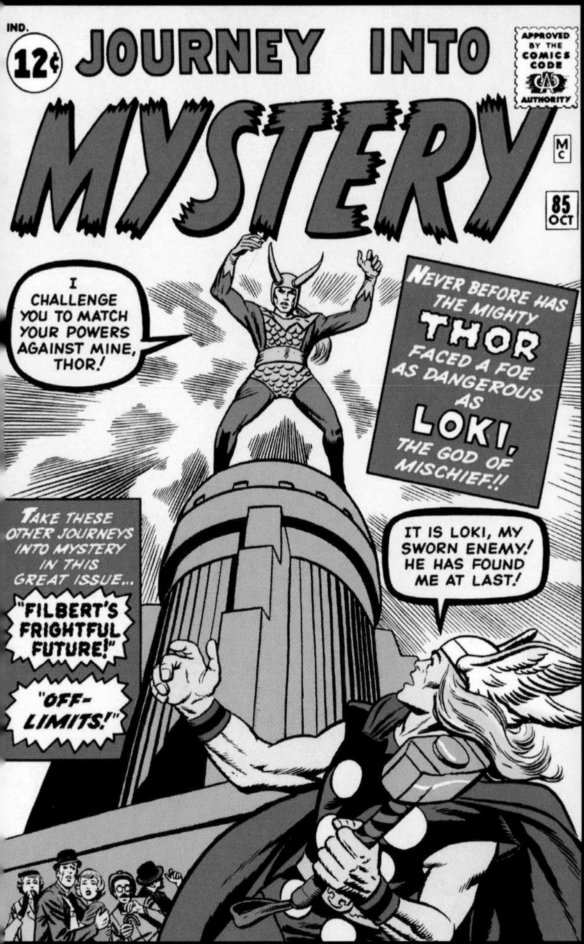
IND.
12¢
JOURNEY INTO MYSTERY
APPROVED BY THE COMICS CODE AUTHORITY
MC
85 OCT
I CHALLENGE YOU TO MATCH YOUR POWERS AGAINST MINE, THOR!
NEVER BEFORE HAS THE MIGHTY THOR FACED A FOE AS DANGEROUS AS LOKI, THE GOD OF MISCHIEF!!
TAKE THESE OTHER JOURNEYS INTO MYSTERY IN THIS GREAT ISSUE...
"FILBERT'S FRIGHTFUL FUTURE!"
"OFF-LIMITS!"
IT IS LOKI, MY SWORN ENEMY! HE HAS FOUND ME AT LAST!

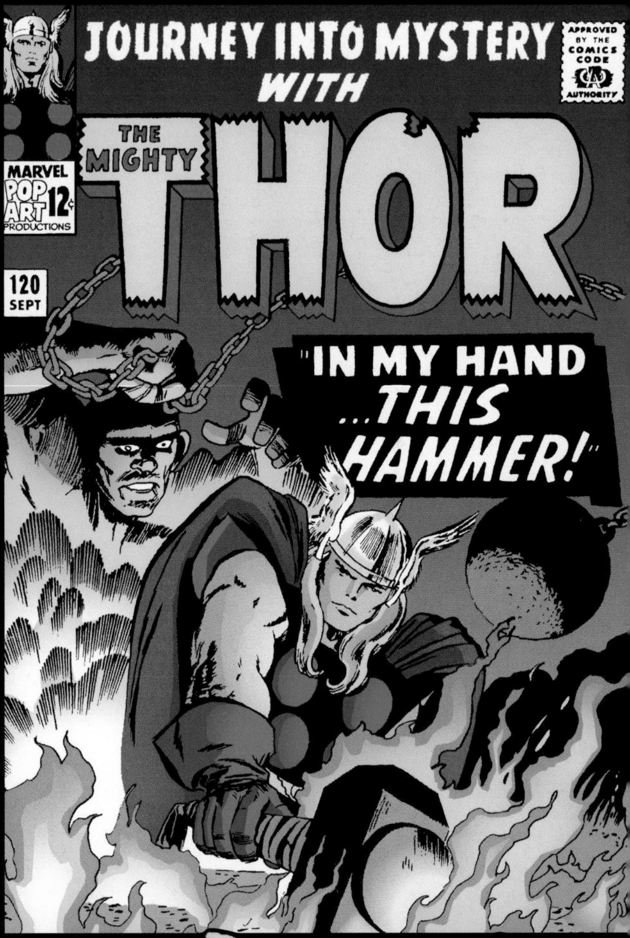
JOURNEY INTO MYSTERY WITH
THE MIGHTY THOR
APPROVED BY THE COMICS CODE AUTHORITY
MARVEL POP ART 12¢ PRODUCTIONS
120 SEPT
"IN MY HAND ...THIS HAMMER!"

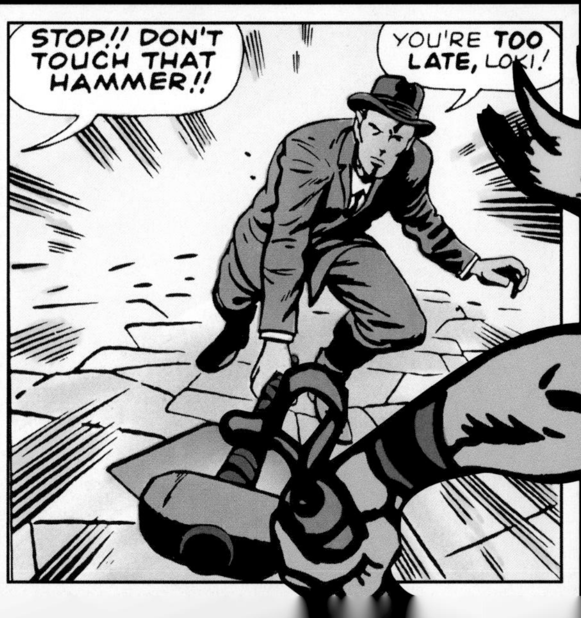
STOP!! DON'T TOUCH THAT HAMMER!!
YOU'RE TOO LATE, LOKI!

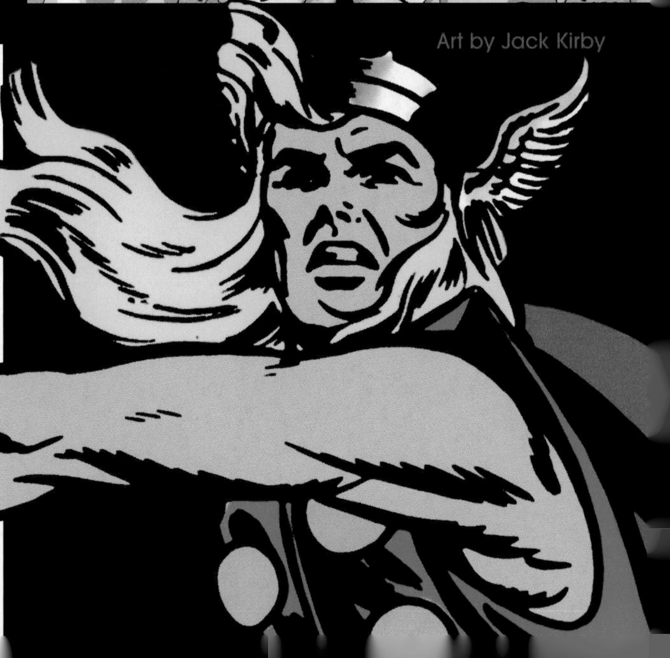
Art by Jack Kirby

IND.

12¢

# TALES OF SUSPENSE

APPROVED BY THE COMICS CODE AUTHORITY

MC

39 MAR.

WHO? OR WHAT, IS THE NEWEST, MOST BREATH-TAKING, MOST SENSATIONAL SUPER HERO OF ALL...?

## "IRON MAN!

HE LIVES!
HE WALKS!
HE CONQUERS!

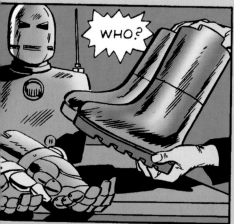

WHO?

WHO?

WHO?

FROM THE TALENTED BULL-PEN WHERE THE FANTASTIC FOUR, SPIDER-MAN, THOR AND YOUR OTHER FAVORITE SUPER-HEROES WERE BORN!

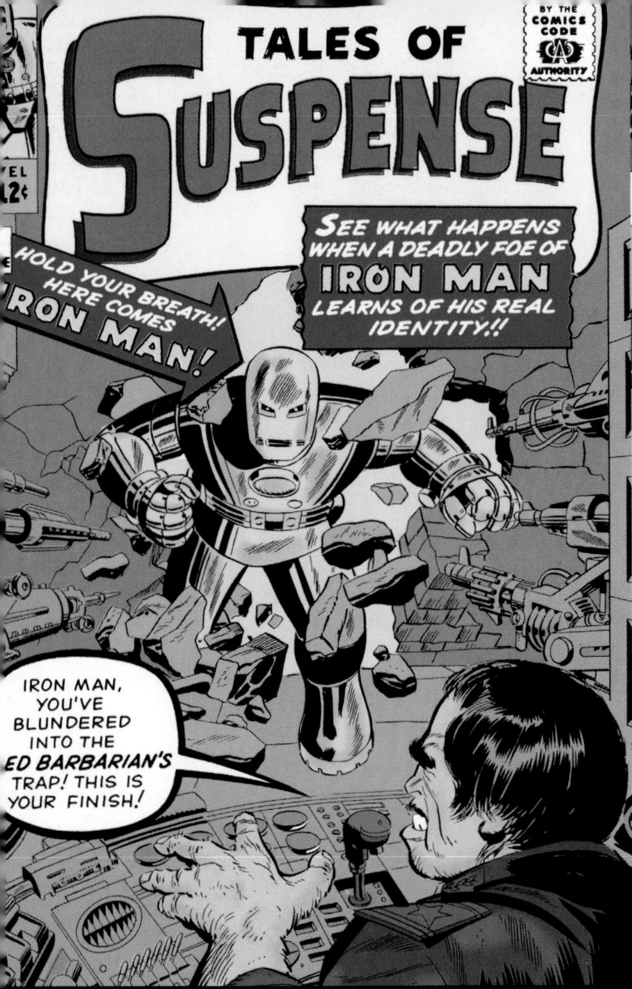
BY THE COMICS CODE AUTHORITY
TALES OF SUSPENSE
SEE WHAT HAPPENS WHEN A DEADLY FOE OF IRON MAN LEARNS OF HIS REAL IDENTITY!!
HOLD YOUR BREATH! HERE COMES RON MAN!
IRON MAN, YOU'VE BLUNDERED INTO THE ED BARBARIAN'S TRAP! THIS IS YOUR FINISH!

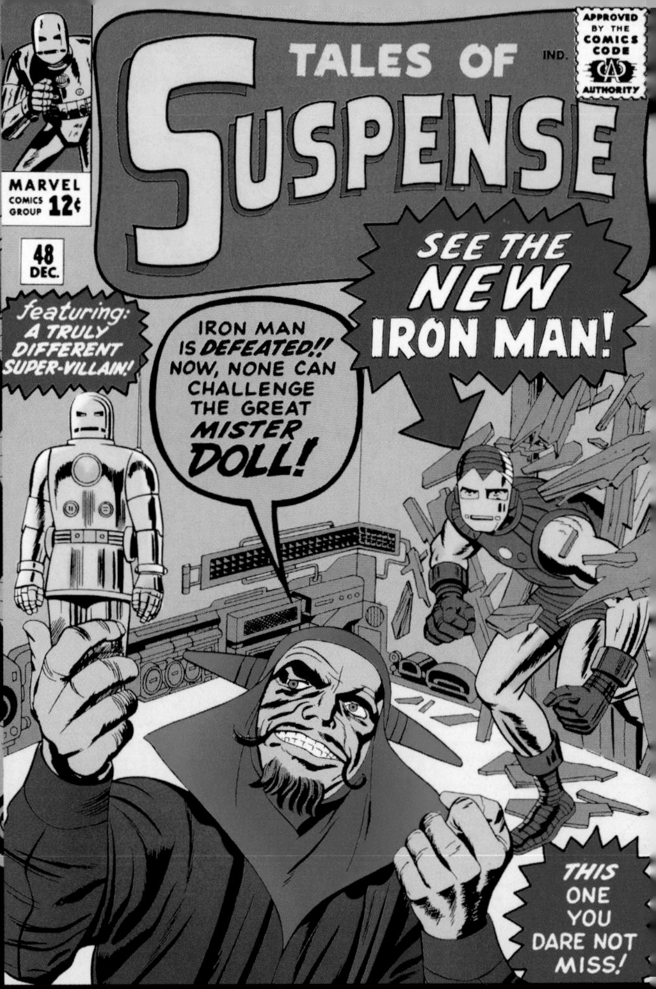
APPROVED BY THE COMICS CODE AUTHORITY
TALES OF SUSPENSE
IND.
MARVEL COMICS GROUP 12¢
48 DEC.
featuring: A TRULY DIFFERENT SUPER-VILLAIN!
IRON MAN IS DEFEATED!! NOW, NONE CAN CHALLENGE THE GREAT MISTER DOLL!
SEE THE NEW IRON MAN!
THIS ONE YOU DARE NOT MISS!

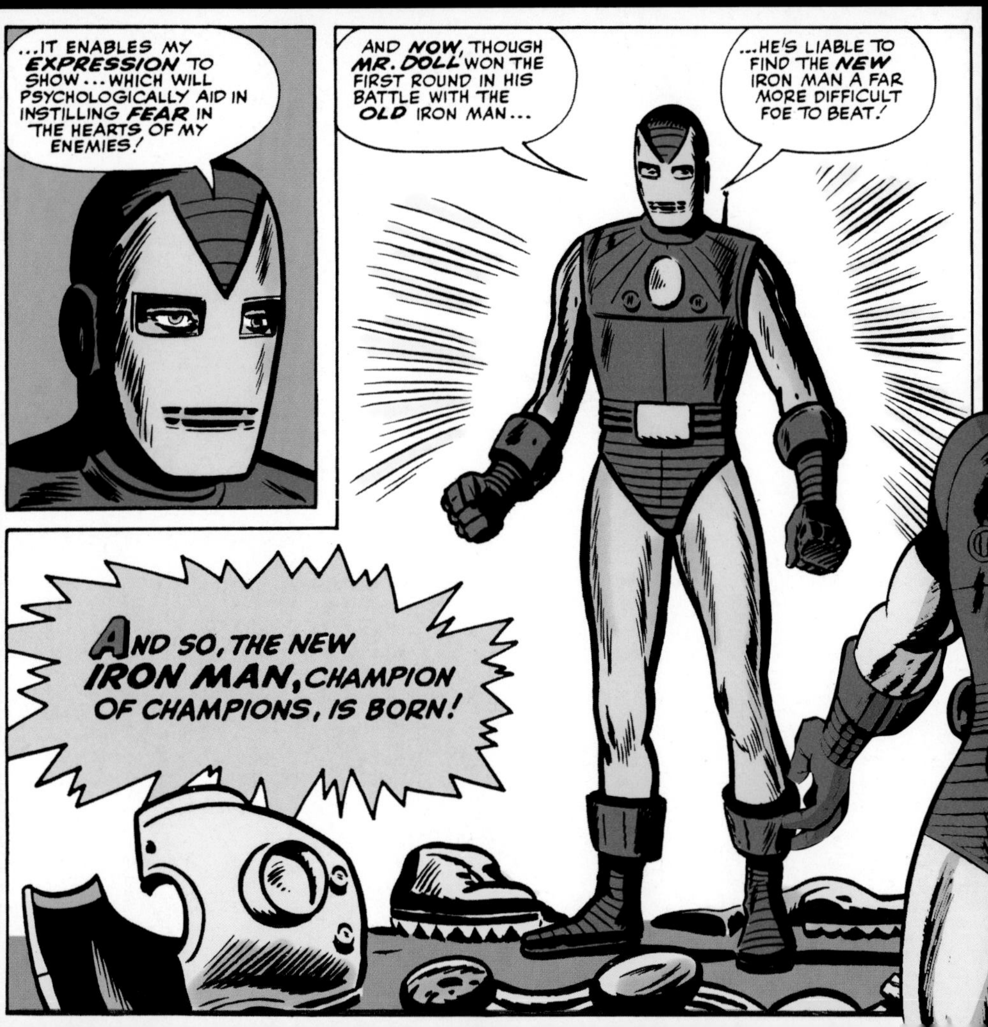
...IT ENABLES MY EXPRESSION TO SHOW... WHICH WILL PSYCHOLOGICALLY AID IN INSTILLING FEAR IN THE HEARTS OF MY ENEMIES!
AND NOW, THOUGH MR. DOLL WON THE FIRST ROUND IN HIS BATTLE WITH THE OLD IRON MAN...
...HE'S LIABLE TO FIND THE NEW IRON MAN A FAR MORE DIFFICULT FOE TO BEAT!
AND SO, THE NEW IRON MAN, CHAMPION OF CHAMPIONS, IS BORN!

Opposite: Art by Jack Kirby. This page: Art by Steve Ditko (interior) and Kirby (covers #42, #48 and Iron Man figure).

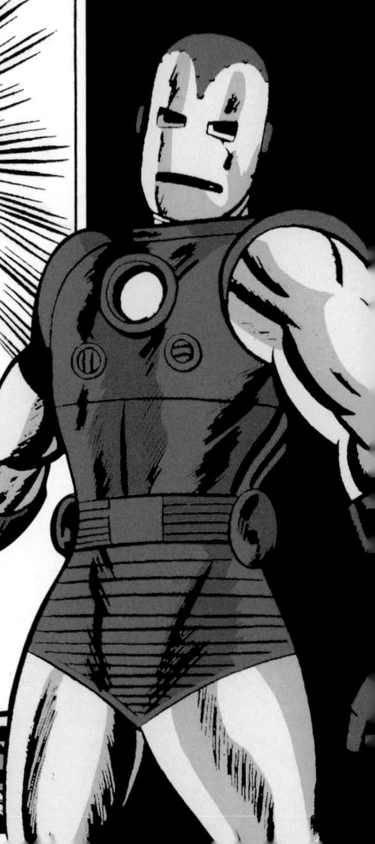

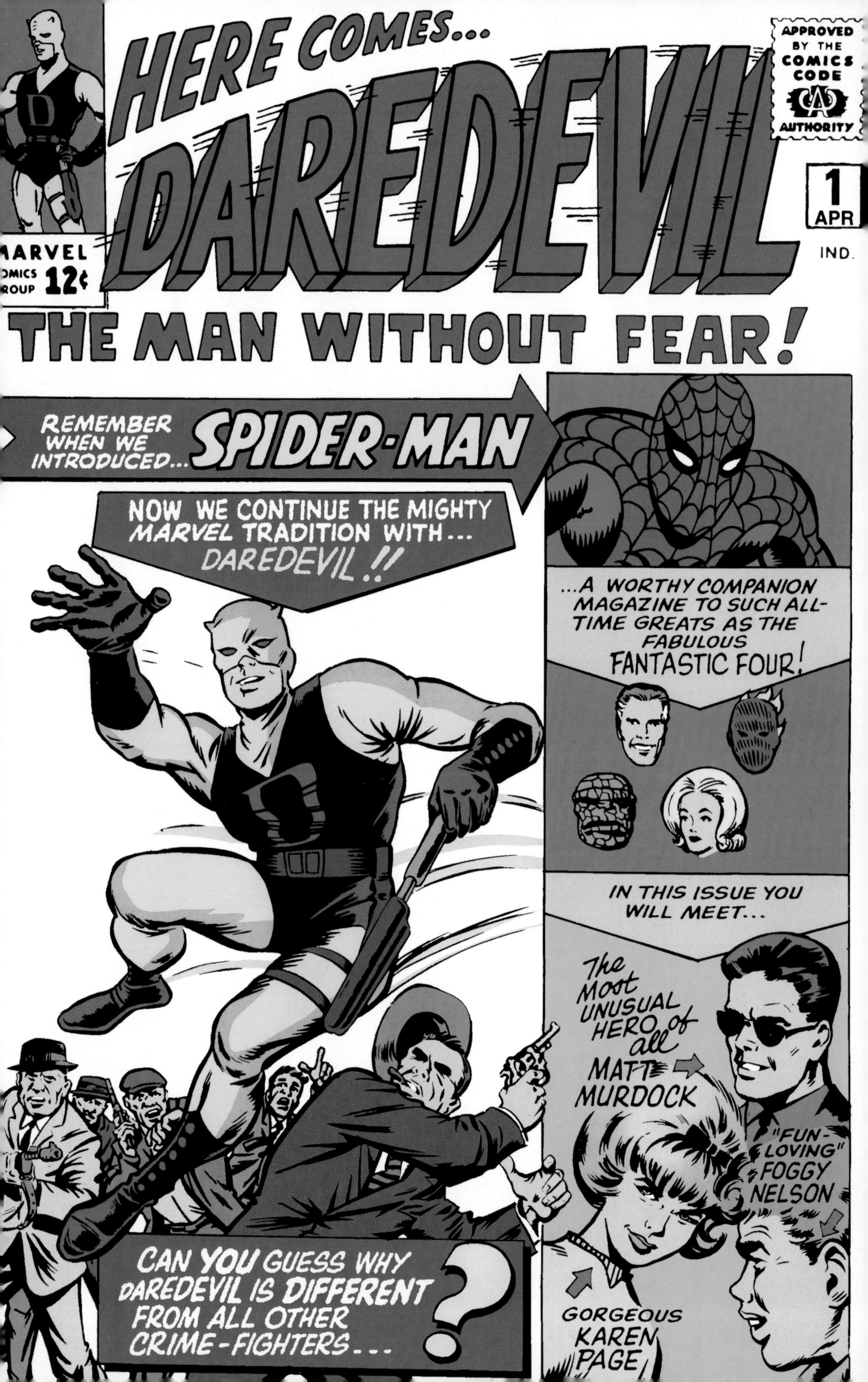

HERE COMES...
DAREDEVIL
APPROVED BY THE COMICS CODE AUTHORITY
1 APR
IND.
MARVEL COMICS GROUP 12¢
THE MAN WITHOUT FEAR!
REMEMBER WHEN WE INTRODUCED... SPIDER-MAN
NOW WE CONTINUE THE MIGHTY MARVEL TRADITION WITH... DAREDEVIL!!
...A WORTHY COMPANION MAGAZINE TO SUCH ALL-TIME GREATS AS THE FABULOUS FANTASTIC FOUR!
IN THIS ISSUE YOU WILL MEET...
The Most UNUSUAL HERO of all MATT MURDOCK
"FUN-LOVING" FOGGY NELSON
GORGEOUS KAREN PAGE
CAN YOU GUESS WHY DAREDEVIL IS DIFFERENT FROM ALL OTHER CRIME-FIGHTERS...?

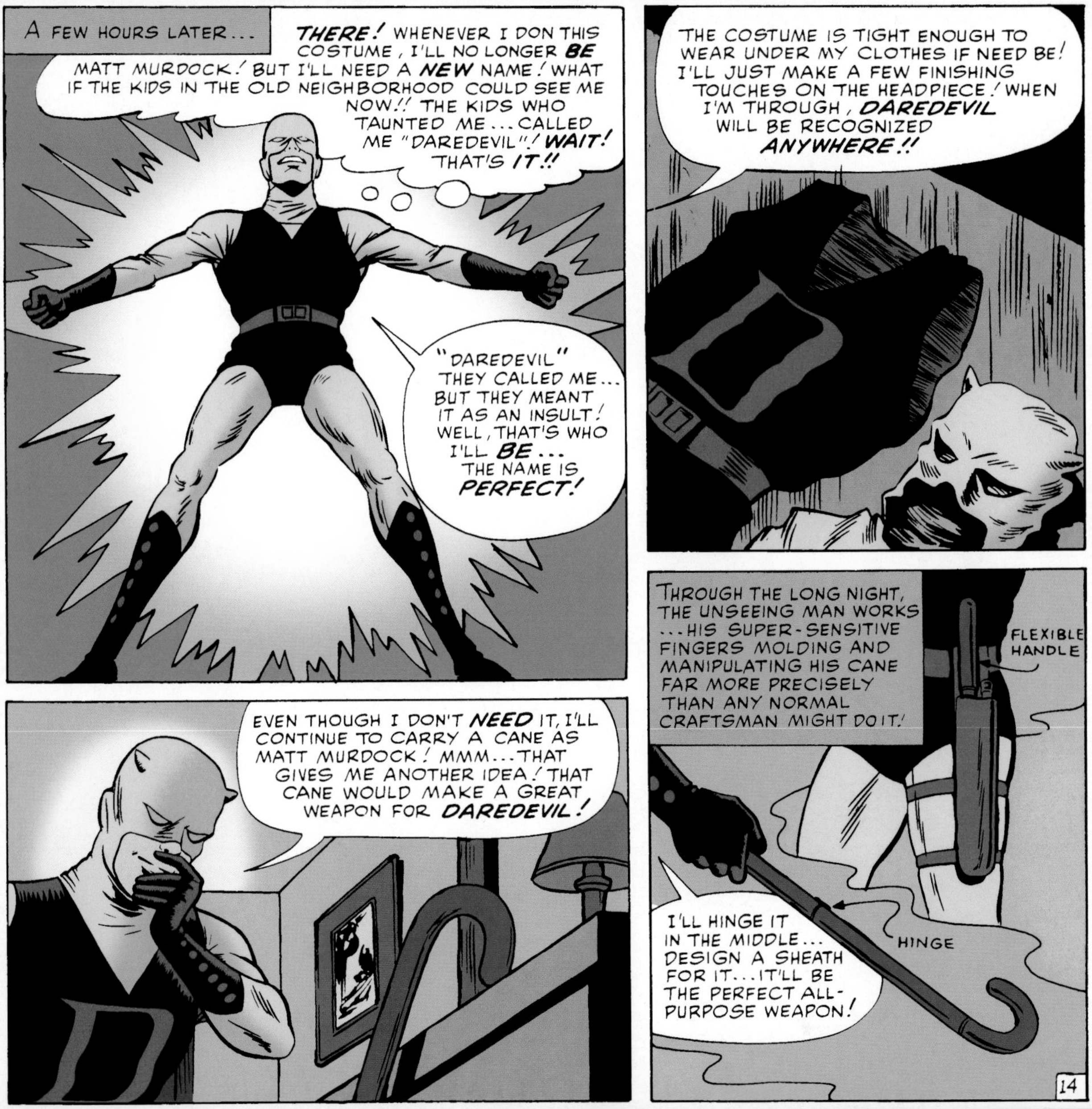
A FEW HOURS LATER...
THERE! WHENEVER I DON THIS COSTUME, I'LL NO LONGER BE MATT MURDOCK! BUT I'LL NEED A NEW NAME! WHAT IF THE KIDS IN THE OLD NEIGHBORHOOD COULD SEE ME NOW!! THE KIDS WHO TAUNTED ME... CALLED ME "DAREDEVIL"! WAIT! THAT'S IT!!
"DAREDEVIL" THEY CALLED ME... BUT THEY MEANT IT AS AN INSULT! WELL, THAT'S WHO I'LL BE... THE NAME IS PERFECT!
THE COSTUME IS TIGHT ENOUGH TO WEAR UNDER MY CLOTHES IF NEED BE! I'LL JUST MAKE A FEW FINISHING TOUCHES ON THE HEADPIECE! WHEN I'M THROUGH, DAREDEVIL WILL BE RECOGNIZED ANYWHERE!!
EVEN THOUGH I DON'T NEED IT, I'LL CONTINUE TO CARRY A CANE AS MATT MURDOCK! MMM... THAT GIVES ME ANOTHER IDEA! THAT CANE WOULD MAKE A GREAT WEAPON FOR DAREDEVIL!
THROUGH THE LONG NIGHT, THE UNSEEING MAN WORKS ...HIS SUPER-SENSITIVE FINGERS MOLDING AND MANIPULATING HIS CANE FAR MORE PRECISELY THAN ANY NORMAL CRAFTSMAN MIGHT DO IT!
FLEXIBLE HANDLE
HINGE
I'LL HINGE IT IN THE MIDDLE... DESIGN A SHEATH FOR IT... IT'LL BE THE PERFECT ALL-PURPOSE WEAPON!
14

Opposite: Art by Bill Everett. This Page: Art by Everett (interior), Wally Wood (cover #9), Jack Kirby (cover #4) and Gene Colan (Daredevil figure).

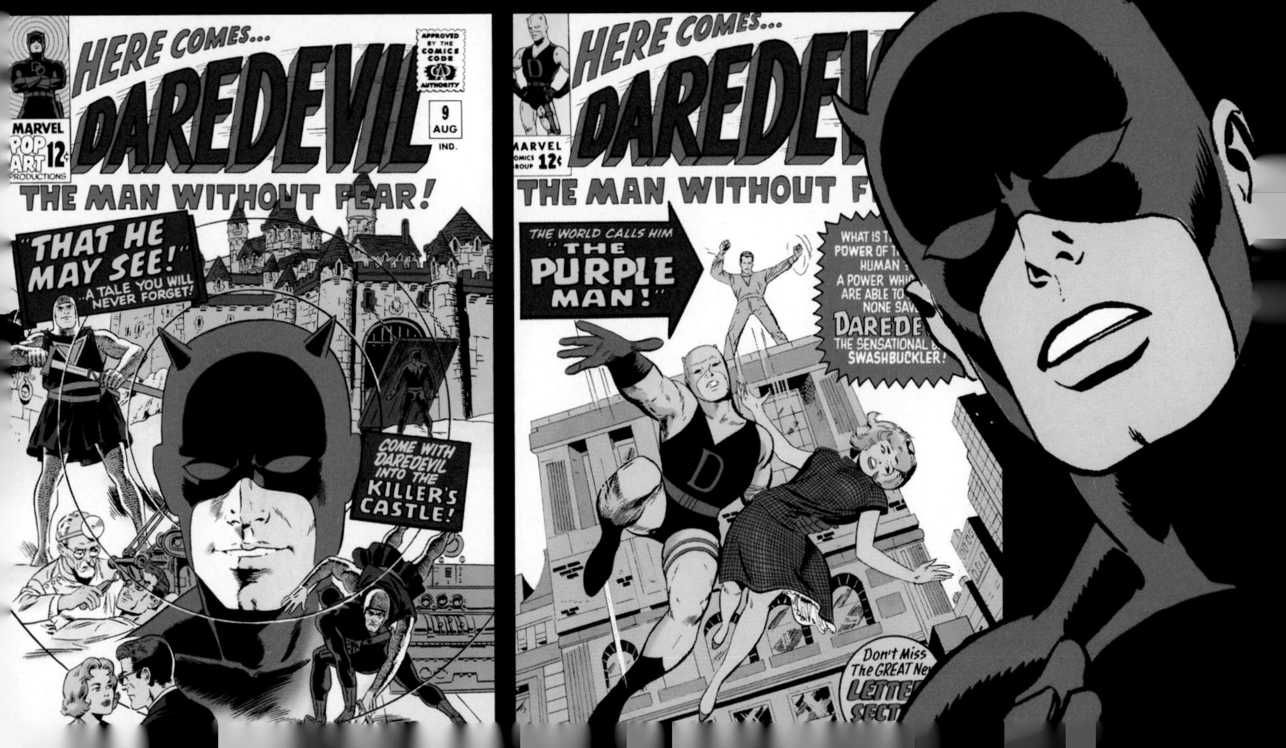
HERE COMES...
DAREDEVIL
THE MAN WITHOUT FEAR!
MARVEL POP ART PRODUCTIONS 12¢
9 AUG
"THAT HE MAY SEE!" ...A TALE YOU WILL NEVER FORGET!
COME WITH DAREDEVIL INTO THE KILLER'S CASTLE!
HERE COMES...
MARVEL COMICS GROUP 12¢
THE WORLD CALLS HIM "THE PURPLE MAN!"
SWASHBUCKLER!
Don't Miss The GREAT New

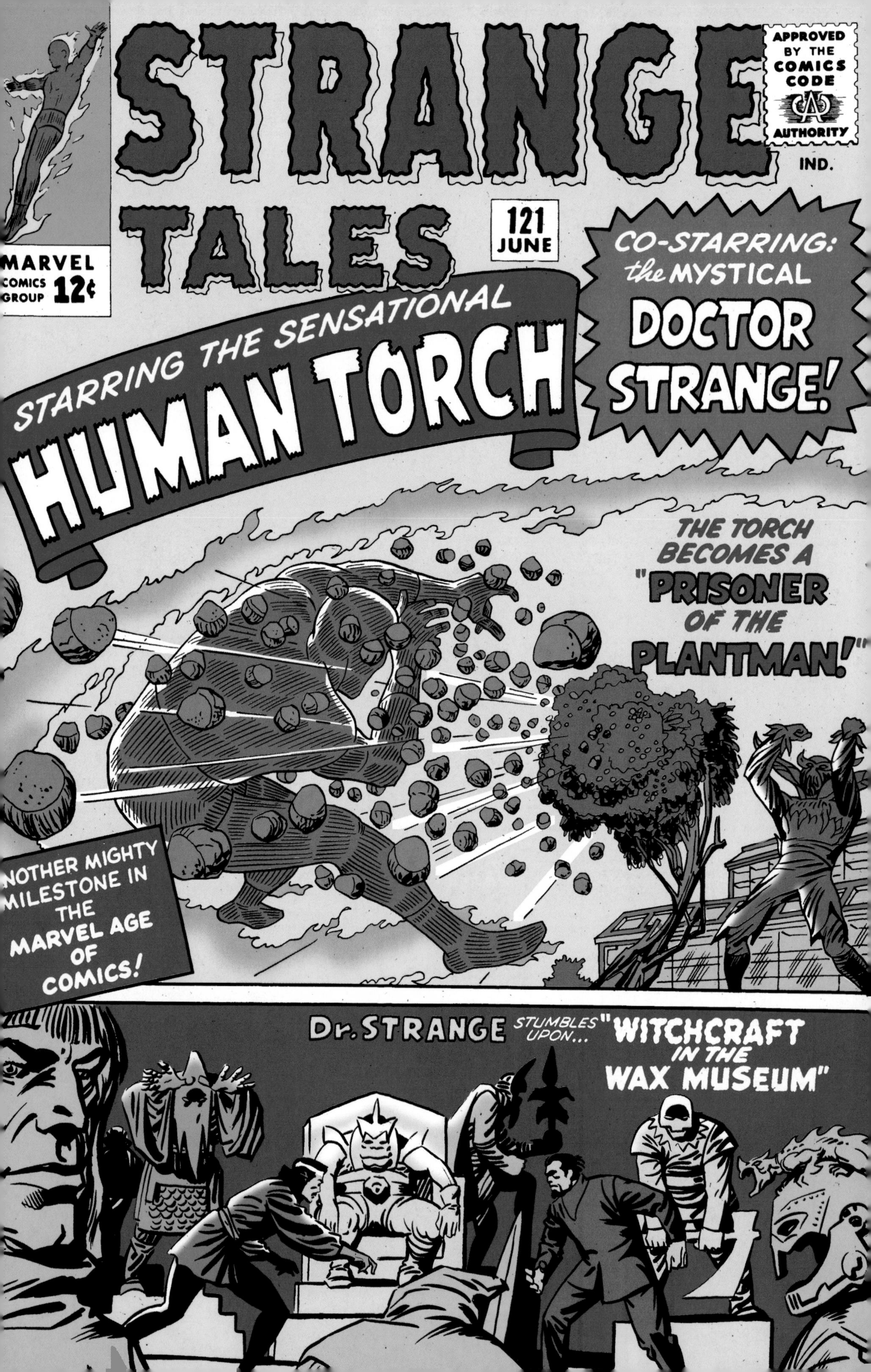

STRANGE TALES
APPROVED BY THE COMICS CODE AUTHORITY
IND.
MARVEL COMICS GROUP 12¢
121 JUNE
STARRING THE SENSATIONAL HUMAN TORCH
CO-STARRING: the MYSTICAL DOCTOR STRANGE!
THE TORCH BECOMES A "PRISONER OF THE PLANTMAN!"
NOTHER MIGHTY MILESTONE IN THE MARVEL AGE OF COMICS!
Dr. STRANGE STUMBLES UPON... "WITCHCRAFT IN THE WAX MUSEUM"

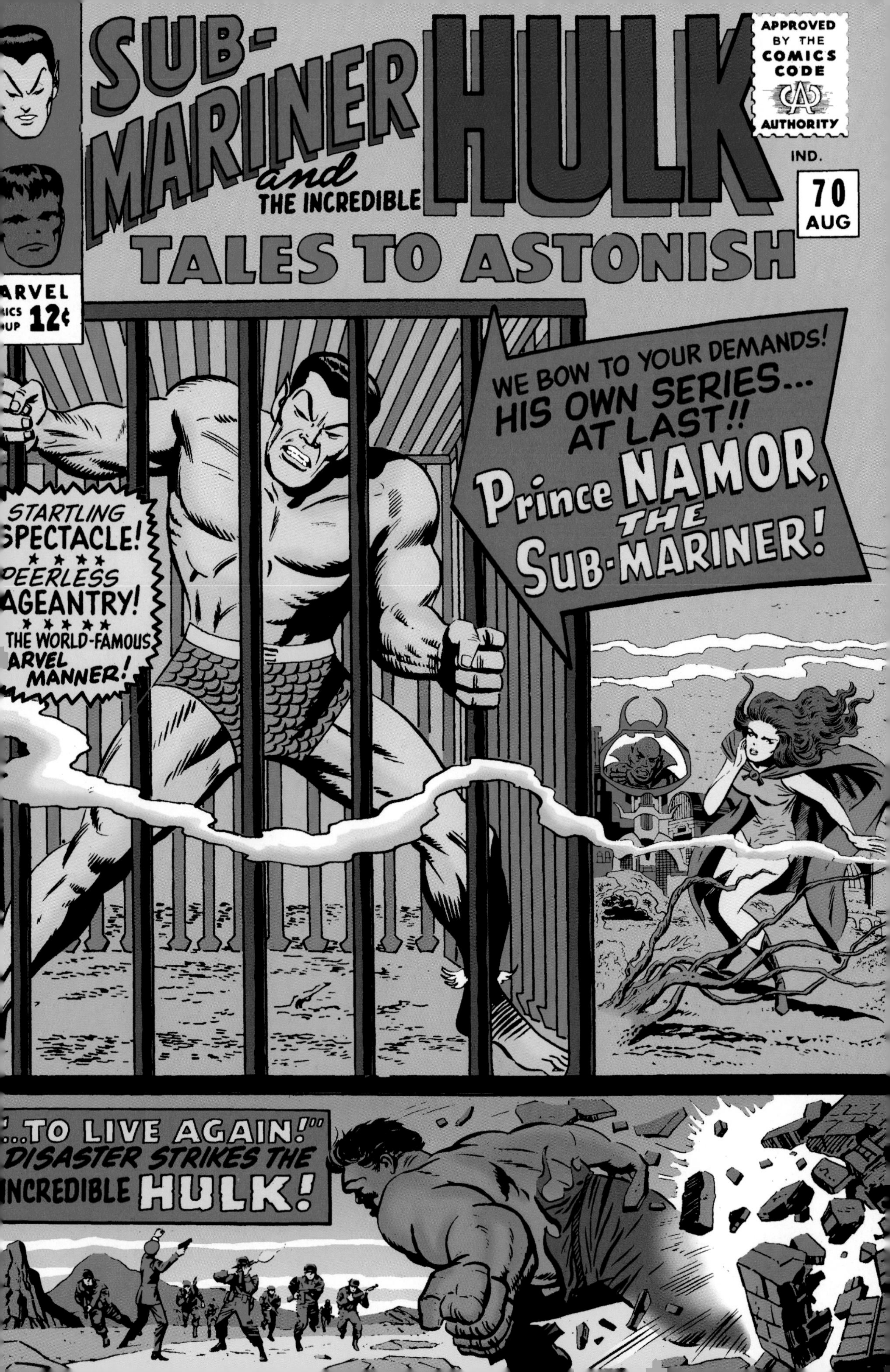

SUB-MARINER and THE INCREDIBLE HULK
TALES TO ASTONISH
APPROVED BY THE COMICS CODE AUTHORITY
IND.
70 AUG
ARVEL
12¢
WE BOW TO YOUR DEMANDS! HIS OWN SERIES... AT LAST!! Prince NAMOR, THE SUB-MARINER!
STARTLING SPECTACLE! ★★★★ EERLESS AGEANTRY! ★★★★★ THE WORLD-FAMOUS ARVEL MANNER!
"...TO LIVE AGAIN!" DISASTER STRIKES THE INCREDIBLE HULK!

# 1970s

"From the ashes of the past there grow the fires of the future!" Marvel experienced a second creative genesis in 1975 with the debut of the All-New, All-Different Uncanny X-Men in the now-legendary *Giant-Size X-Men #1*. These weren't the Merry Mutants of a decade earlier. Gone were the troubled teens that had honed their powers at Xavier's School for Gifted Youngsters. These new X-Men were older, wiser — and more diverse — heroes sworn to protect a world in which they were hated and feared.

In addition to Wolverine's claw-popping debut in the pages of *Incredible Hulk #181*, the seventies saw another sensational character find: The Punisher, scourge of the underworld, set his sights on a certain world-famous wall-crawler in *Amazing Spider-Man #129*. In another first, Daredevil, the Man without Fear, first teamed with sexy secret agent Black Widow in *Daredevil #81*. And Doctor Strange, Master of the Mystic Arts, set out to strengthen the barriers between our world and countless other hostile realms in his very own monthly mag.

Not to be outdone, Marvel's mainstays showed no signs of slowing down. "King" Kirby returned to *Captain America* to run the star-spangled Sentinel of Liberty through a gauntlet of Bicentennial battles. And death returned to *Amazing Spider-Man*, times two, as the untimely departures of both paternal police captain George Stacy and his daughter, Gwen, the first great love of Peter Parker's young life, left the web-slinger's world a colder, more lonely place.

Death visited Marvel in other forms, as well. Dracula, the legendary Lord of the Undead, came to life in *Tomb of Dracula*, the most popular of the House's heralded seventies horror titles, which also introduced Blade, the Vampire-Slayer. In the same vein, Marvel unleashed *Monster of Frankenstein* and a host of black-and-white horror magazines able to target a more mature audience by being exempt from the Comics Code.

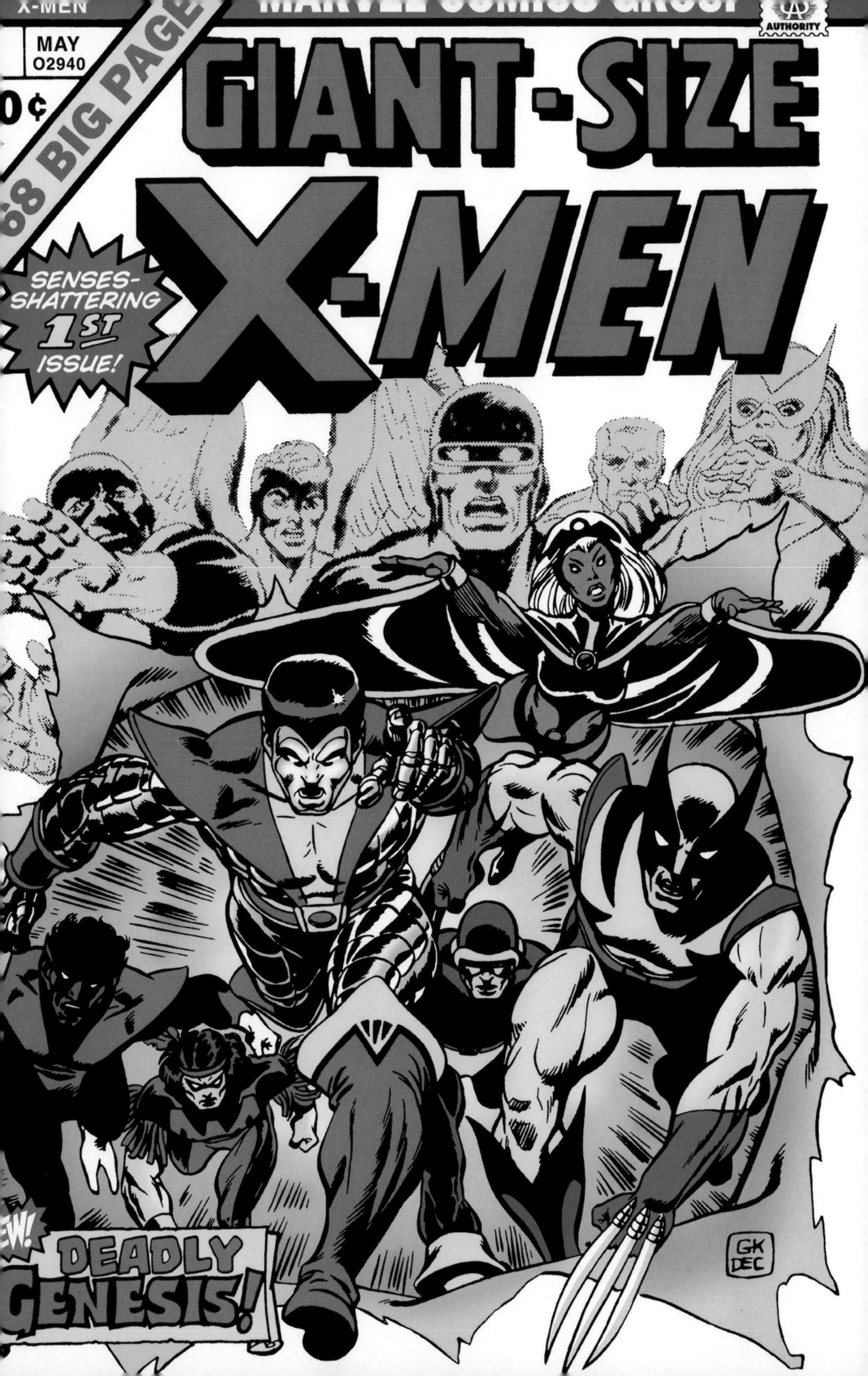
X-MEN
MARVEL COMICS GROUP
AUTHORITY
MAY
O2940
0¢
68 BIG PAGES
GIANT-SIZE
X-MEN
SENSES-SHATTERING 1ST ISSUE!
NEW!
DEADLY GENESIS!
GK DEC

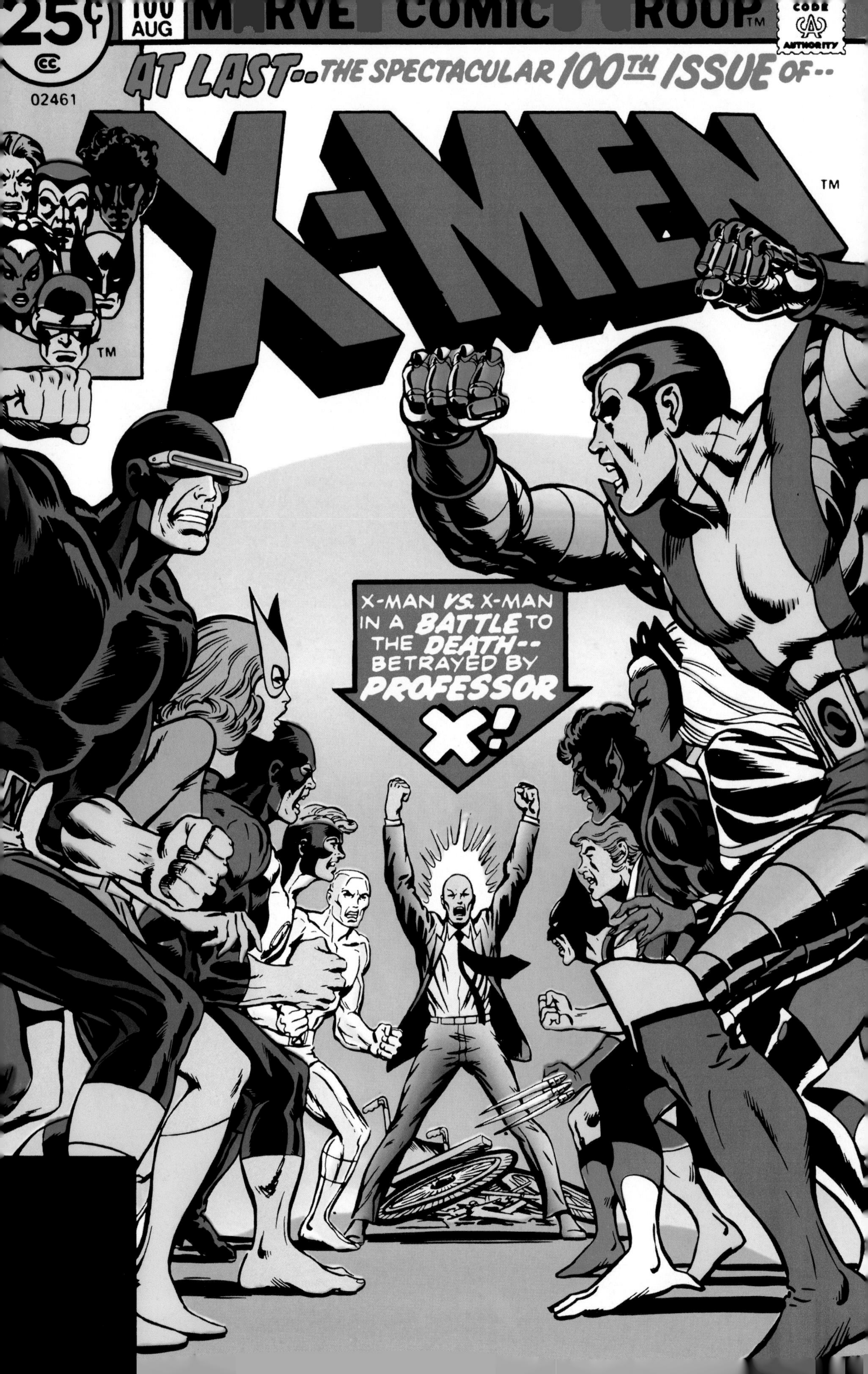

25¢
100
AUG
CODE
AUTHORITY
02461
AT LAST--THE SPECTACULAR 100TH ISSUE OF--
X-MEN
X-MAN VS. X-MAN IN A BATTLE TO THE DEATH-- BETRAYED BY PROFESSOR X!

Opposite: Art by Dave Cockrum. This page: Art by Cockrum (covers #101 and #104) and John Byrne (cover #112 and interior).

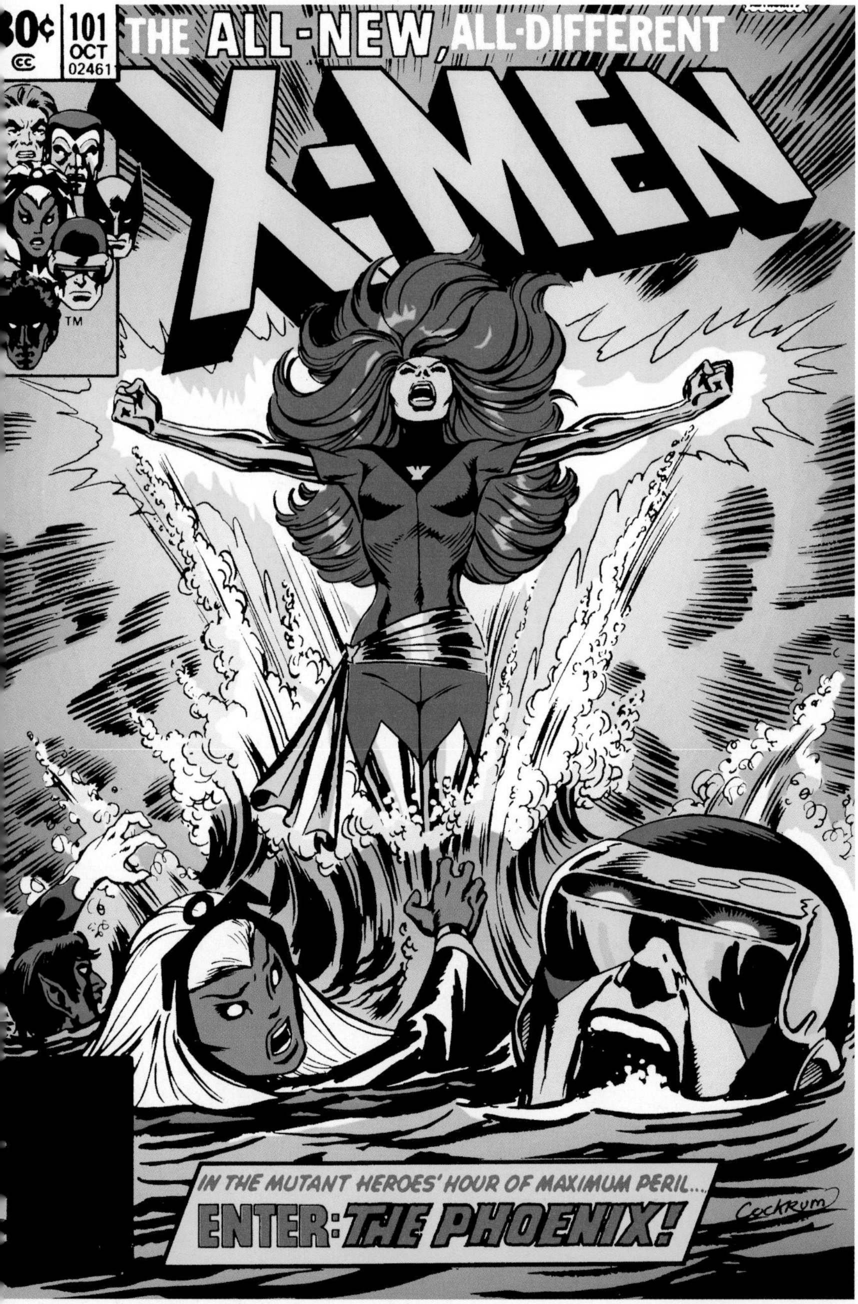
101 OCT 02461
THE ALL-NEW, ALL-DIFFERENT
X-MEN
IN THE MUTANT HEROES' HOUR OF MAXIMUM PERIL...
ENTER: THE PHOENIX!
Cockrum

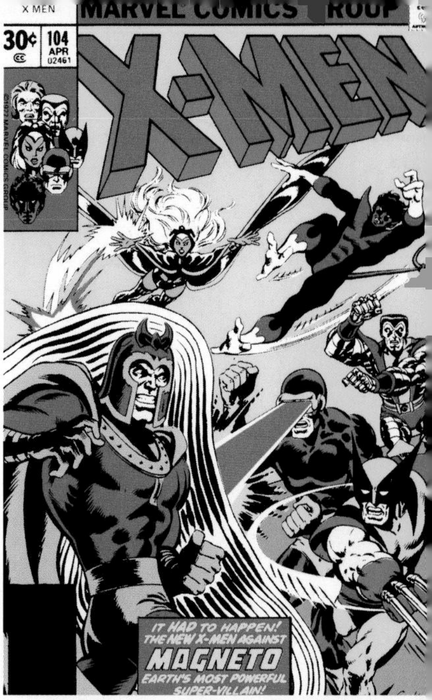
X MEN
30¢ 104 APR 02461
X-MEN
IT HAD TO HAPPEN! THE NEW X-MEN AGAINST
MAGNETO
EARTH'S MOST POWERFUL SUPER-VILLAIN!

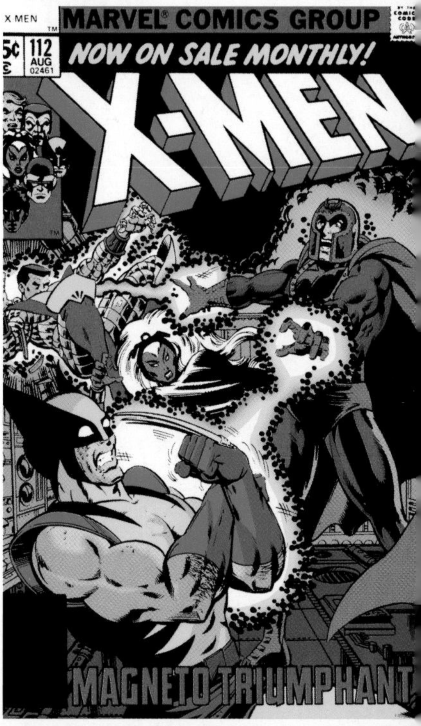
X MEN
MARVEL COMICS GROUP
112 AUG 02461
NOW ON SALE MONTHLY!
MAGNETO TRIUMPHANT

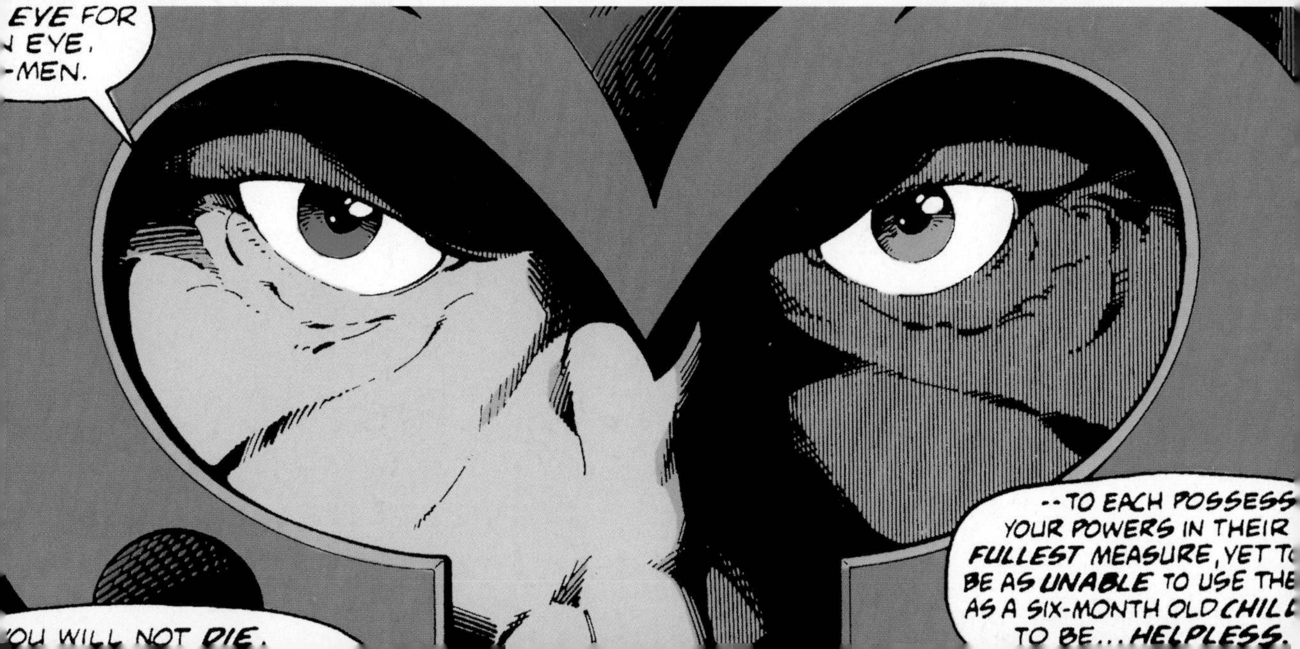
EYE FOR
EYE,
-MEN.
OU WILL NOT DIE.
--TO EACH POSSESS
YOUR POWERS IN THEIR
FULLEST MEASURE, YET T
BE AS UNABLE TO USE THE
AS A SIX-MONTH OLD CHIL
TO BE... HELPLESS.

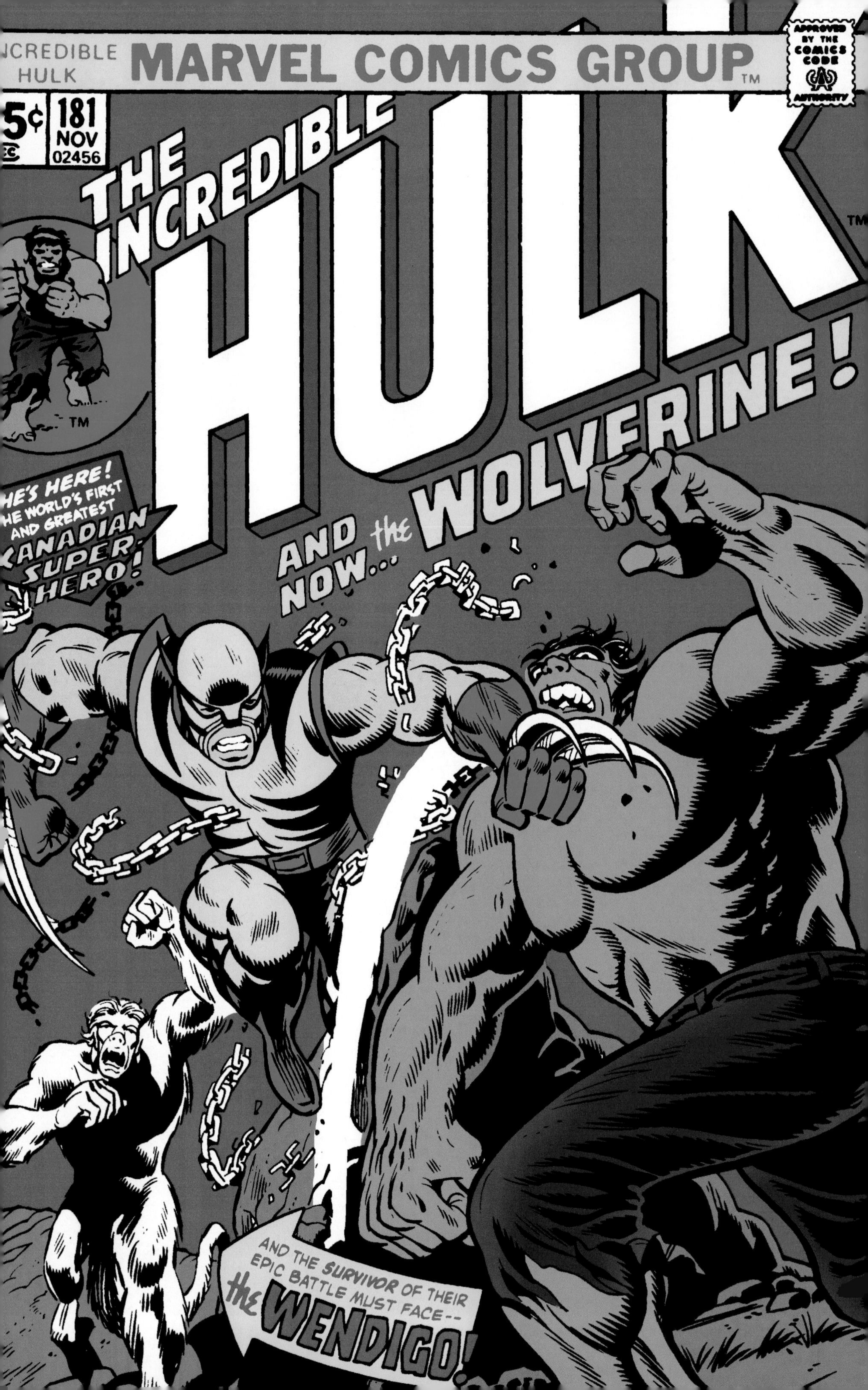
INCREDIBLE HULK
MARVEL COMICS GROUP
APPROVED BY THE COMICS CODE AUTHORITY
25¢ 181 NOV 02456
THE INCREDIBLE HULK
HE'S HERE! THE WORLD'S FIRST AND GREATEST CANADIAN SUPER-HERO!
AND NOW... THE WOLVERINE!
AND THE SURVIVOR OF THEIR EPIC BATTLE MUST FACE-- THE WENDIGO!

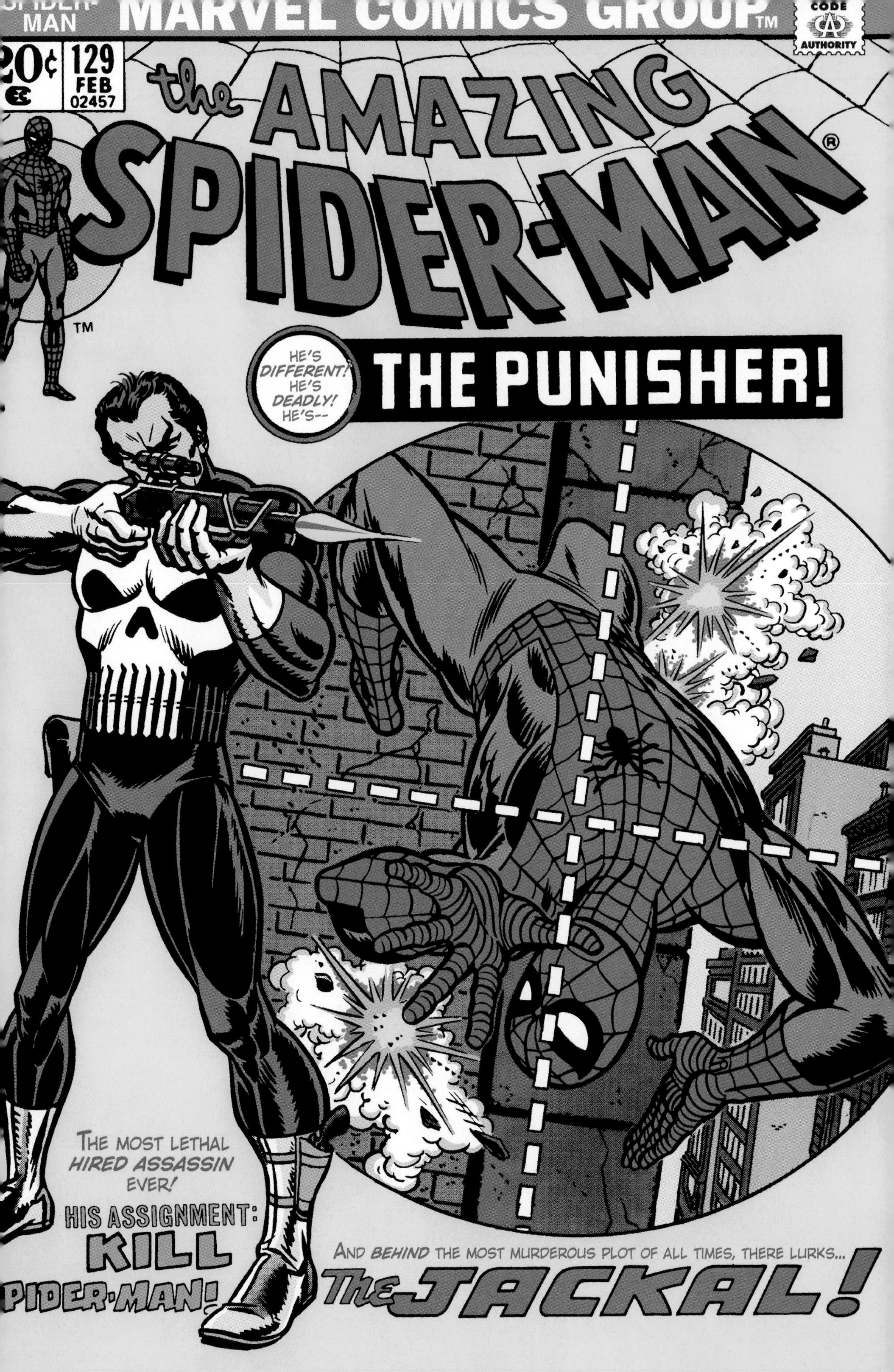
SPIDER-MAN
MARVEL COMICS GROUP™
APPROVED BY THE COMICS CODE AUTHORITY
20¢
129 FEB 02457
the AMAZING SPIDER-MAN®
™
HE'S DIFFERENT! HE'S DEADLY! HE'S--
THE PUNISHER!
THE MOST LETHAL HIRED ASSASSIN EVER!
HIS ASSIGNMENT: KILL SPIDER-MAN!
AND BEHIND THE MOST MURDEROUS PLOT OF ALL TIMES, THERE LURKS...
The JACKAL!

Art by Gil Kane. Opposite: Art by Herb Trimpe.

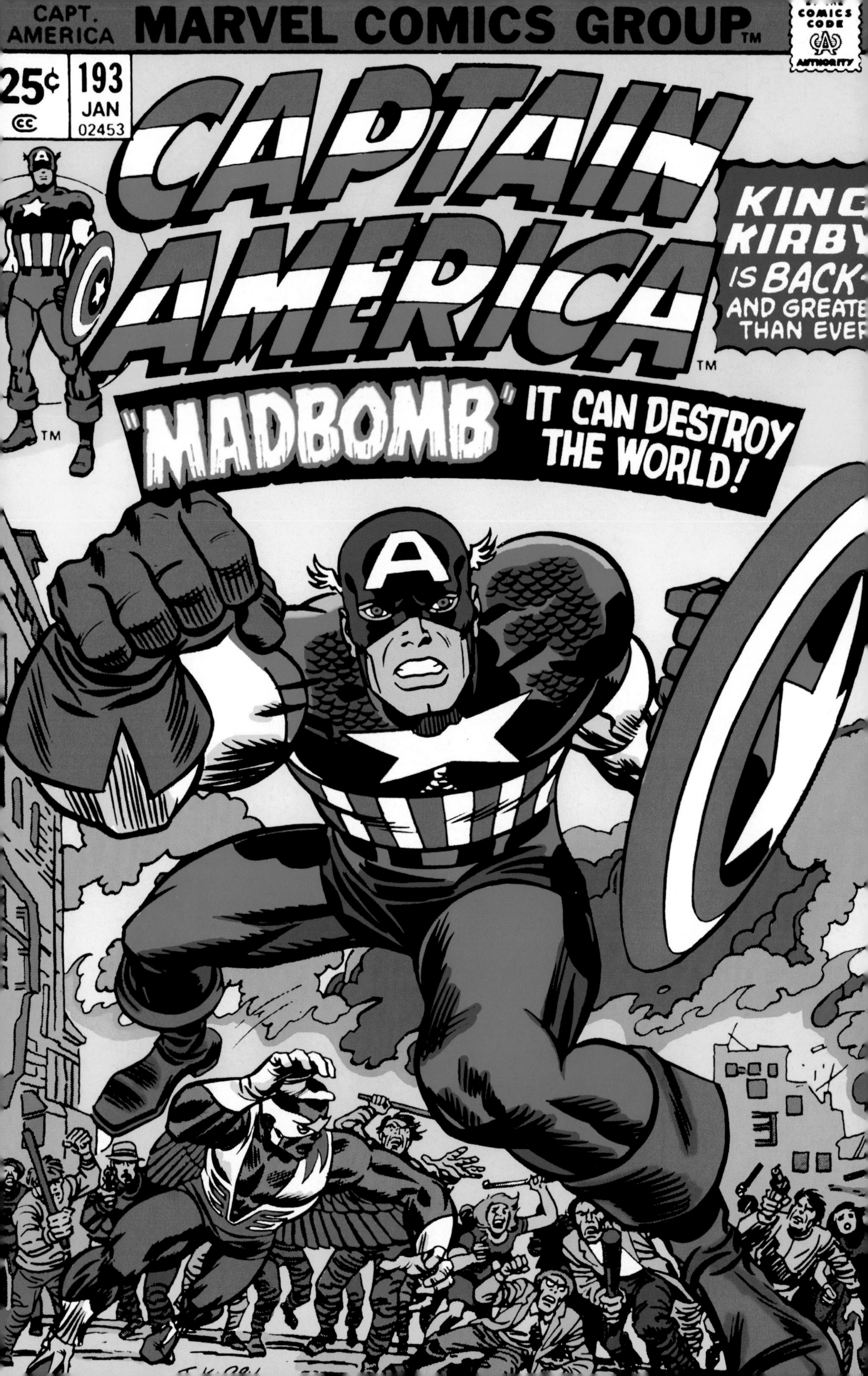
CAPT. AMERICA
MARVEL COMICS GROUP
APPROVED BY THE COMICS CODE AUTHORITY
25¢
193
JAN
02453
CAPTAIN AMERICA
KING KIRBY IS BACK— AND GREATER THAN EVER
"MADBOMB" IT CAN DESTROY THE WORLD!

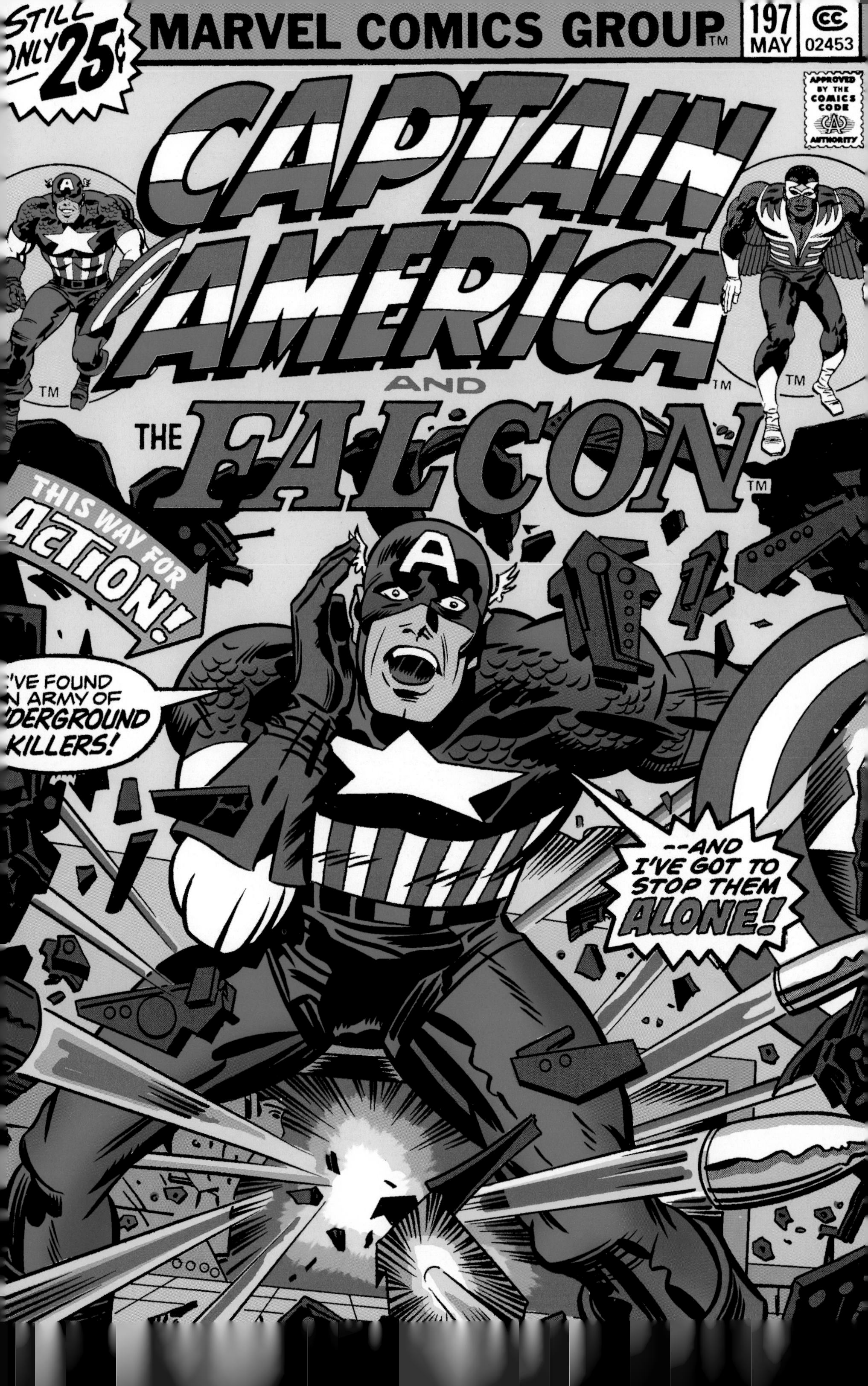
STILL ONLY 25¢
MARVEL COMICS GROUP™
197
MAY
CC
02453
APPROVED BY THE COMICS CODE AUTHORITY
CAPTAIN AMERICA
AND
THE FALCON™
THIS WAY FOR ACTION!
I'VE FOUND AN ARMY OF UNDERGROUND KILLERS!
--AND I'VE GOT TO STOP THEM ALONE!

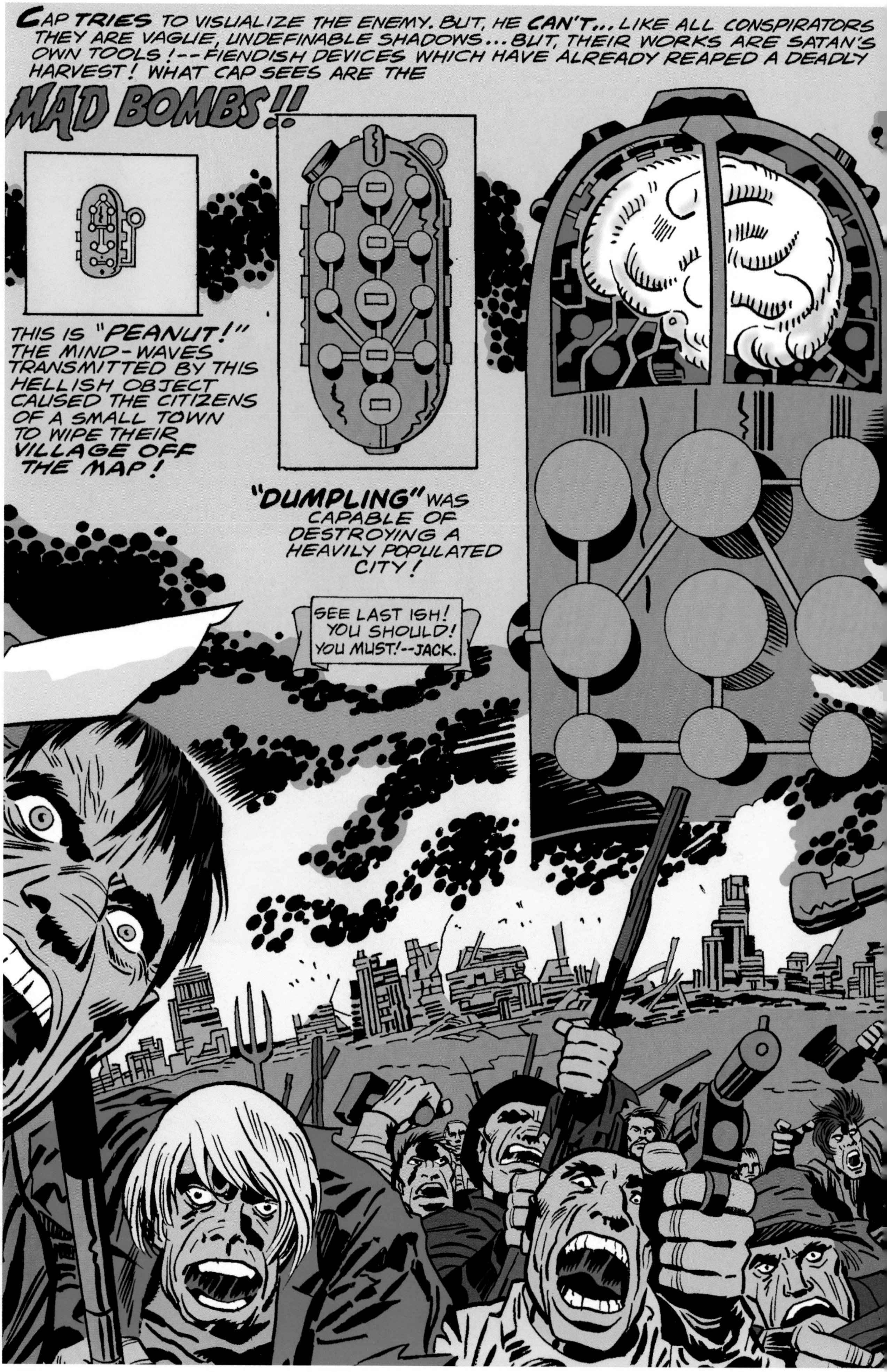
CAP TRIES TO VISUALIZE THE ENEMY. BUT, HE CAN'T... LIKE ALL CONSPIRATORS THEY ARE VAGUE, UNDEFINABLE SHADOWS... BUT, THEIR WORKS ARE SATAN'S OWN TOOLS! -- FIENDISH DEVICES WHICH HAVE ALREADY REAPED A DEADLY HARVEST! WHAT CAP SEES ARE THE
MAD BOMBS!!
THIS IS "PEANUT!" THE MIND-WAVES TRANSMITTED BY THIS HELLISH OBJECT CAUSED THE CITIZENS OF A SMALL TOWN TO WIPE THEIR VILLAGE OFF THE MAP!
"DUMPLING" WAS CAPABLE OF DESTROYING A HEAVILY POPULATED CITY!
SEE LAST ISH! YOU SHOULD! YOU MUST! --JACK.

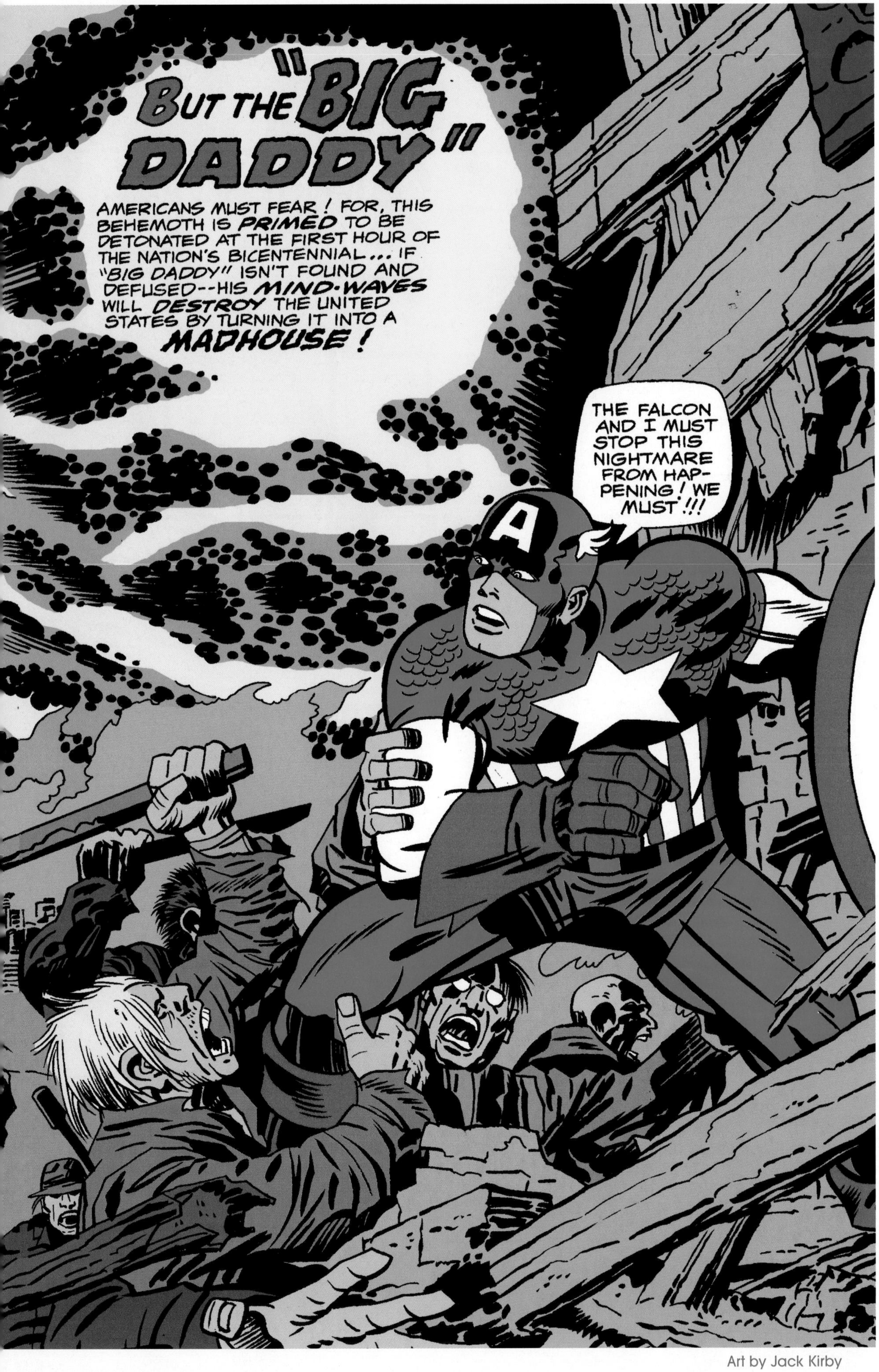

BUT THE "BIG DADDY"
AMERICANS MUST FEAR! FOR, THIS BEHEMOTH IS PRIMED TO BE DETONATED AT THE FIRST HOUR OF THE NATION'S BICENTENNIAL... IF "BIG DADDY" ISN'T FOUND AND DEFUSED--HIS MIND-WAVES WILL DESTROY THE UNITED STATES BY TURNING IT INTO A MADHOUSE!
THE FALCON AND I MUST STOP THIS NIGHTMARE FROM HAPPENING! WE MUST!!!


Art by Jack Kirby

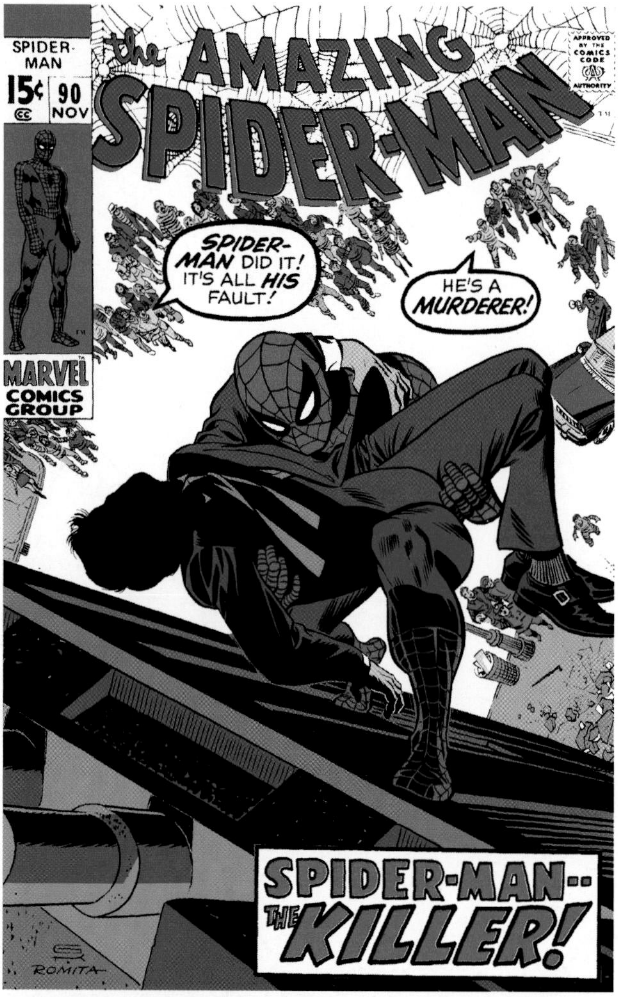
SPIDER-MAN
15¢ 90 NOV
APPROVED BY THE COMICS CODE AUTHORITY
the AMAZING SPIDER-MAN
MARVEL COMICS GROUP
SPIDER-MAN DID IT! IT'S ALL HIS FAULT!
HE'S A MURDERER!
SPIDER-MAN-- THE KILLER!
ROMITA

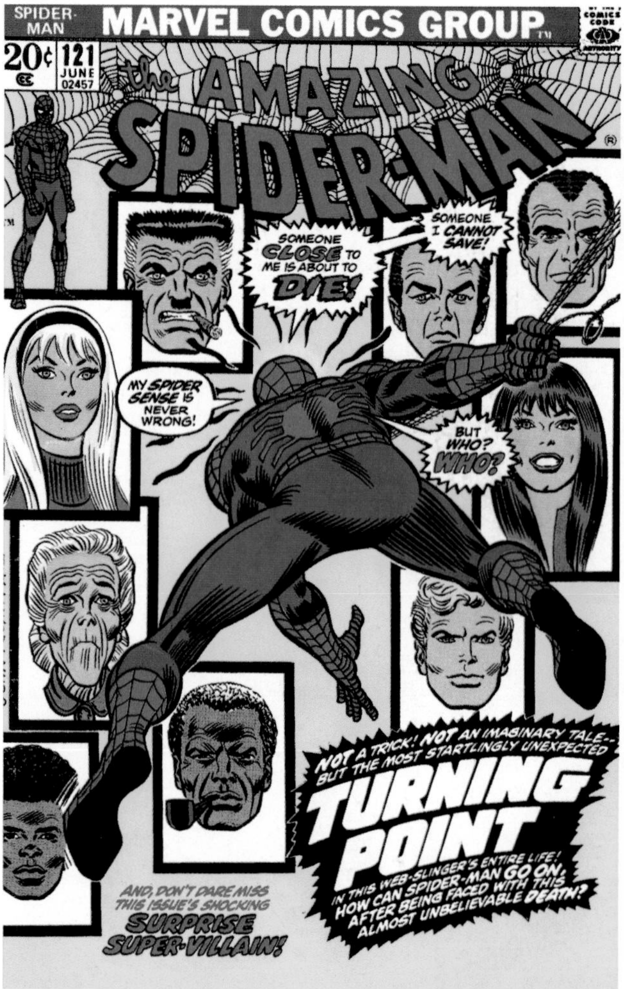
SPIDER-MAN
MARVEL COMICS GROUP
20¢ 121 JUNE 02457
the AMAZING SPIDER-MAN
SOMEONE CLOSE TO ME IS ABOUT TO DIE!
SOMEONE I CANNOT SAVE!
MY SPIDER SENSE IS NEVER WRONG!
BUT WHO? WHO?
NOT A TRICK! NOT AN IMAGINARY TALE-- BUT THE MOST STARTLINGLY UNEXPECTED
TURNING POINT
IN THIS WEB-SLINGER'S ENTIRE LIFE! HOW CAN SPIDER-MAN GO ON, AFTER BEING FACED WITH THIS ALMOST UNBELIEVABLE DEATH?
AND, DON'T DARE MISS THIS ISSUE'S SHOCKING SURPRISE SUPER-VILLAIN!

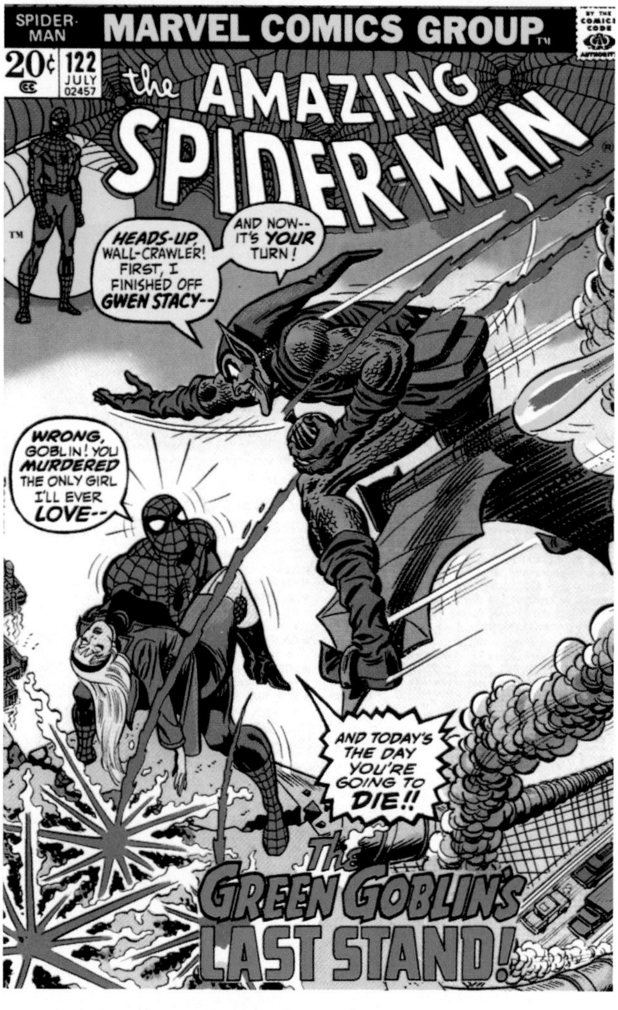
SPIDER-MAN
MARVEL COMICS GROUP
20¢ 122 JULY 02457
the AMAZING SPIDER-MAN
HEADS-UP, WALL-CRAWLER! FIRST, I FINISHED OFF GWEN STACY--
AND NOW-- IT'S YOUR TURN!
WRONG, GOBLIN! YOU MURDERED THE ONLY GIRL I'LL EVER LOVE--
AND TODAY'S THE DAY YOU'RE GOING TO DIE!!
The GREEN GOBLIN'S LAST STAND!

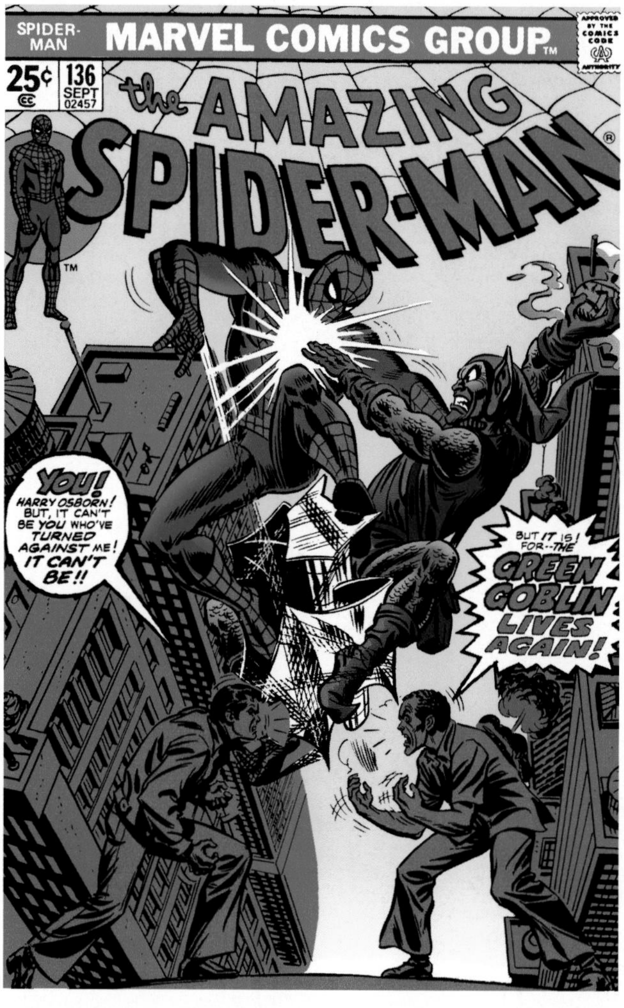
SPIDER-MAN
MARVEL COMICS GROUP
APPROVED BY THE COMICS CODE AUTHORITY
25¢ 136 SEPT 02457
the AMAZING SPIDER-MAN
YOU! HARRY OSBORN! BUT, IT CAN'T BE YOU WHO'VE TURNED AGAINST ME! IT CAN'T BE!!
BUT IT IS! FOR--THE GREEN GOBLIN LIVES AGAIN!

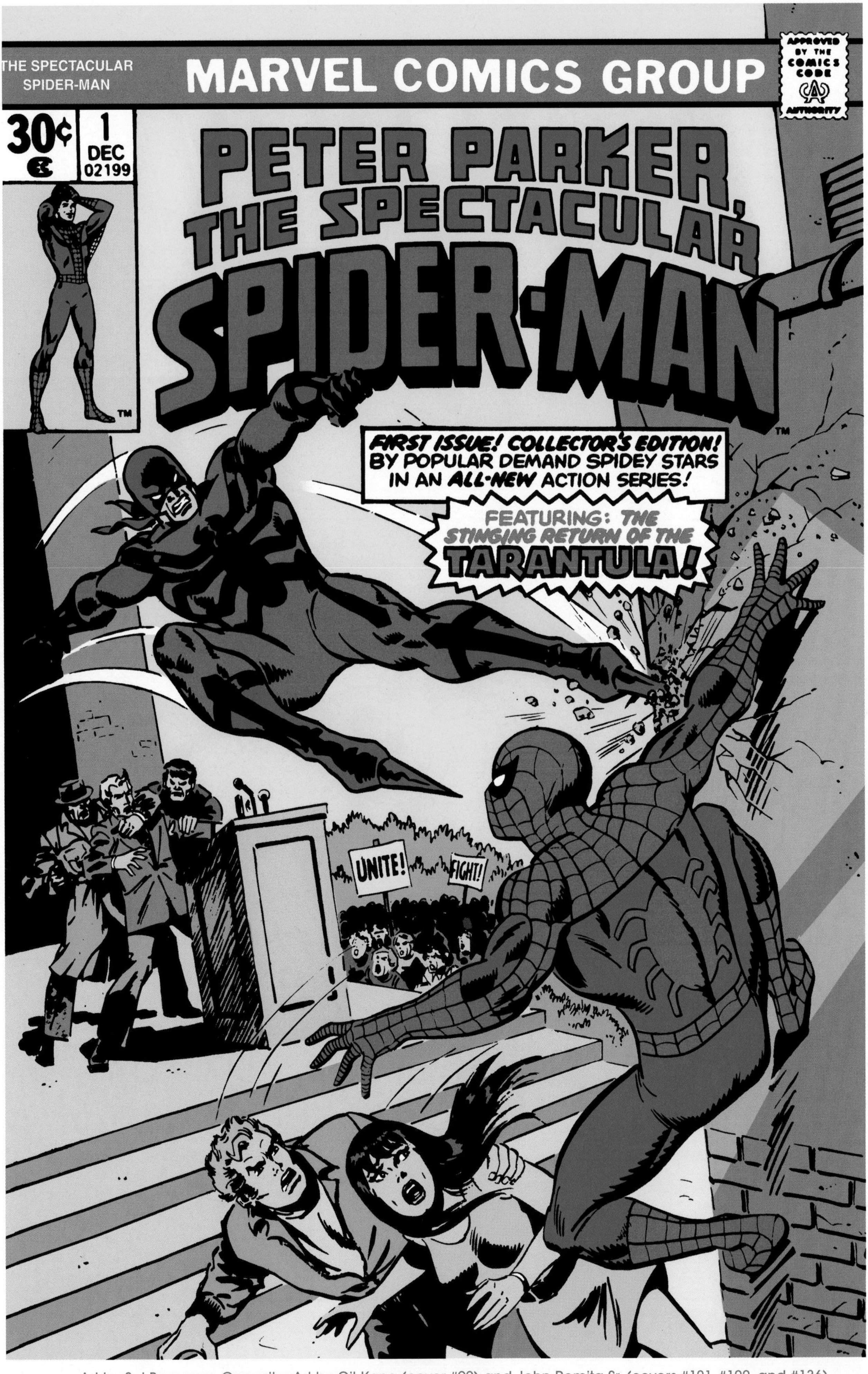
THE SPECTACULAR
SPIDER-MAN
MARVEL COMICS GROUP
APPROVED BY THE COMICS CODE AUTHORITY
30¢
1
DEC
02199
PETER PARKER, THE SPECTACULAR SPIDER-MAN
FIRST ISSUE! COLLECTOR'S EDITION! BY POPULAR DEMAND SPIDEY STARS IN AN ALL-NEW ACTION SERIES!
FEATURING: THE STINGING RETURN OF THE TARANTULA!
UNITE!
FIGHT!

Art by Sal Buscema. Opposite: Art by Gil Kane (cover #90) and John Romita Sr. (covers #121, #122, and #136).

Art by Gil Kane. Opposite: Art by Frank Brunner.

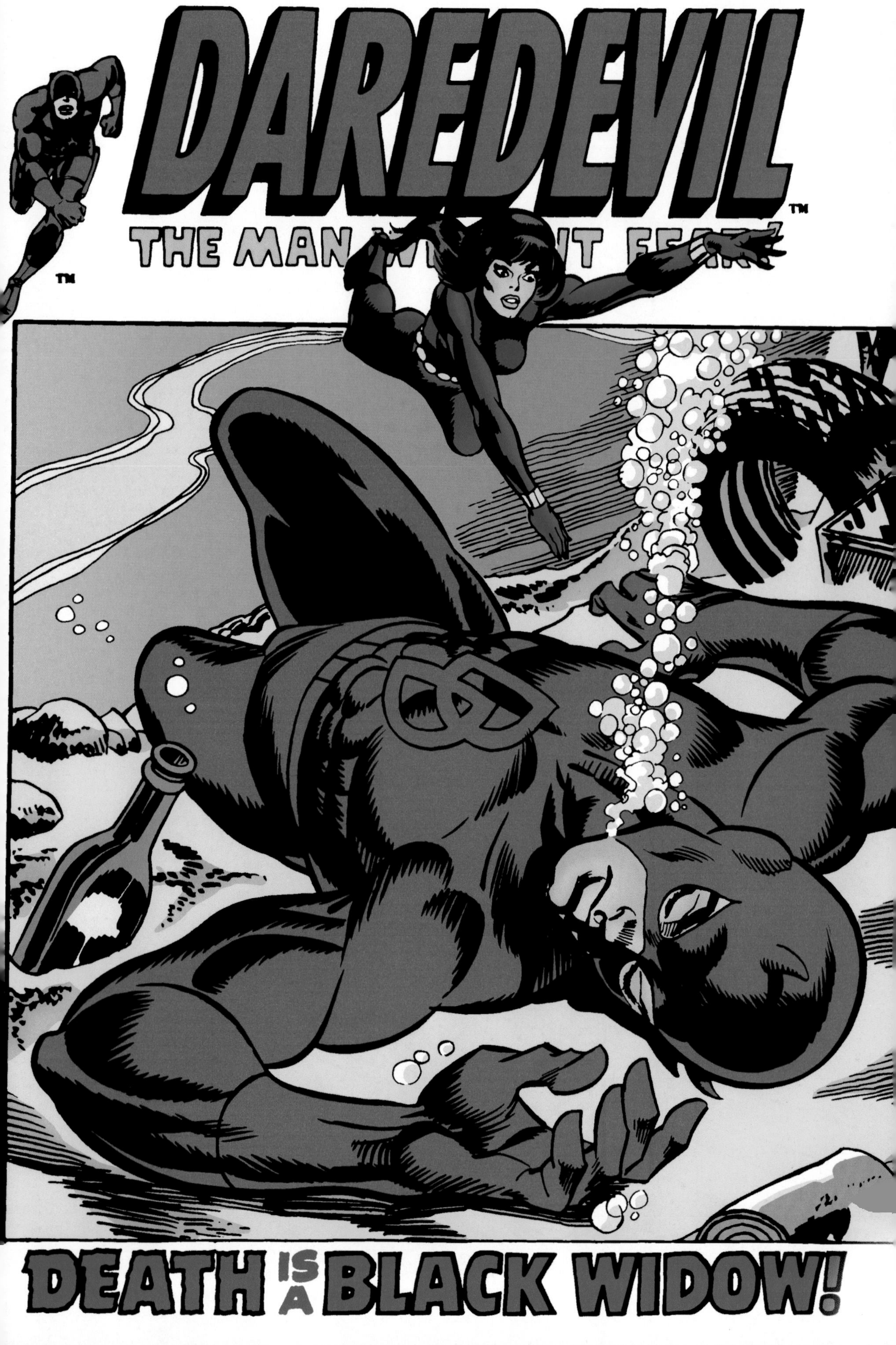
DAREDEVIL
THE MAN
DEATH IS A BLACK WIDOW!

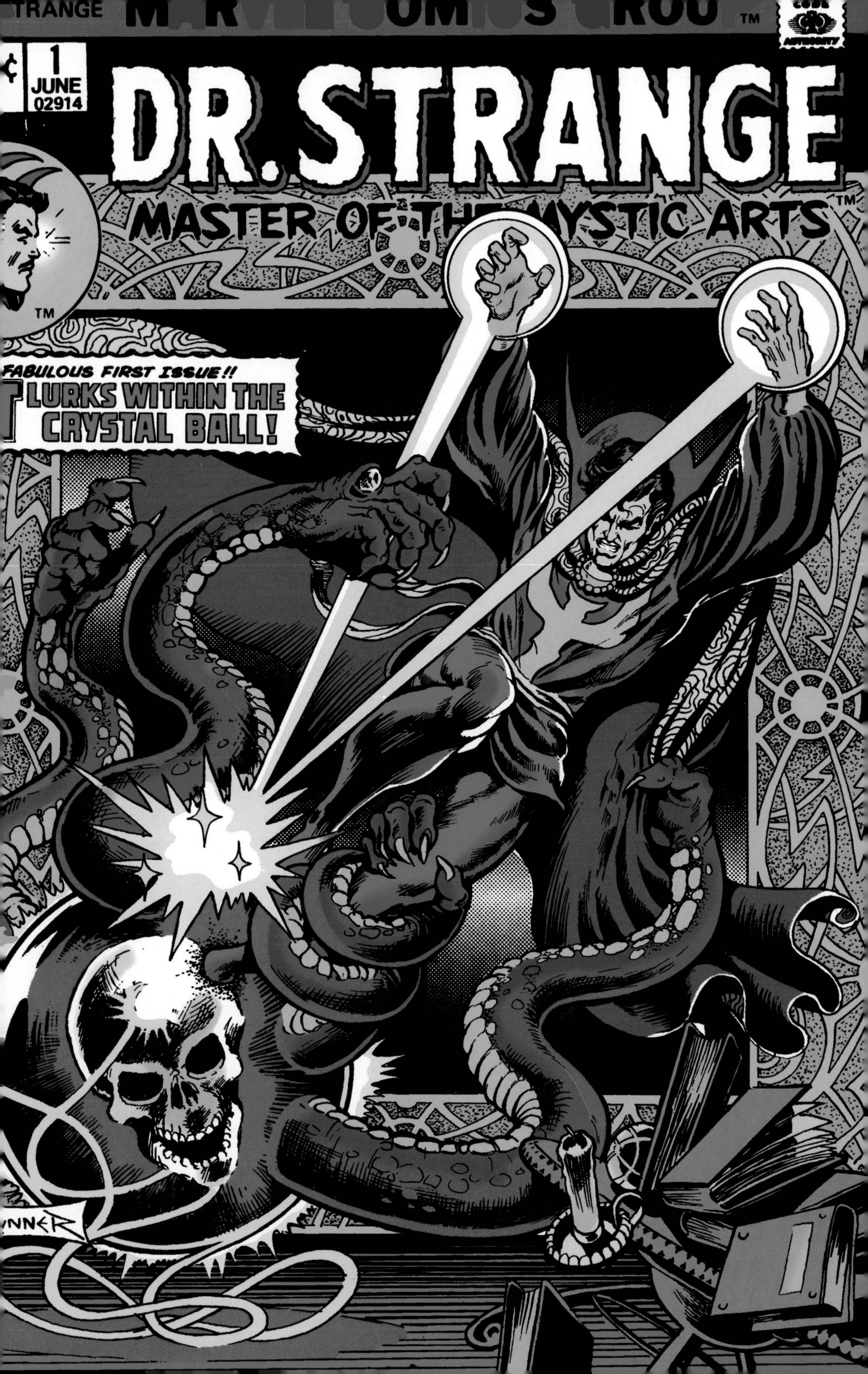

STRANGE
TM
1
JUNE
02914
DR. STRANGE
MASTER OF THE MYSTIC ARTS
TM
TM
FABULOUS FIRST ISSUE!!
LURKS WITHIN THE CRYSTAL BALL!

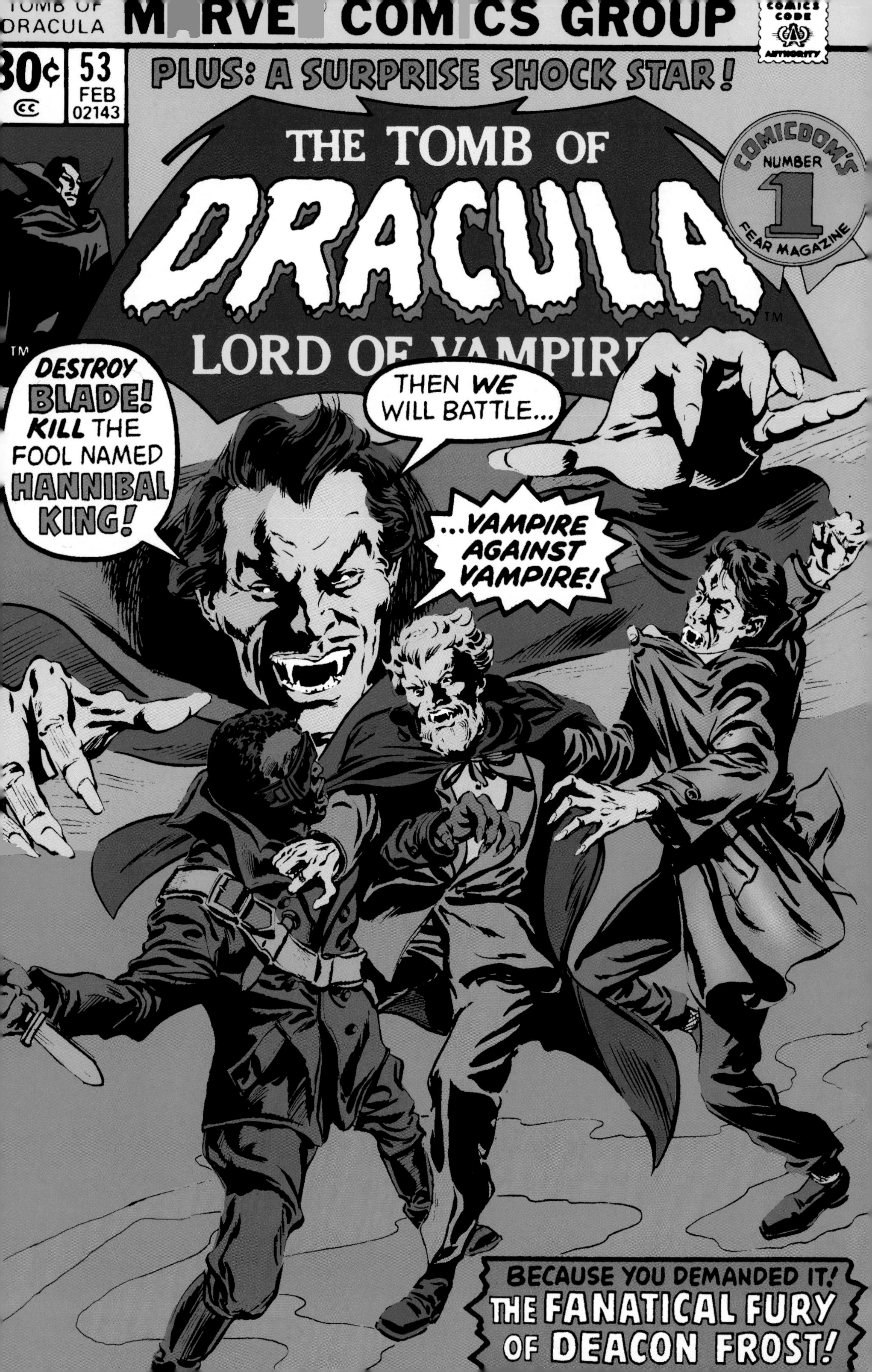
TOMB OF DRACULA
MARVEL COMICS GROUP
COMICS CODE AUTHORITY
30¢
53 FEB 02143
PLUS: A SURPRISE SHOCK STAR!
THE TOMB OF
DRACULA
LORD OF VAMPIRES
COMICDOM'S NUMBER 1 FEAR MAGAZINE
DESTROY BLADE! KILL THE FOOL NAMED HANNIBAL KING!
THEN WE WILL BATTLE...
...VAMPIRE AGAINST VAMPIRE!
BECAUSE YOU DEMANDED IT!
THE FANATICAL FURY OF DEACON FROST!

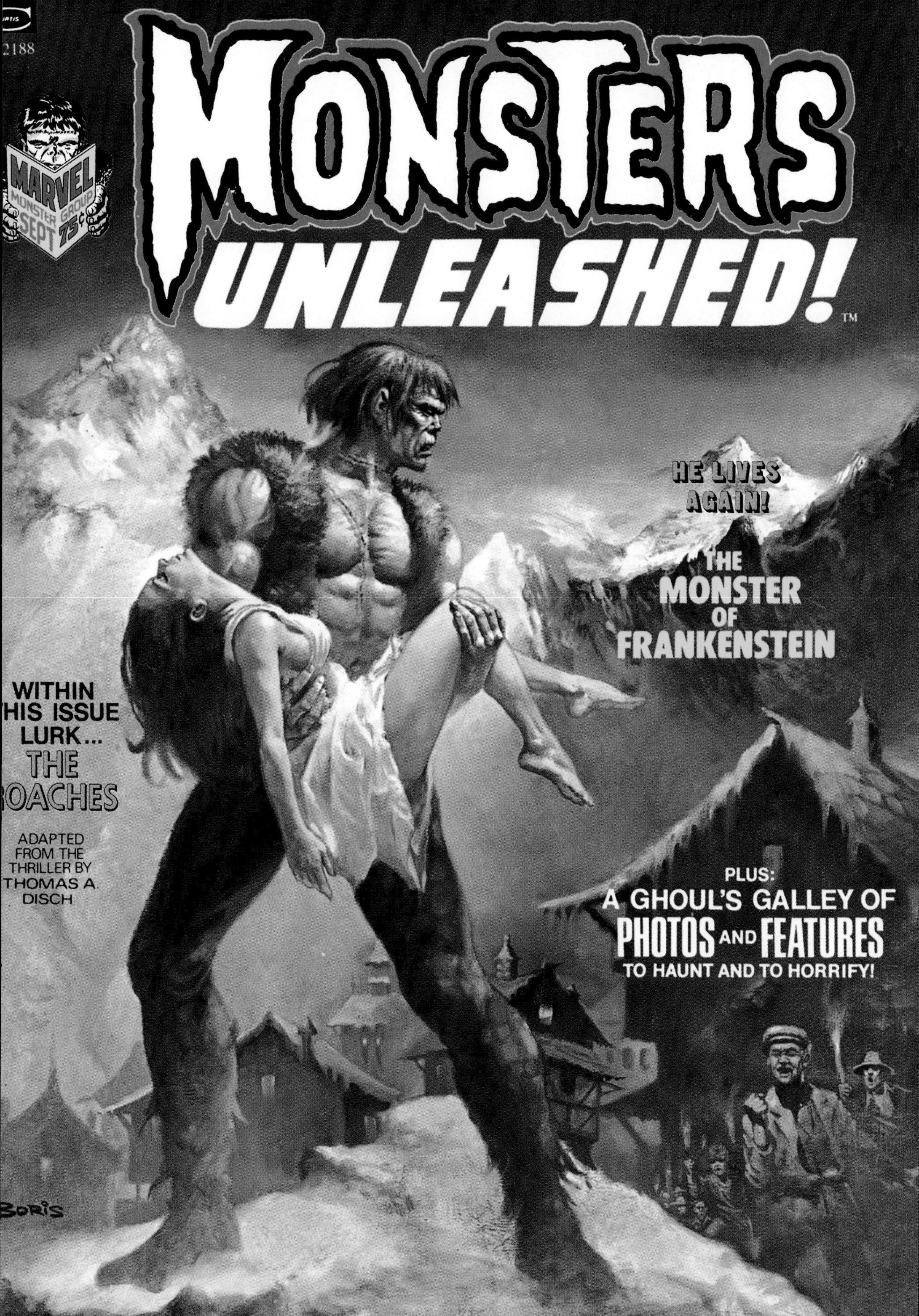

2188
MONSTERS
UNLEASHED!
TM
MARVEL
MONSTER GROUP
SEPT
75¢
HE LIVES AGAIN!
THE MONSTER OF FRANKENSTEIN
WITHIN
HIS ISSUE
LURK...
THE
OACHES
ADAPTED FROM THE THRILLER BY THOMAS A. DISCH
PLUS:
A GHOUL'S GALLEY OF
PHOTOS AND FEATURES
TO HAUNT AND TO HORRIFY!
BORIS

# 1980s

He's always been the best there is at what he does — and the man named Logan first staked his claim to the title of world's most famous mutant during the 1980s, when writer Chris Claremont teamed with artist Frank Miller to deliver the first-ever Wolverine solo series. Packed with realistic martial-arts-inspired action and intrigue, this is the landmark story that vaulted the feral X-Man to fan-favorite status.

Miller, meanwhile, became the driving force behind *Daredevil*, embarking on an historic three-year run that forever defined Marvel's Man Without Fear as the grim guardian devil of New York City's Hell's Kitchen. During his tenure on the title, Miller created the ninja assassin known as Elektra; her untimely demise at the hands of the hitman Bullseye left an indelible impression on fans everywhere — and on Daredevil himself, who had hoped to help his former lover reclaim her soul. Miller later resurrected the character in *Elektra: Assassin*, a groundbreaking graphic-novel collaboration with *New Mutants* artist Bill Sienkiewicz. And proving that lightning can strike twice, Miller returned to *Daredevil* later in the decade to write the "Born Again" storyline, illustrated by David Mazzucchelli — which many still consider the definitive Daredevil tale.

The X-Men continued their creative renaissance, under the guidance of Claremont and a host of equally visionary artistic collaborators — including John Byrne, Arthur Adams and Alan Davis, with whom the author also teamed on *Excalibur*.

Other visionary creators left a lasting impression, as well. Writer/artist Walter Simonson's work on *Thor* swept the Norse God of Thunder to heights never before seen and rarely achieved in his wake; writer/artist Byrne perfectly captured the intense mood, cosmic style and classic sense of adventure of *Fantastic Four*; and artist Mike Zeck — also famous for adding heft to the likes of Captain America, Wolverine and Spider-Man — took aim at the Punisher with writer Steven Grant, setting the vengeance-seeking vigilante down his own dark path.

The '80s also saw the debut of fresh talents that would propel Marvel into the next decade and beyond. In the mid 1960s, legendary illustrator John Romita Sr. established Spider-Man's distinctive look, setting an artistic trend that would remain consistent for more than two decades. In the late '80s, Todd McFarlane boldly redefined the web-slinger's appearance. It was during McFarlane's run on *Amazing Spider-Man* that a new villain — Venom — challenged the popularity of Spider-Man's classic foes. *Amazing* soon doubled its circulation, becoming Marvel's first biweekly comics magazine.

Art by Alex Ross. Opposite: *Wolverine #1* cover by Frank Miller.

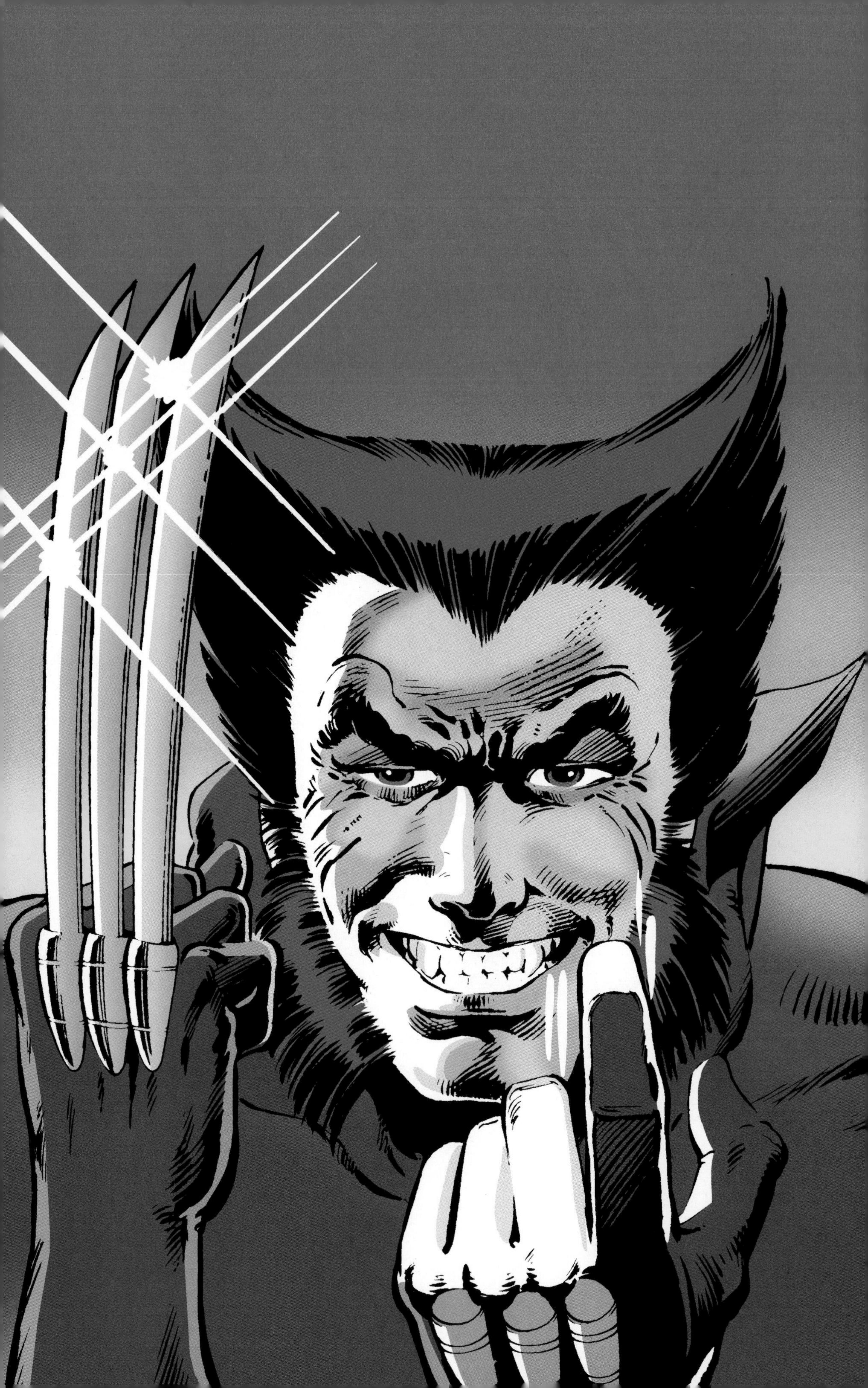

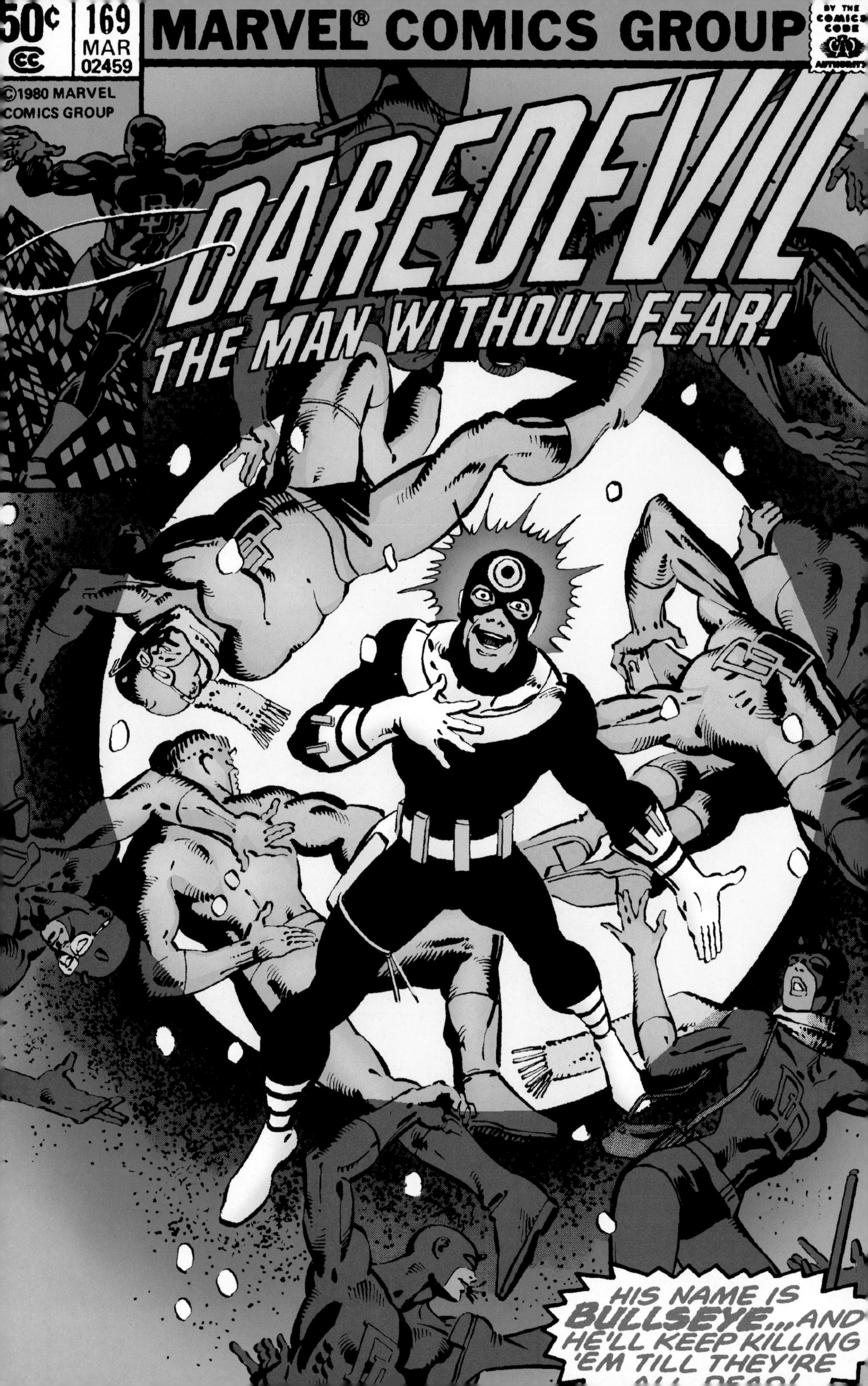
50¢
169
MAR
02459
MARVEL® COMICS GROUP
BY THE COMICS CODE AUTHORITY
©1980 MARVEL COMICS GROUP
DAREDEVIL
THE MAN WITHOUT FEAR!
HIS NAME IS BULLSEYE... AND HE'LL KEEP KILLING 'EM TILL THEY'RE

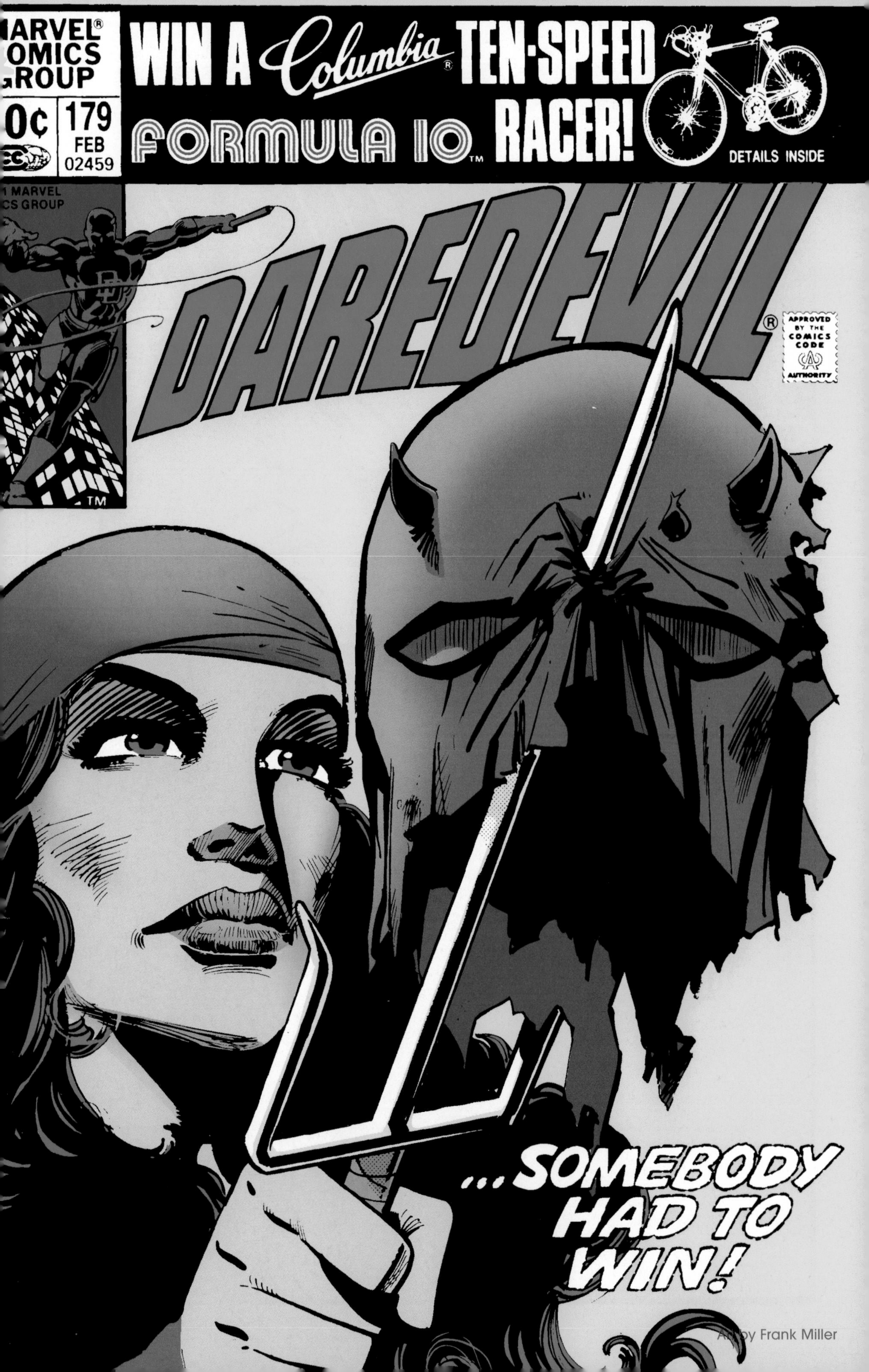
ARVEL® OMICS ROUP
0¢
179
FEB
02459
WIN A Columbia® TEN-SPEED
FORMULA 10™ RACER!
DETAILS INSIDE
DAREDEVIL®
APPROVED BY THE COMICS CODE AUTHORITY
...SOMEBODY HAD TO WIN!

Art by Frank Miller

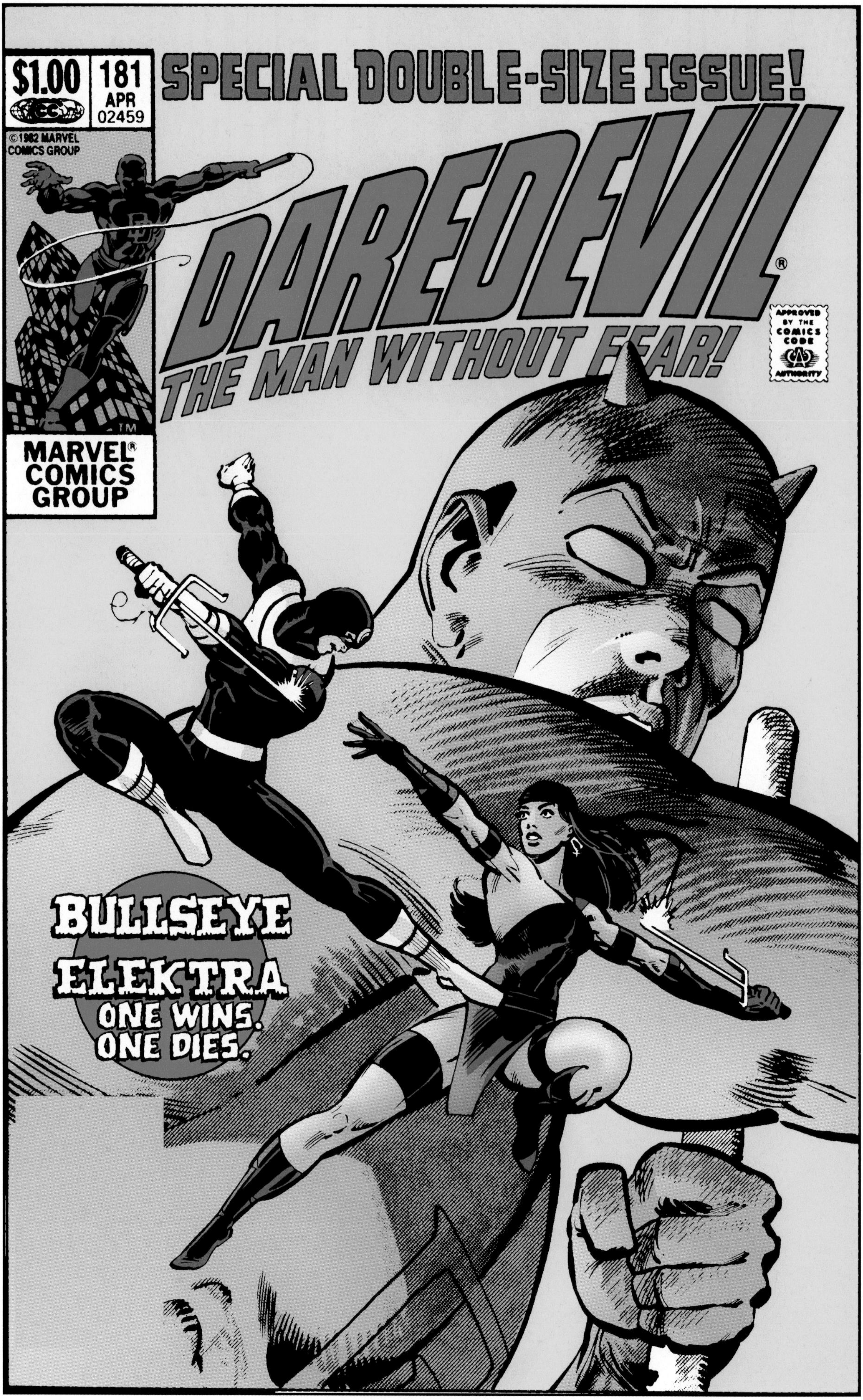
$1.00
181
APR
02459
©1982 MARVEL COMICS GROUP
SPECIAL DOUBLE-SIZE ISSUE!
DAREDEVIL
THE MAN WITHOUT FEAR!
MARVEL COMICS GROUP
APPROVED BY THE COMICS CODE AUTHORITY
BULLSEYE
ELEKTRA
ONE WINS.
ONE DIES.

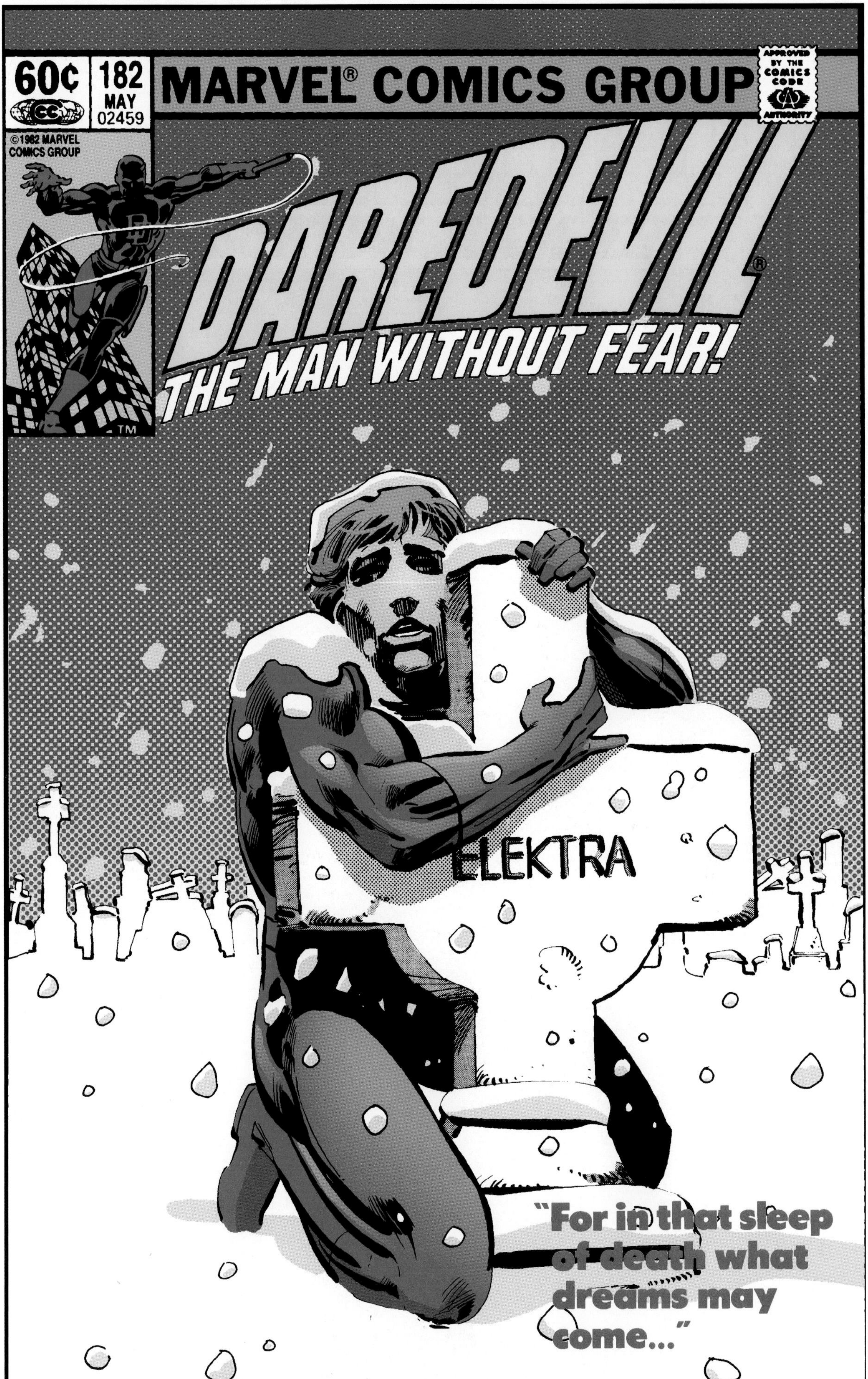

60¢
182
MAY
02459
MARVEL® COMICS GROUP
APPROVED BY THE COMICS CODE AUTHORITY
©1982 MARVEL COMICS GROUP
DAREDEVIL®
THE MAN WITHOUT FEAR!
TM
ELEKTRA
"For in that sleep of death what dreams may come..."


Art by Frank Miller

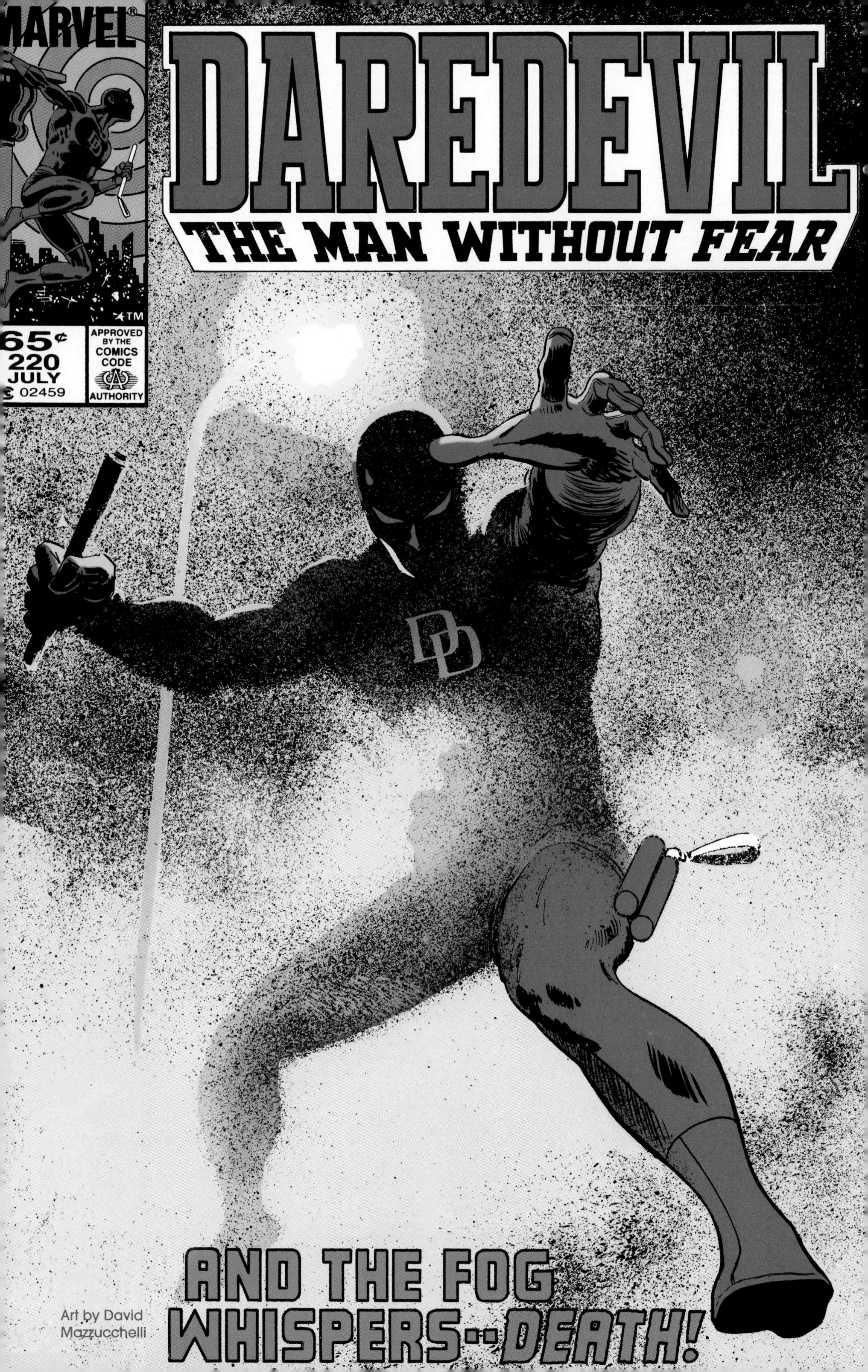
MARVEL®
DAREDEVIL
THE MAN WITHOUT FEAR
TM
65¢
220
JULY
02459
APPROVED BY THE COMICS CODE AUTHORITY
AND THE FOG WHISPERS--DEATH!
Art by David Mazzucchelli

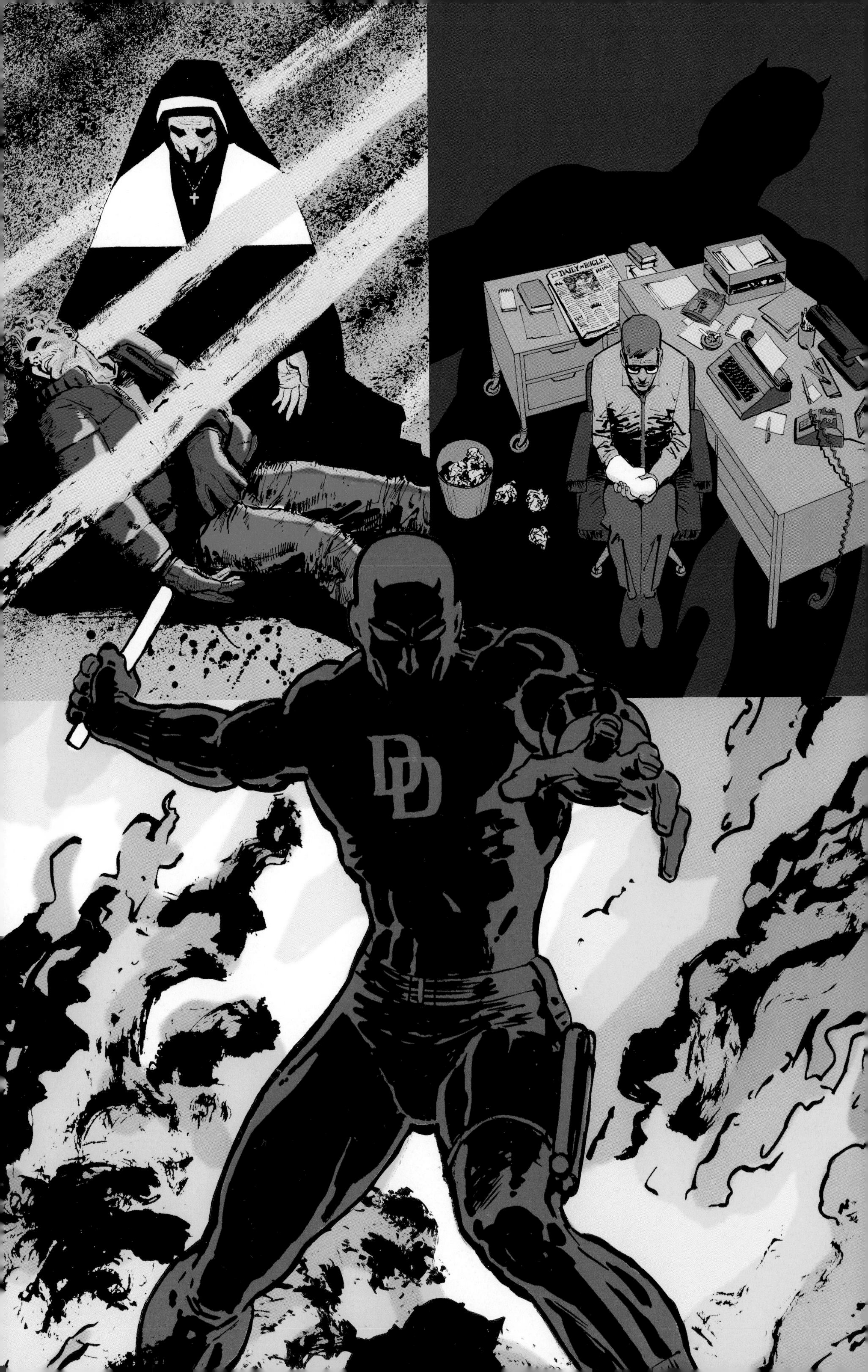
DAILY BUGLE

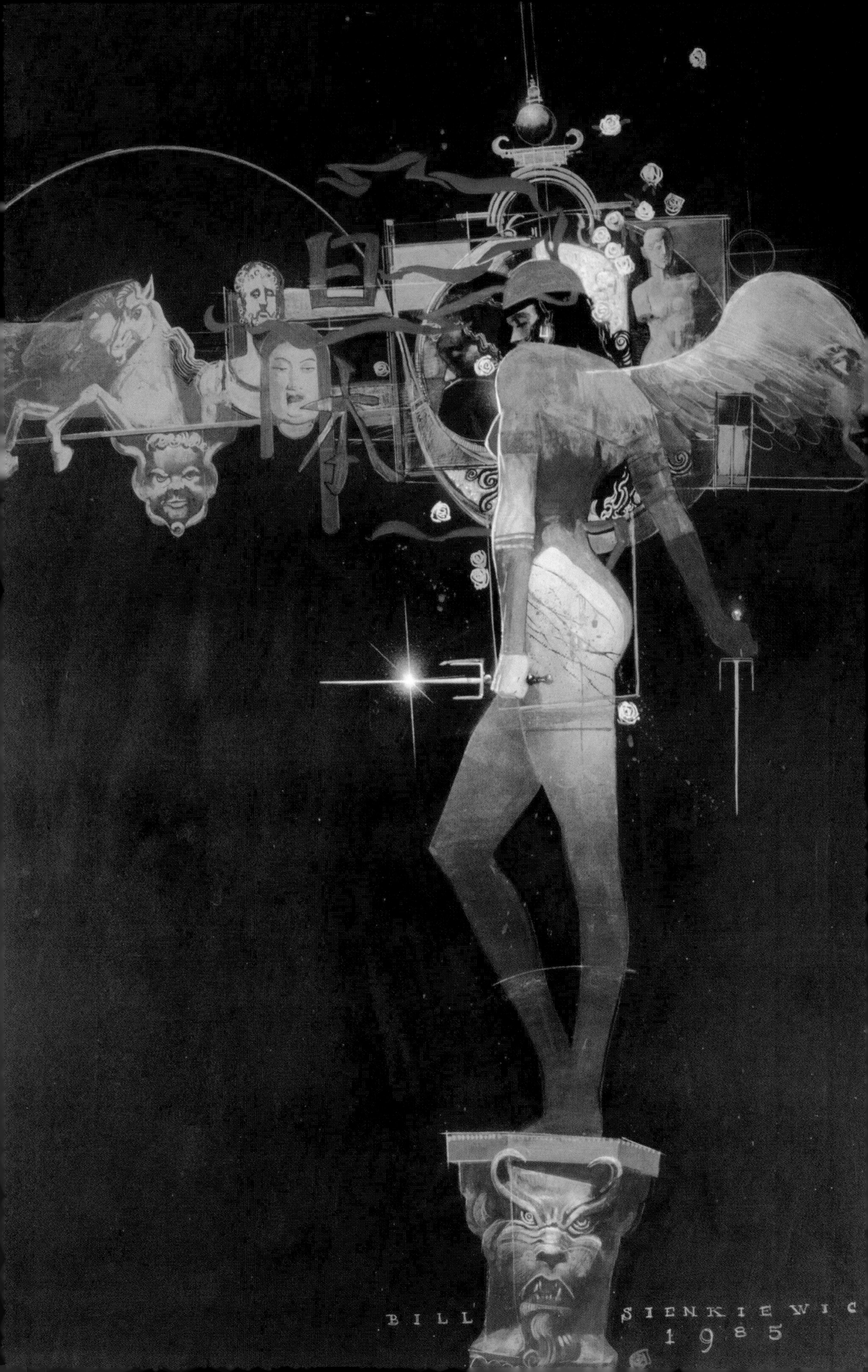
BILL SIENKIEWICZ
1985

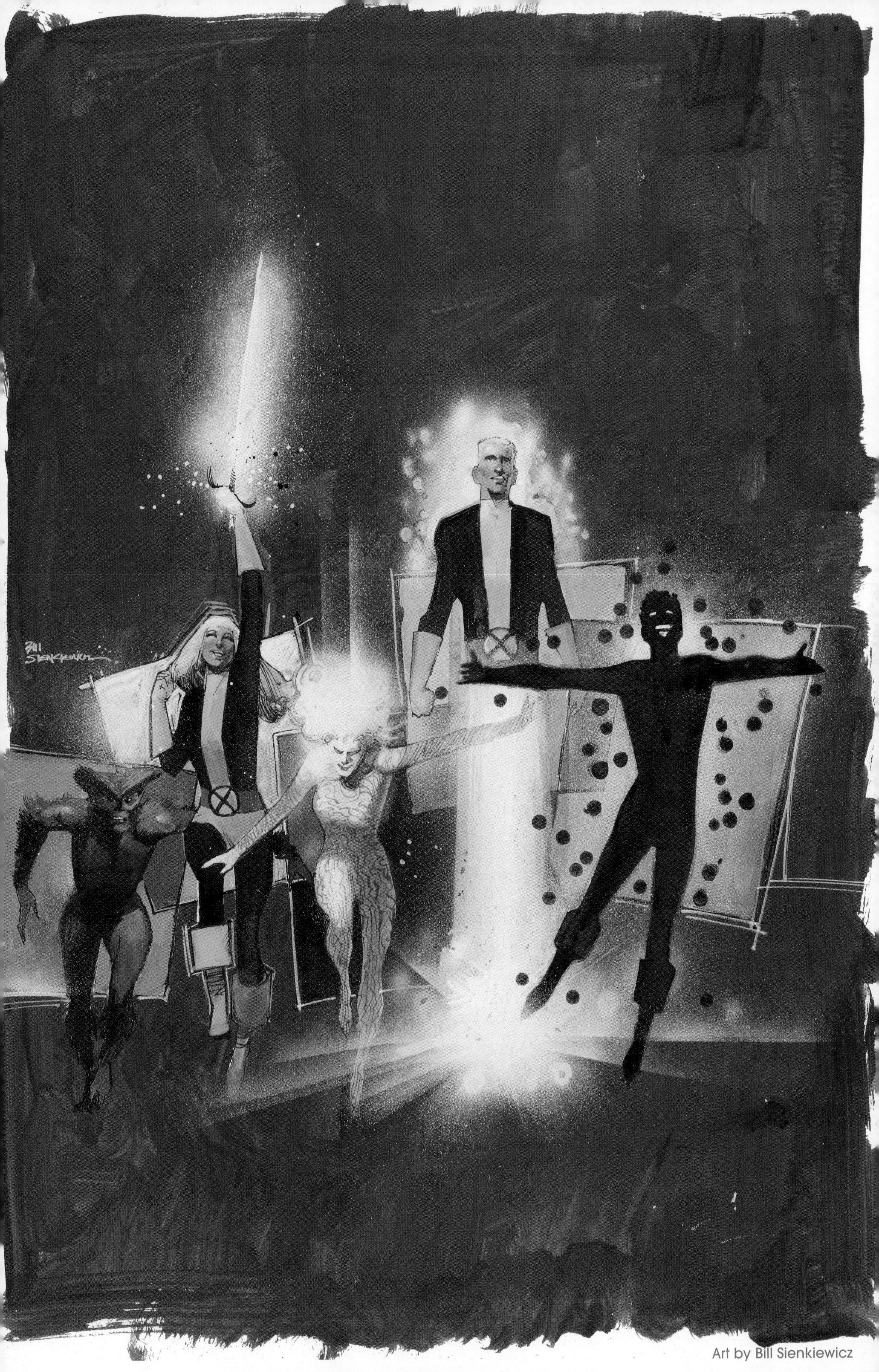
BILL SIENKIEWICZ

Art by Bill Sienkiewicz

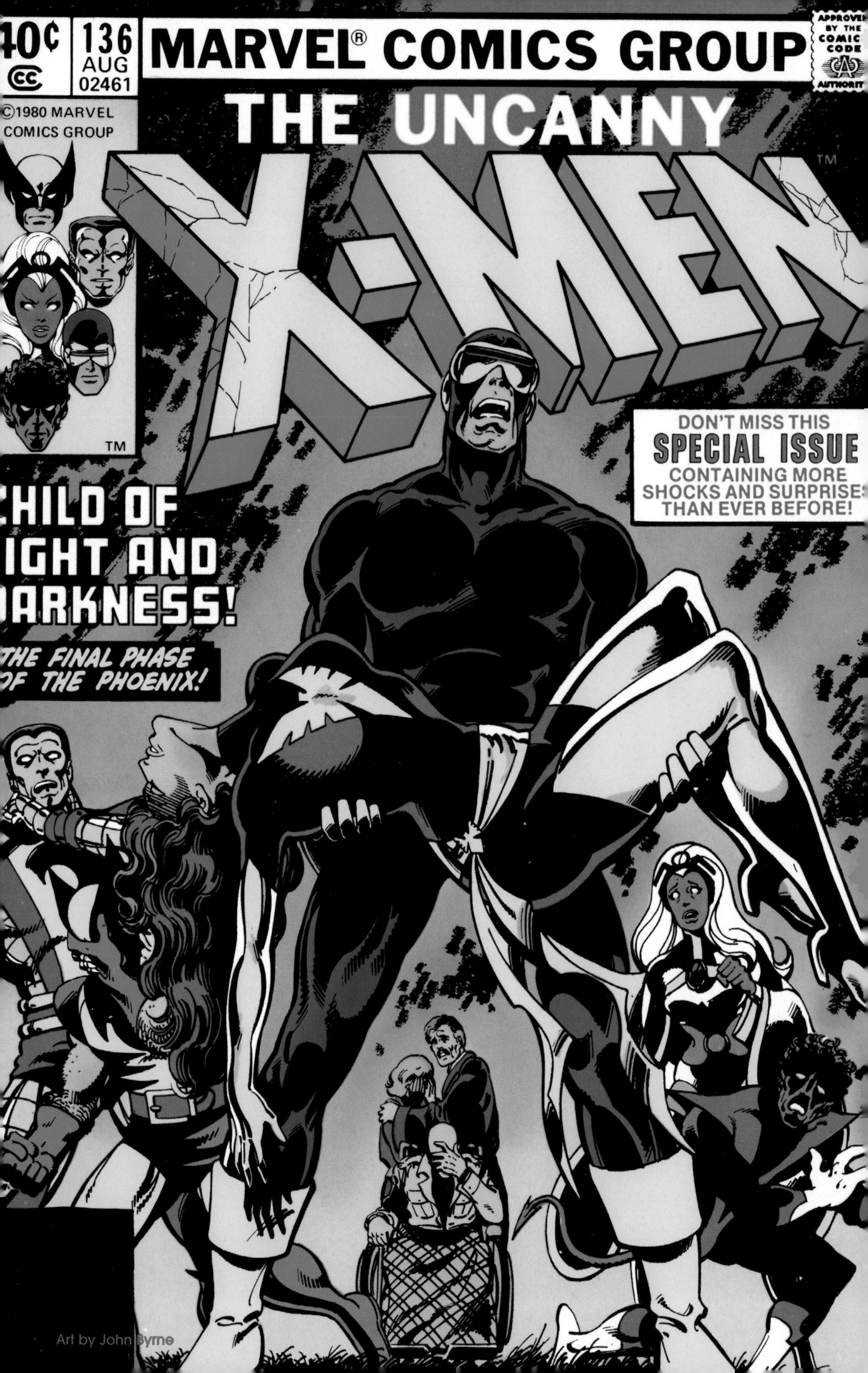
40¢
136
AUG
02461
MARVEL® COMICS GROUP
APPROVED BY THE COMIC CODE AUTHORITY
©1980 MARVEL COMICS GROUP
THE UNCANNY
X-MEN™
TM
DON'T MISS THIS
SPECIAL ISSUE
CONTAINING MORE
SHOCKS AND SURPRISES
THAN EVER BEFORE!
CHILD OF LIGHT AND DARKNESS!
THE FINAL PHASE OF THE PHOENIX!

Art by John Byrne

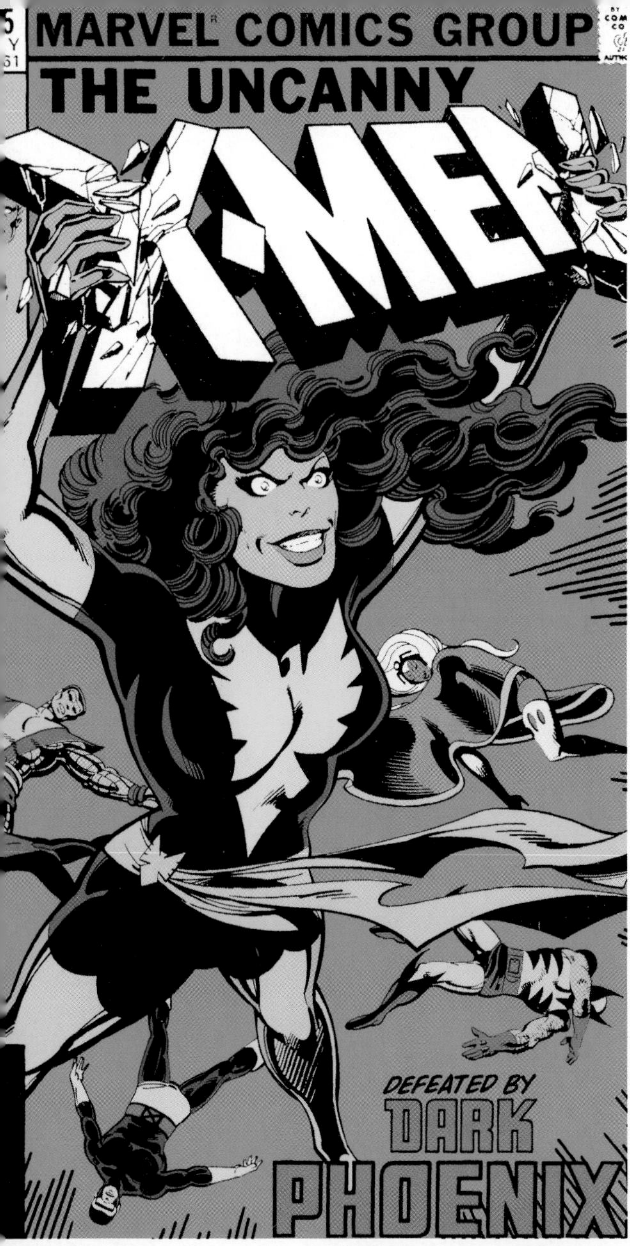
MARVEL COMICS GROUP
THE UNCANNY
X-MEN
DEFEATED BY
DARK
PHOENIX

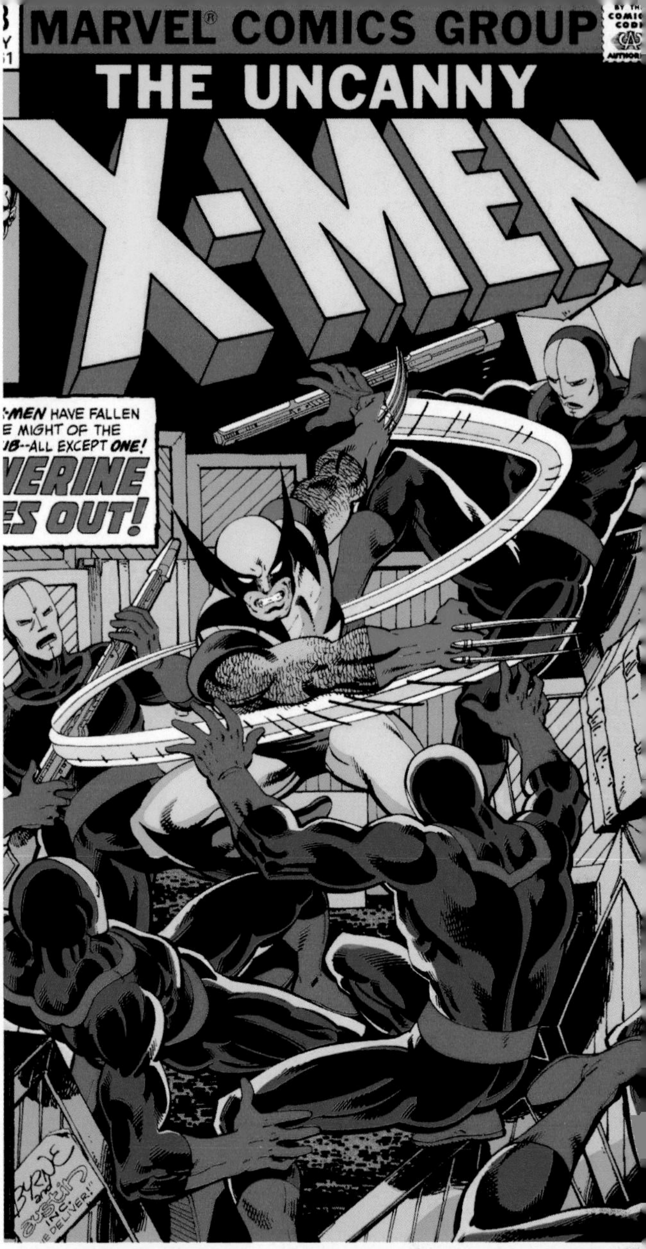
MARVEL COMICS GROUP
THE UNCANNY
X-MEN
HAVE FALLEN
MIGHT OF THE
ALL EXCEPT ONE!

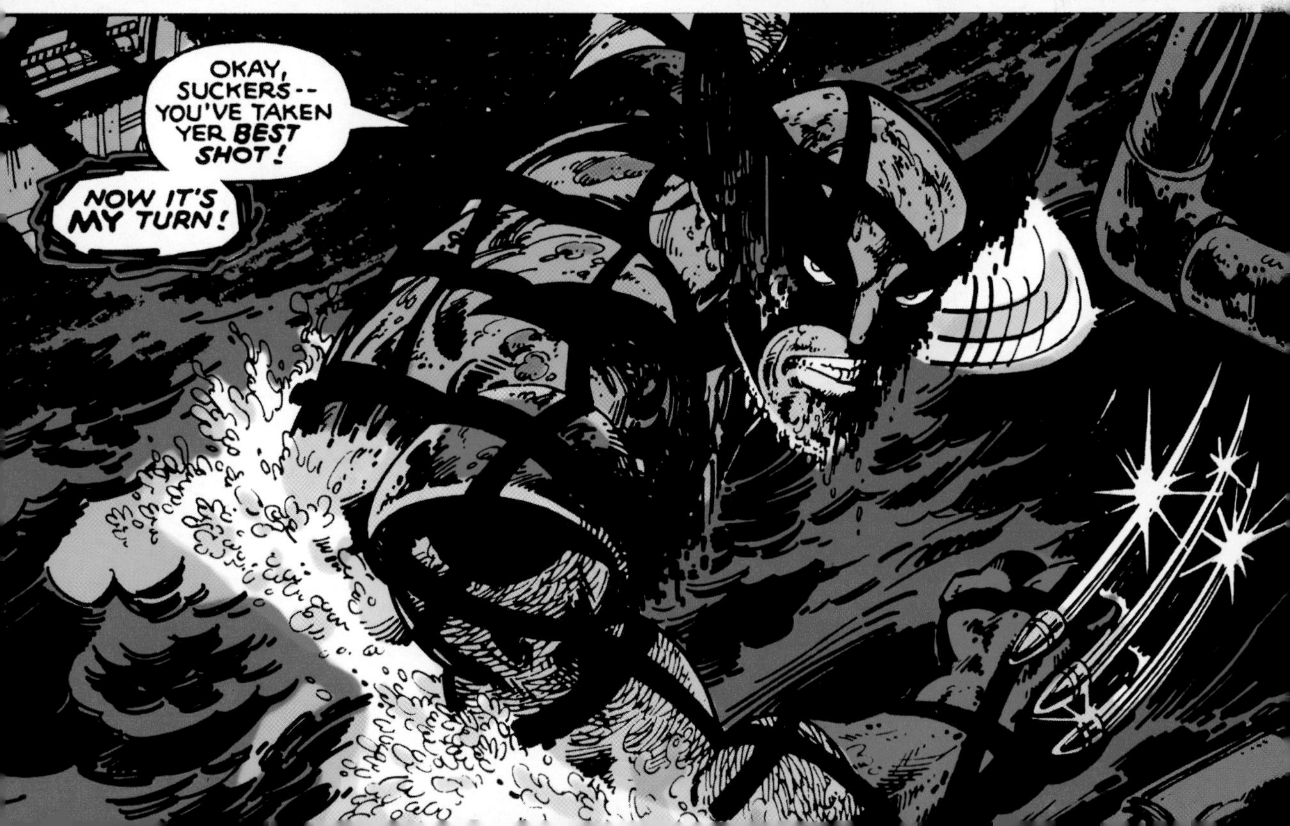
OKAY, SUCKERS-- YOU'VE TAKEN YER BEST SHOT!
NOW IT'S MY TURN!

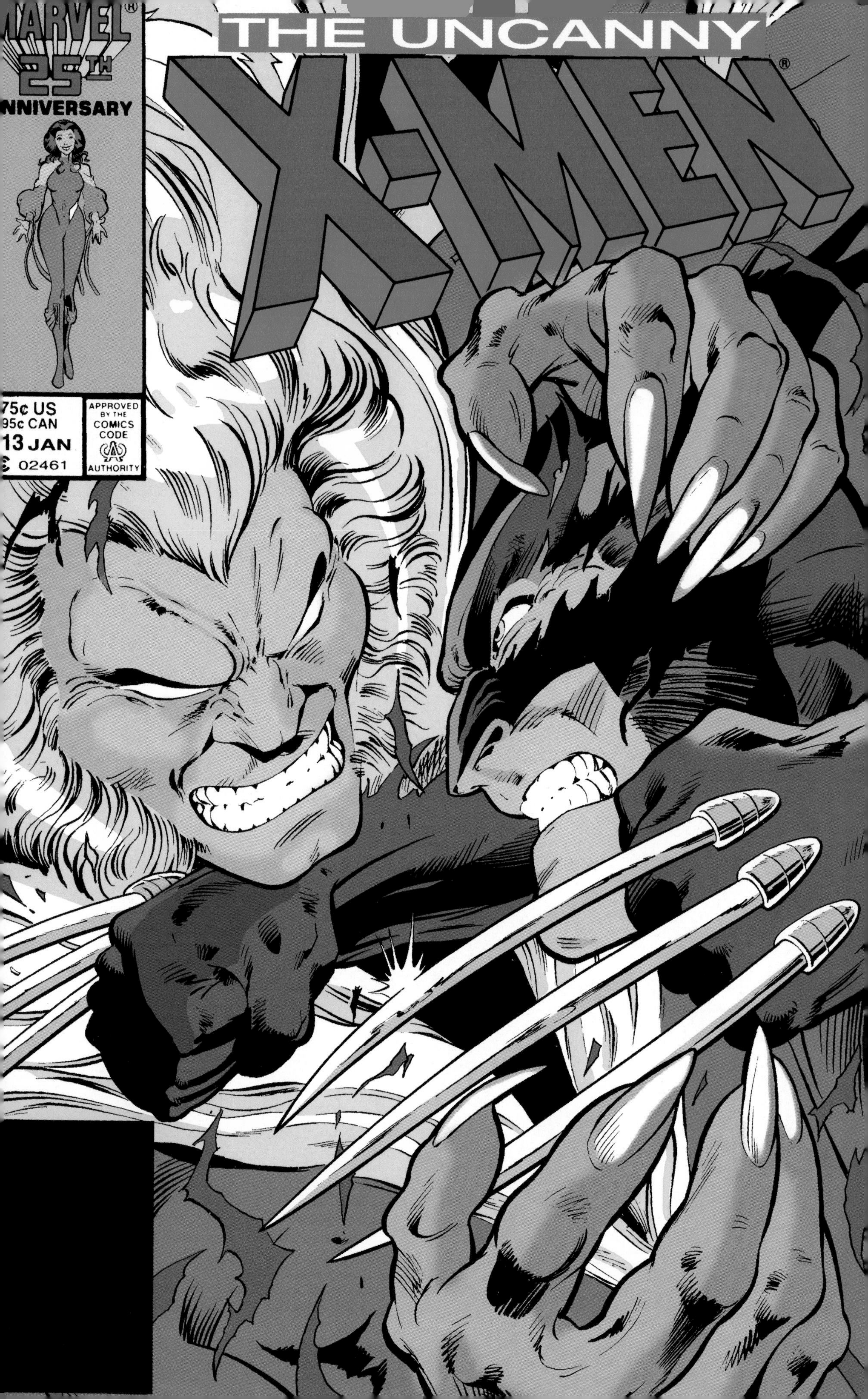
MARVEL
25TH ANNIVERSARY
THE UNCANNY
X-MEN
75¢ US
95¢ CAN
13 JAN
02461
APPROVED BY THE COMICS CODE AUTHORITY

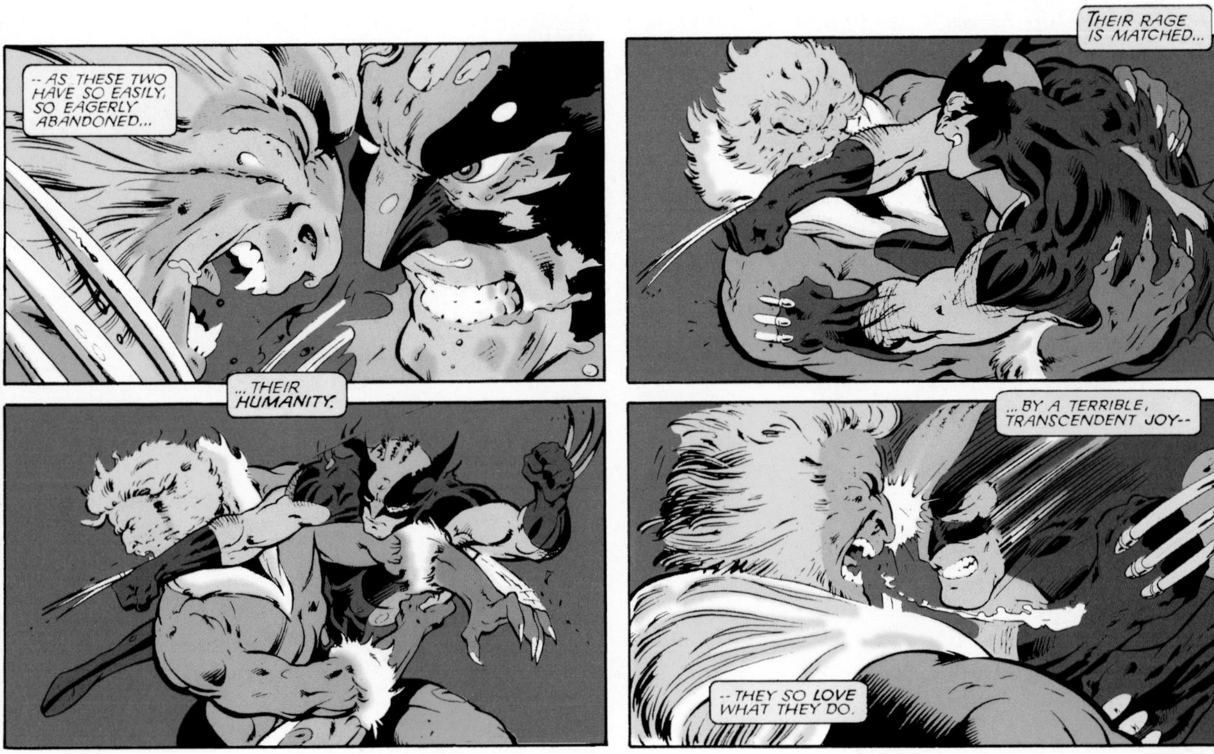
-- AS THESE TWO HAVE SO EASILY, SO EAGERLY ABANDONED...
THEIR RAGE IS MATCHED...
...THEIR HUMANITY.
...BY A TERRIBLE, TRANSCENDENT JOY--
--THEY SO LOVE WHAT THEY DO.

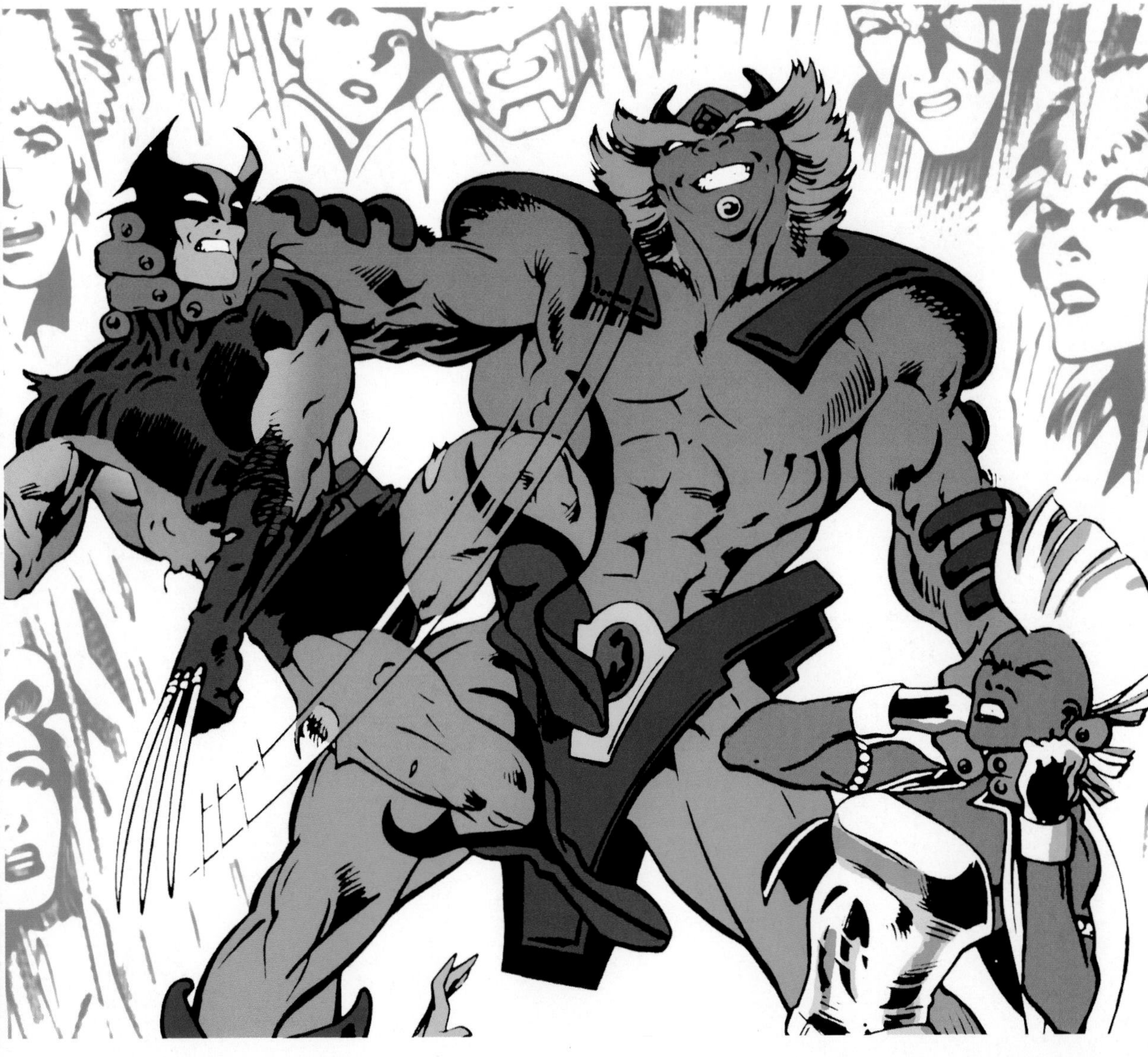

Art by Alan Davis

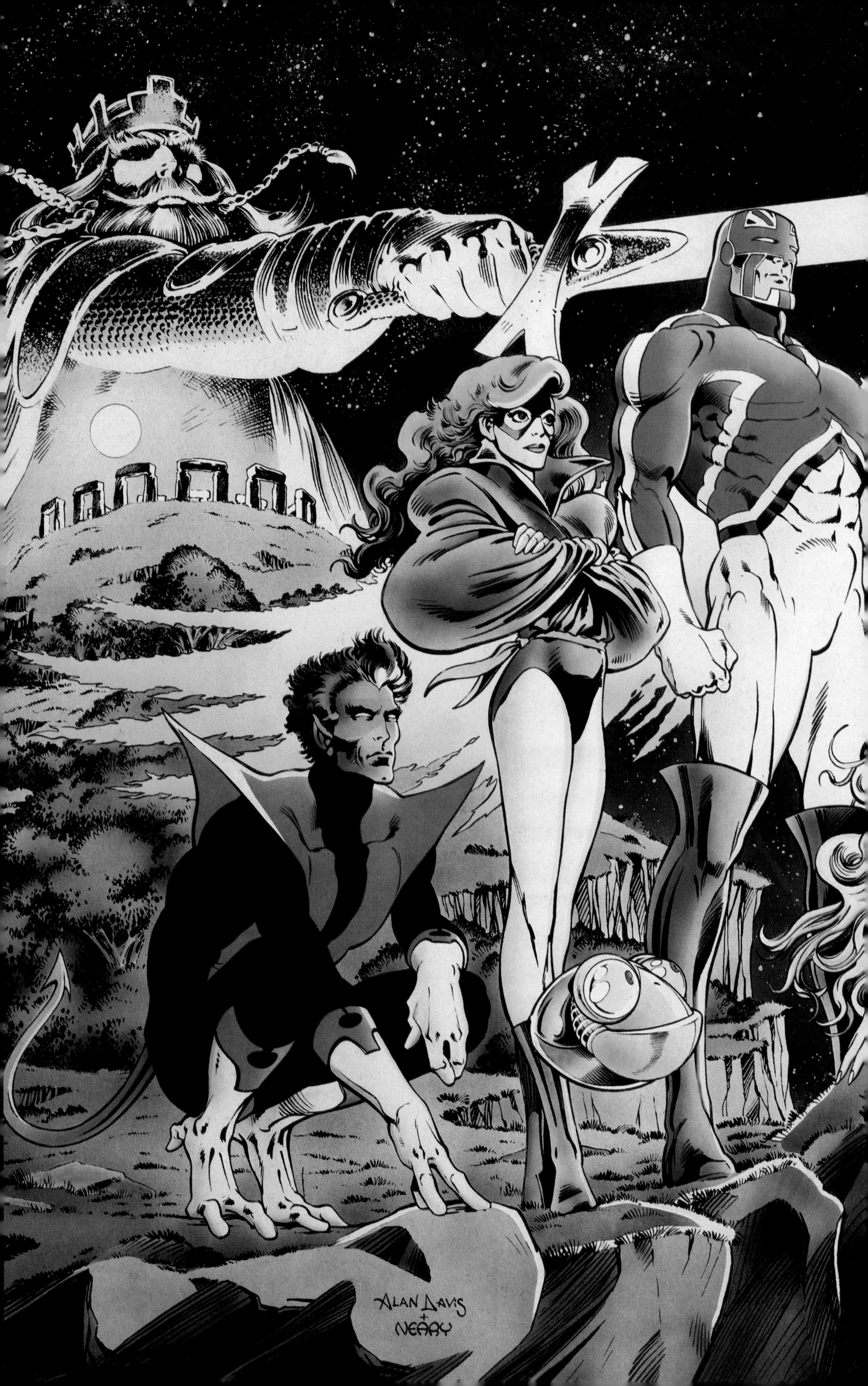
ALAN DAVIS
+
NEARY

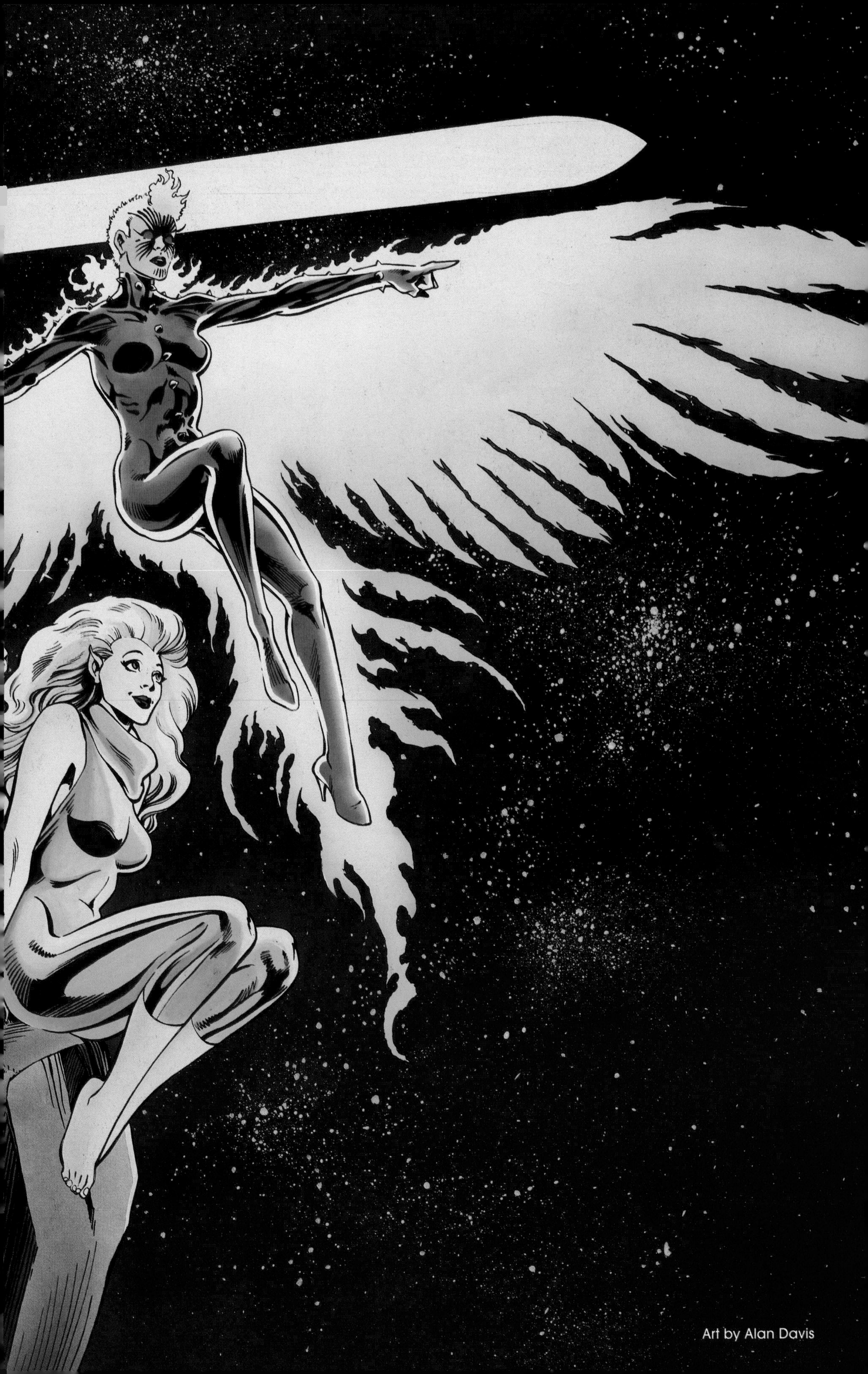

Art by Alan Davis

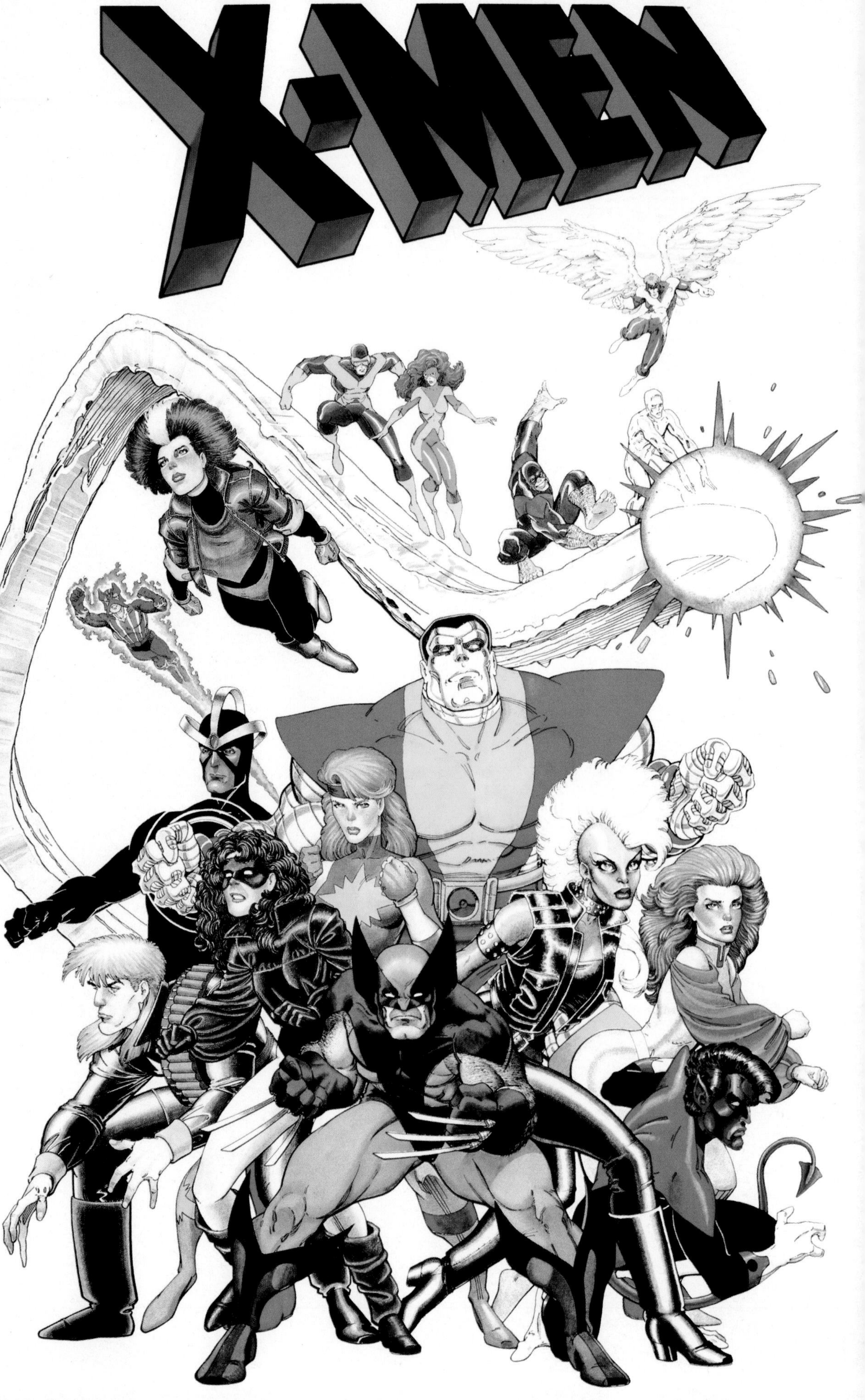
X-MEN

Art by Arthur Adams

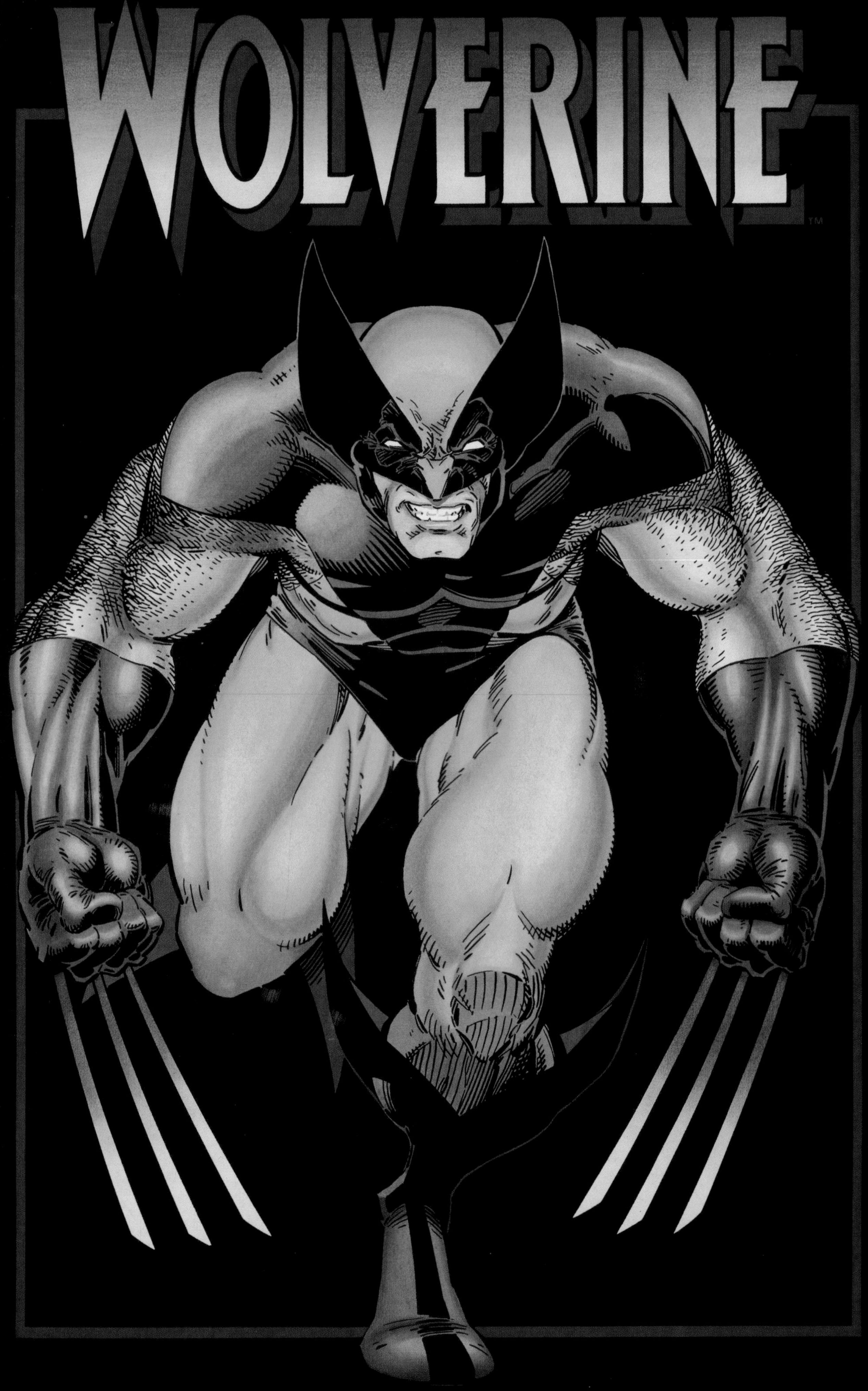
WOLVERINE™

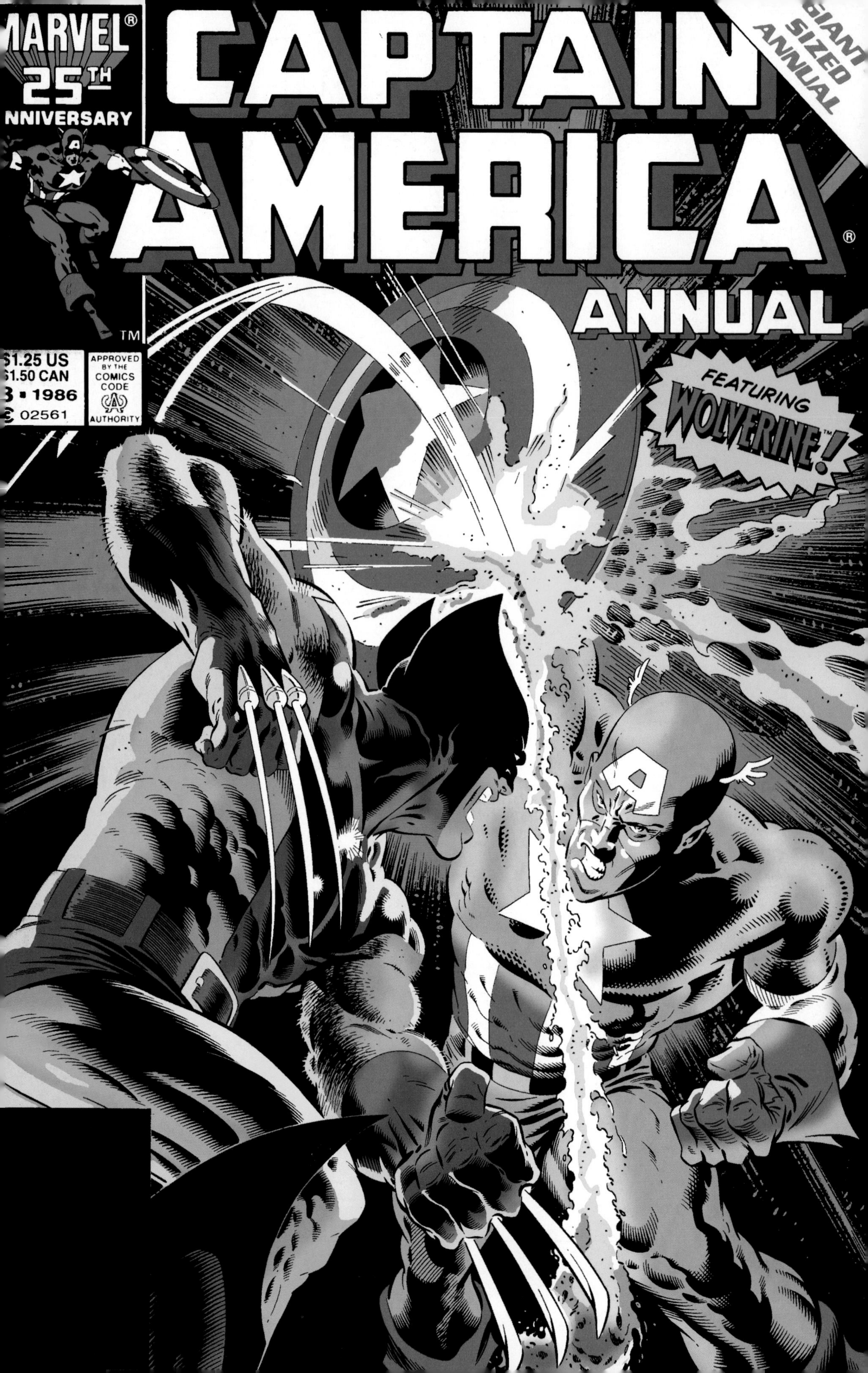
MARVEL
25TH ANNIVERSARY
CAPTAIN AMERICA
ANNUAL
GIANT SIZED ANNUAL
$1.25 US
$1.50 CAN
8 • 1986
02561
APPROVED BY THE COMICS CODE AUTHORITY
FEATURING WOLVERINE!

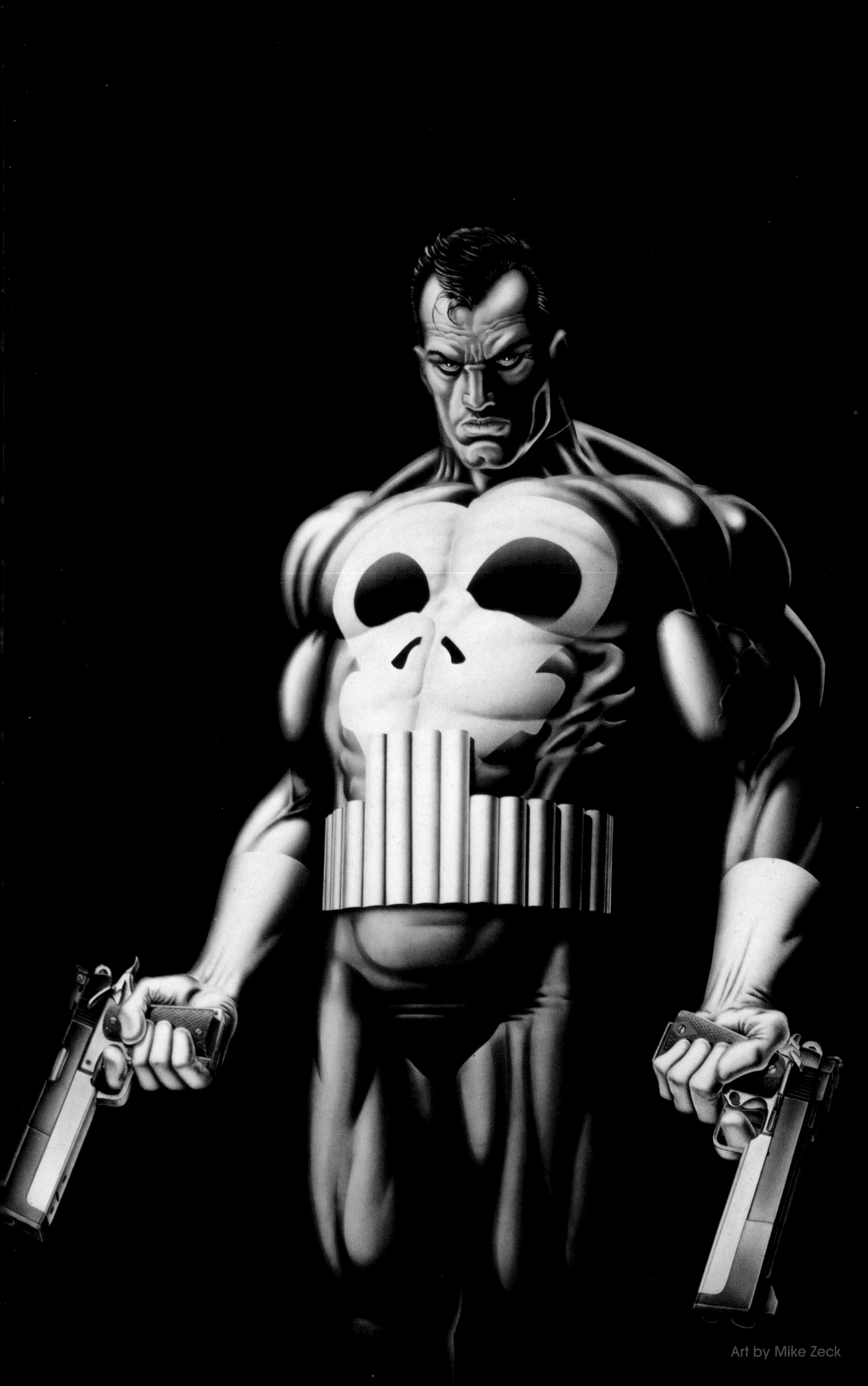

Art by Mike Zeck

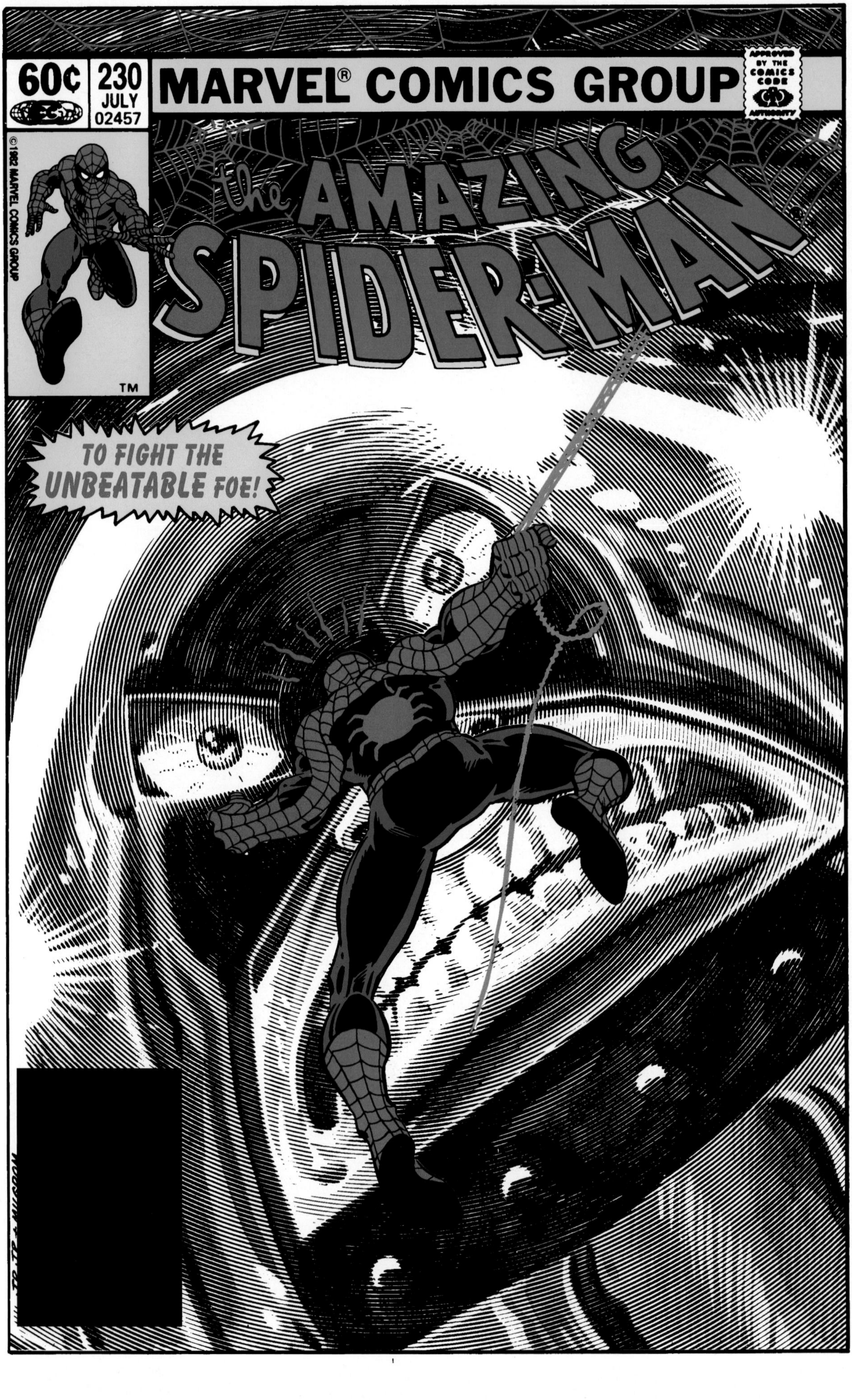
60¢
230
JULY
02457
MARVEL® COMICS GROUP
APPROVED BY THE COMICS CODE AUTHORITY
©1982 MARVEL COMICS GROUP
the AMAZING SPIDER-MAN®
TM
TO FIGHT THE UNBEATABLE FOE!

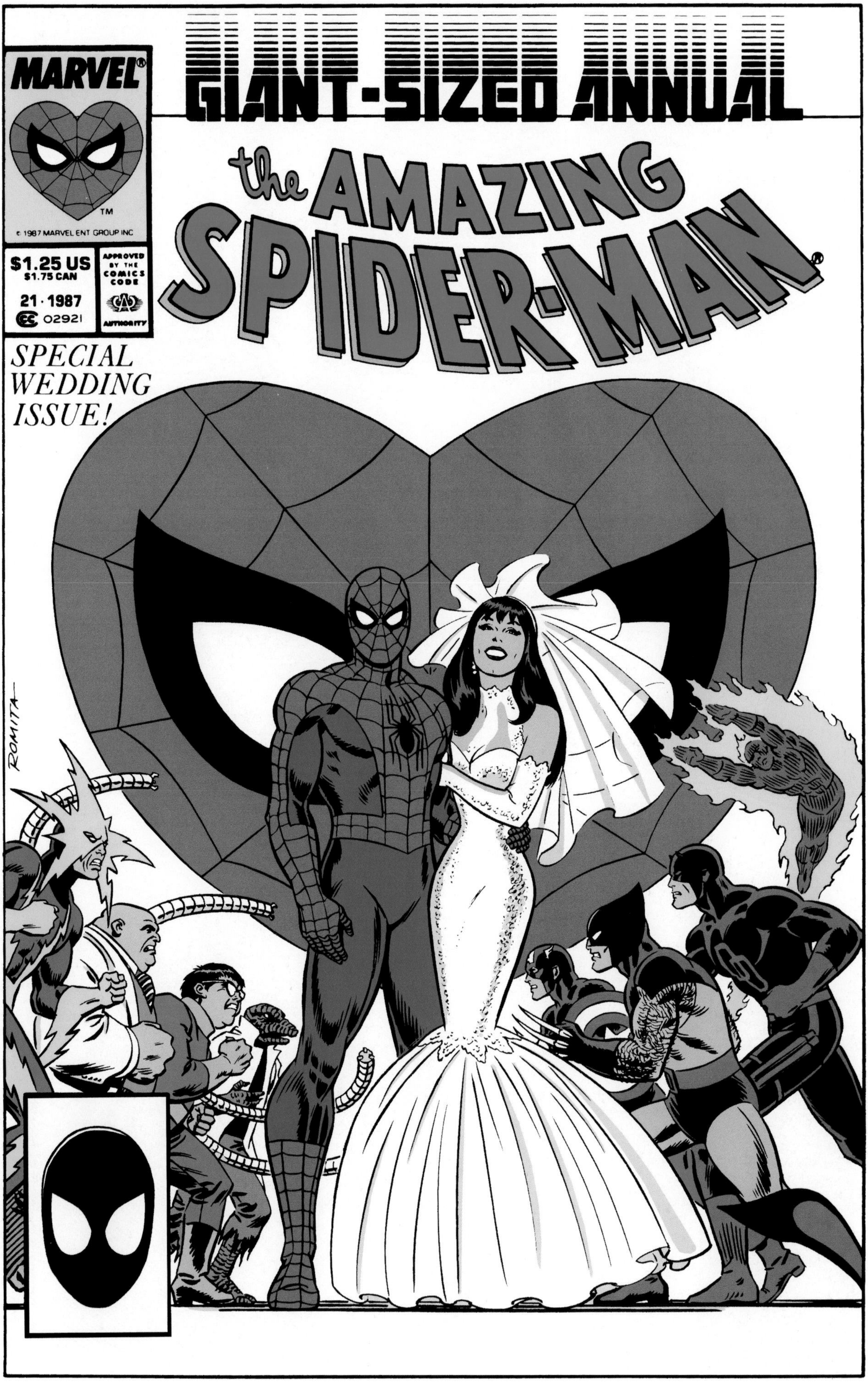
GIANT-SIZED ANNUAL
MARVEL®
TM
© 1987 MARVEL ENT GROUP INC
$1.25 US
$1.75 CAN
21 · 1987
02921
APPROVED BY THE COMICS CODE AUTHORITY
the AMAZING SPIDER-MAN®
SPECIAL WEDDING ISSUE!
ROMITA

Art by John Romita Sr. Opposite: Art by John Romita Jr.

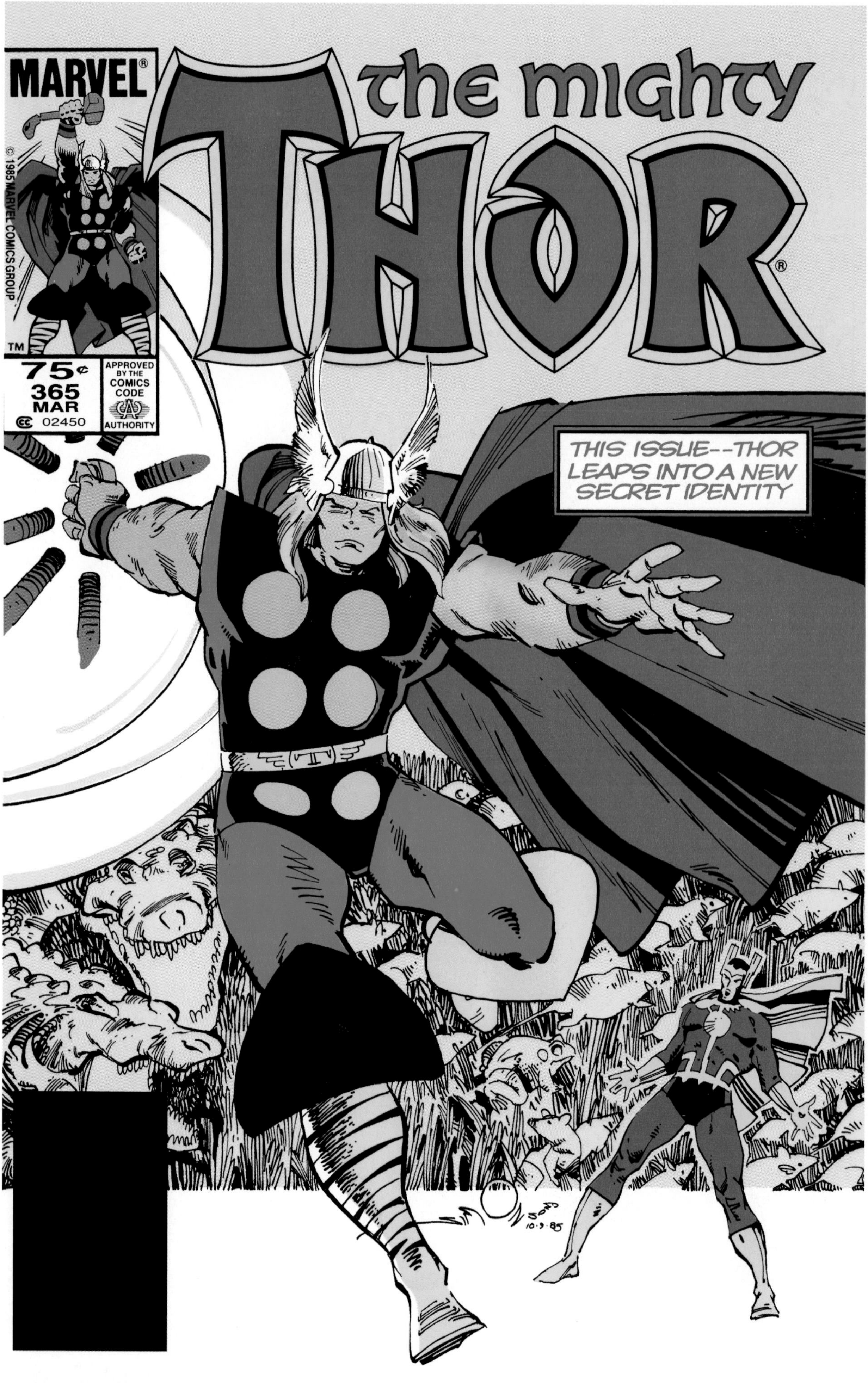
MARVEL
the mighty
THOR
© 1985 MARVEL COMICS GROUP
TM
75¢
365
MAR
02450
APPROVED BY THE COMICS CODE AUTHORITY
THIS ISSUE--THOR LEAPS INTO A NEW SECRET IDENTITY

Art by Walter Simonson. Opposite: Art by John Byrne.

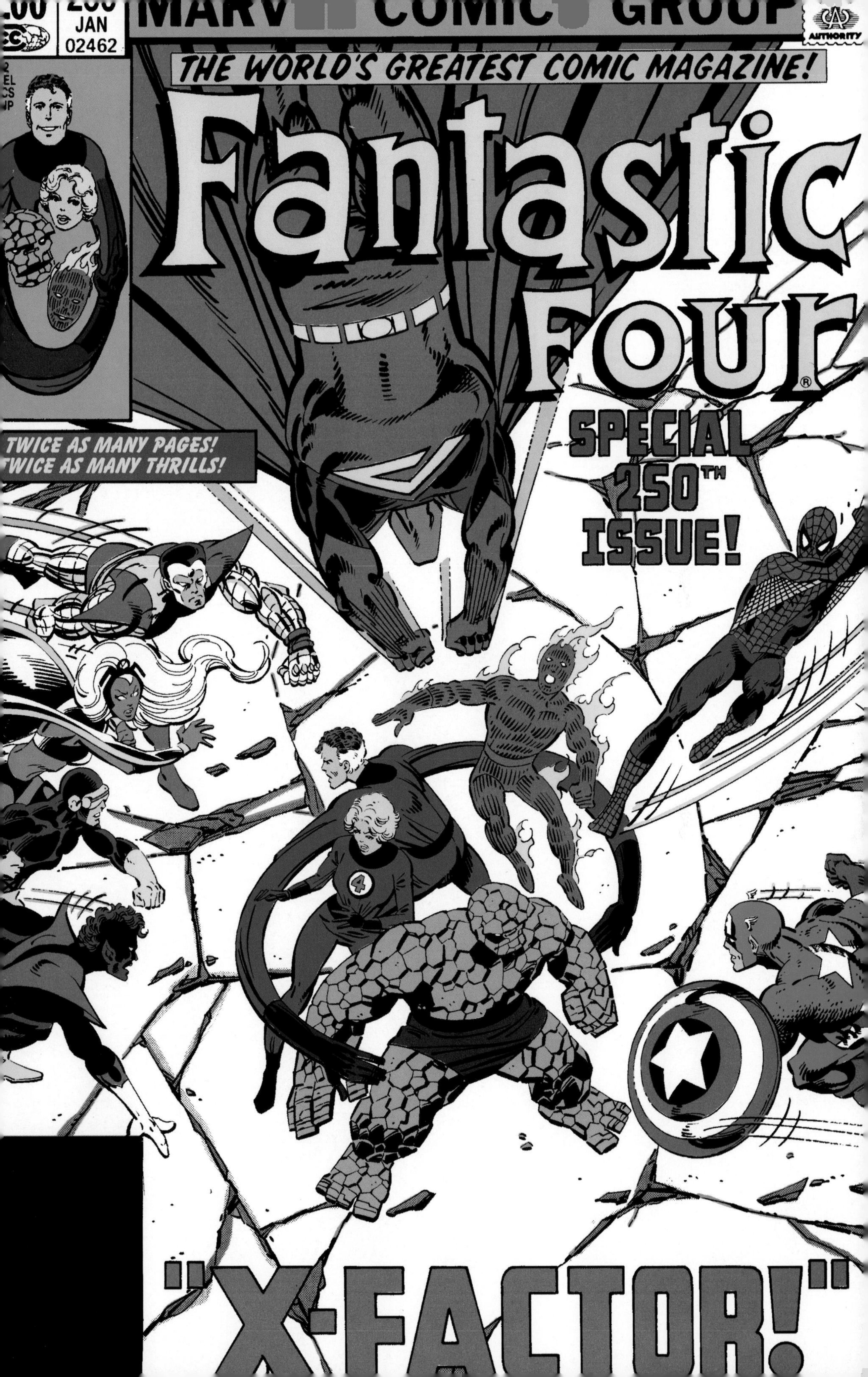
250
JAN
02462
AUTHORITY
THE WORLD'S GREATEST COMIC MAGAZINE!
Fantastic Four
TWICE AS MANY PAGES!
TWICE AS MANY THRILLS!
SPECIAL 250TH ISSUE!
"X-FACTOR!"

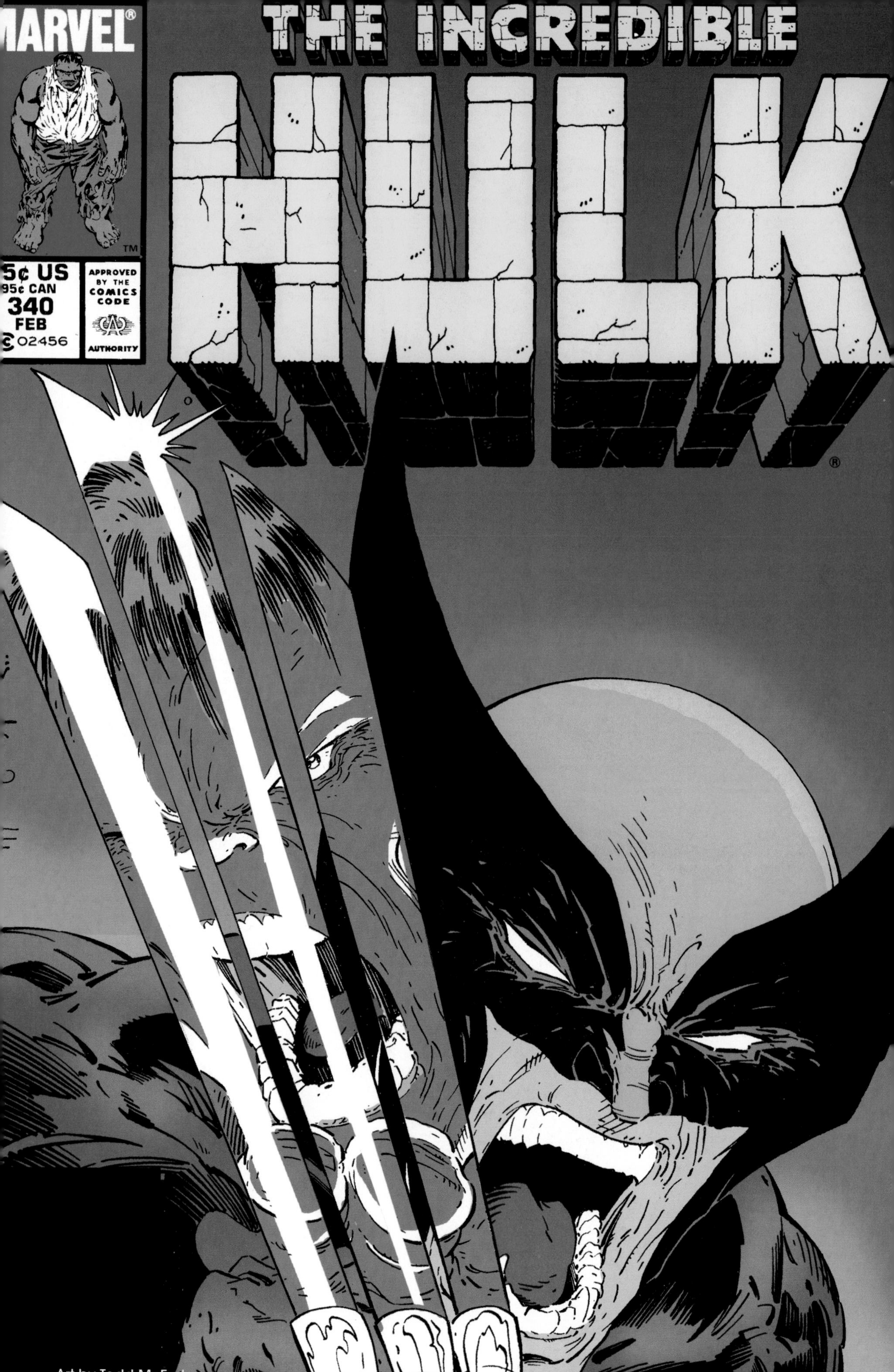
MARVEL
THE INCREDIBLE HULK
5¢ US
95¢ CAN
340
FEB
APPROVED BY THE COMICS CODE AUTHORITY

Art by Todd McFarlane

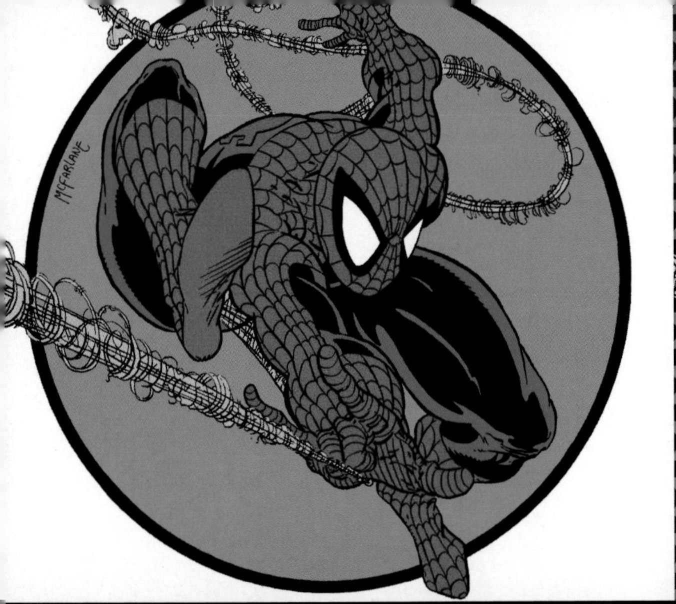
McFARLANE

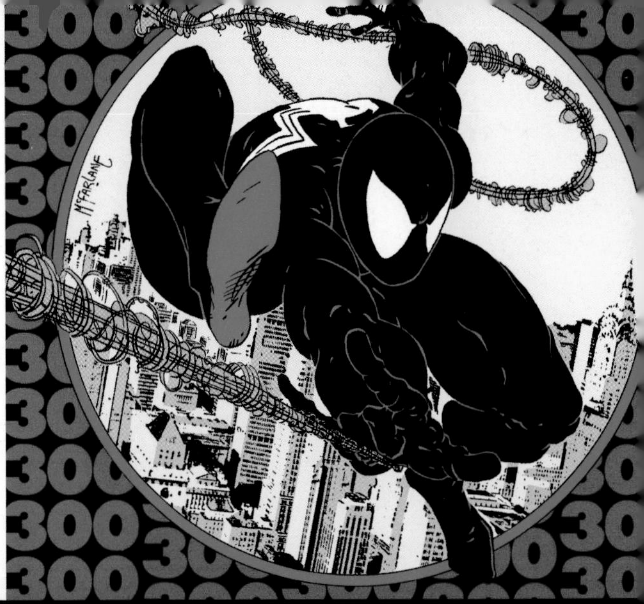
McFARLANE
300

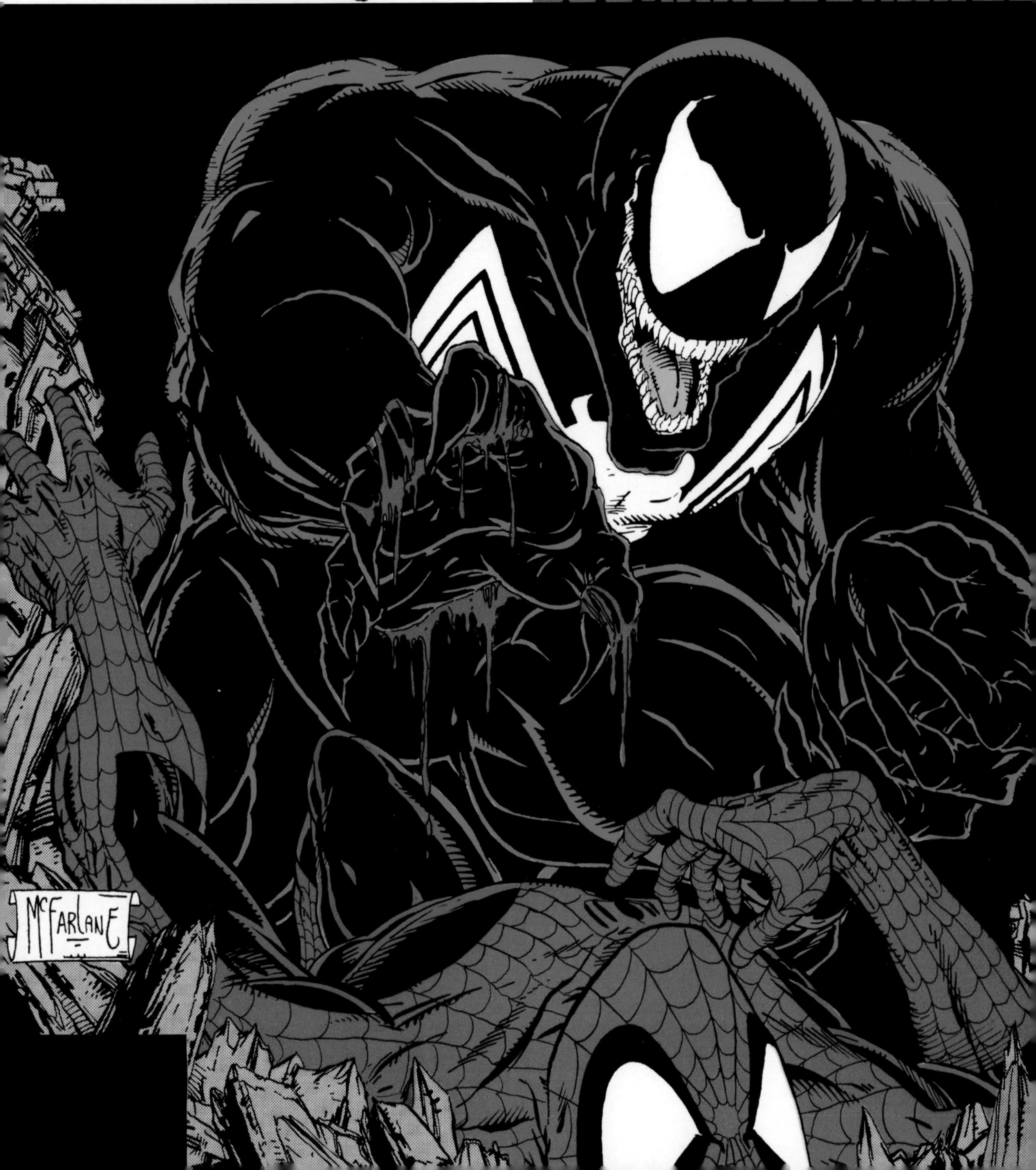
McFARLANE

# 1990s

Writers may have had their day during previous decades, but the 1990s were defined by the artists. Todd McFarlane's work continued to capture the imaginations of fans worldwide — sparking a craze not seen since the web-slinger's debut, and launching the artist to a stratospheric popularity that continues to the present day. Marvel unleashed a total of eight versions of the debut issue of his new series, *Spider-Man* — including silver-ink covers, gold-foil covers, and signed-and-numbered variants. The hype was unbelievable, with total circulation surpassing one million copies.

After dazzling readers and critics alike with his stunning artwork on *Uncanny X-Men*, artist Jim Lee did McFarlane one better — helping writer Chris Claremont make *X-Men #1*, with its five variant covers, the best-selling comic book of all time. Spawning countless imitators and inspiring a legion of fans, Lee later joined with other hot, young artists of the day — including Rob Liefeld and Whilce Portacio — to reinvigorate Marvel mainstays such as Captain America, Thor, Iron Man, the Avengers and the Fantastic Four. The House's most popular heroes were reborn with a bold new look, their origins re-envisioned with a raw vitality and contemporary sensibility.

Also new to the scene was artist Mark Bagley, whose career had begun with an unusual twist. As winner of the legendary *Marvel Try-Out Book*, he beat out thousands of other hopefuls to land his first professional assignment on *Visionaries*, a comic book based on an '80s toy line. Bagley's talent led him to a five-year run on *Amazing Spider-Man*, beginning in 1991. Since then, he has drawn more than 200 Spider-Man-related comics.

Not to be outdone by the decade's young guns, rock-steady John Romita Jr. added power and prestige to two of Marvel's grittiest heroes, Punisher and Daredevil — in *The Punisher: War Zone*, an old-school shoot-'em-up penned by action auteur Chuck Dixon; and *Daredevil: Man Without Fear*, the tour-de-force origin of Matt Murdock's crimson-clad alter ego as told by Frank Miller, the only man who could. And following the Heroes Reborn experiment of Lee, Liefeld & Co., writer Kurt Busiek and artist George Pérez ushered in a bold new era for Earth's Mightiest Heroes, reassembling the classic Avengers in the mainline Marvel Universe for an epic storyline uniting every member of the team, past and present.

Art by Alex Ross. Opposite: *Spider-Man #1* cover by Todd McFarlane.

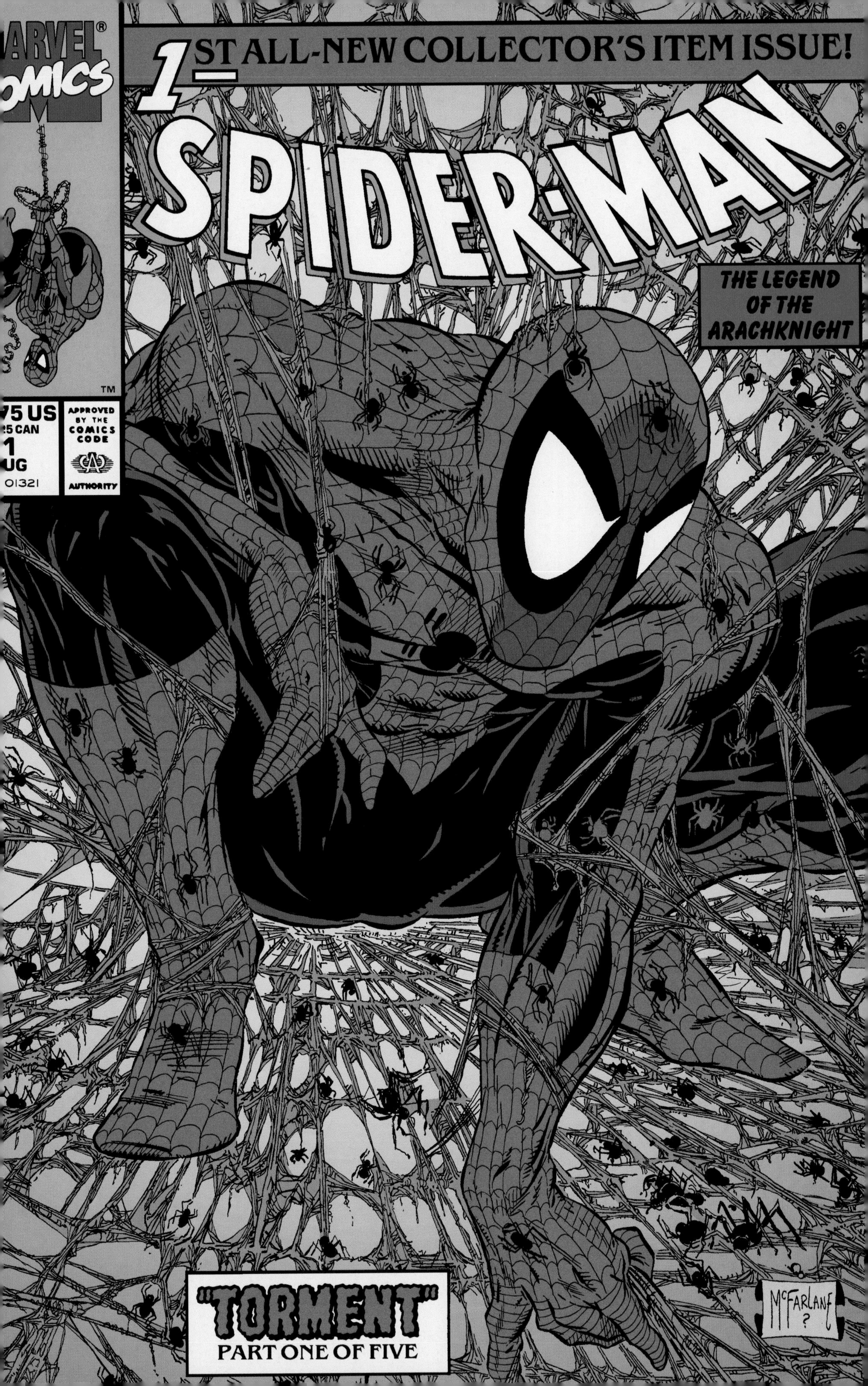
MARVEL COMICS
1ST ALL-NEW COLLECTOR'S ITEM ISSUE!
SPIDER-MAN
THE LEGEND OF THE ARACHKNIGHT
75 US
25 CAN
1
UG
APPROVED BY THE COMICS CODE AUTHORITY
"TORMENT"
PART ONE OF FIVE
McFARLANE

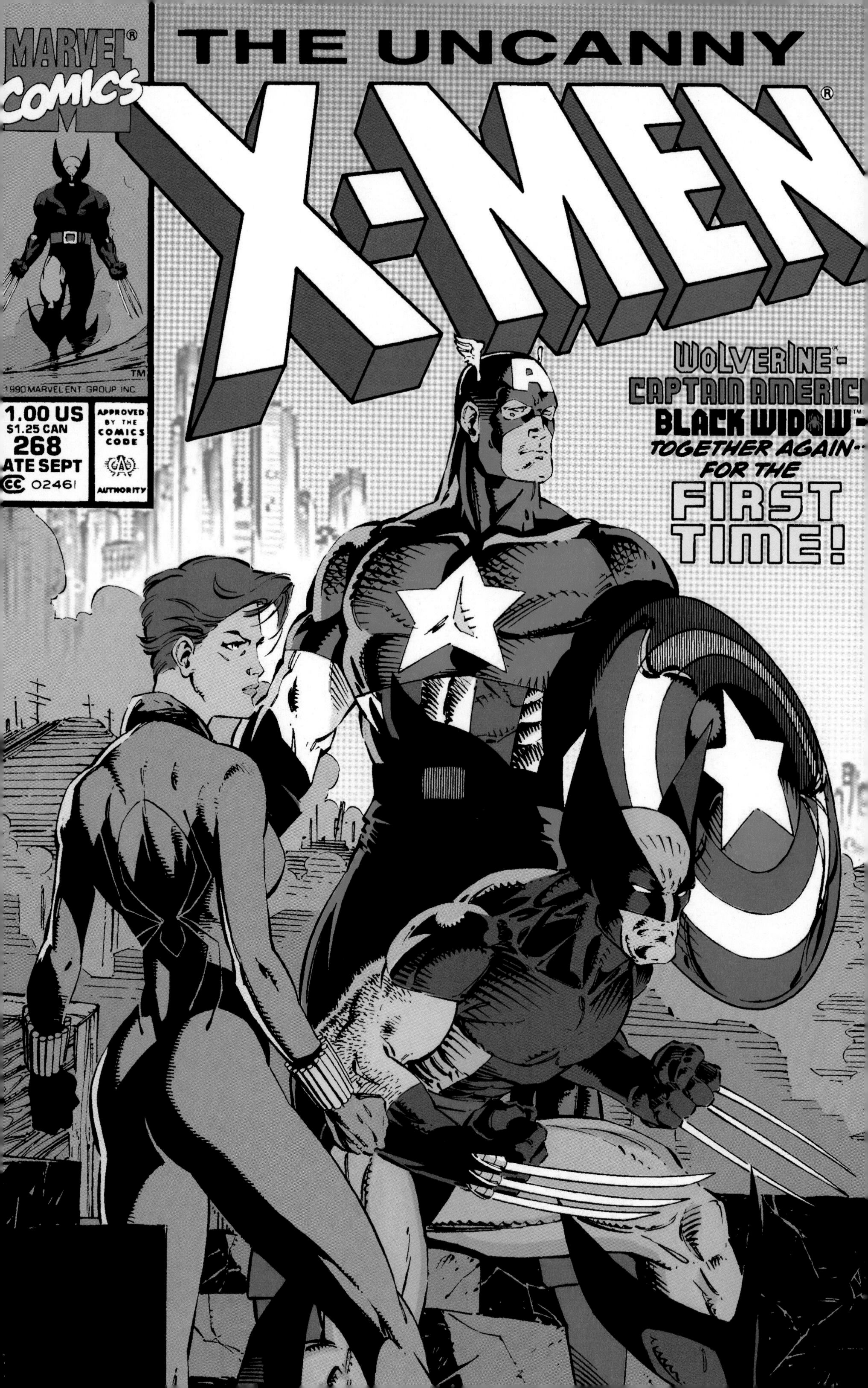
MARVEL® COMICS
THE UNCANNY
X-MEN®
TM
1990 MARVEL ENT GROUP INC
1.00 US
$1.25 CAN
268
ATE SEPT
APPROVED BY THE COMICS CODE AUTHORITY
WOLVERINE® -
CAPTAIN AMERIC
BLACK WIDOW™ -
TOGETHER AGAIN--
FOR THE
FIRST
TIME!

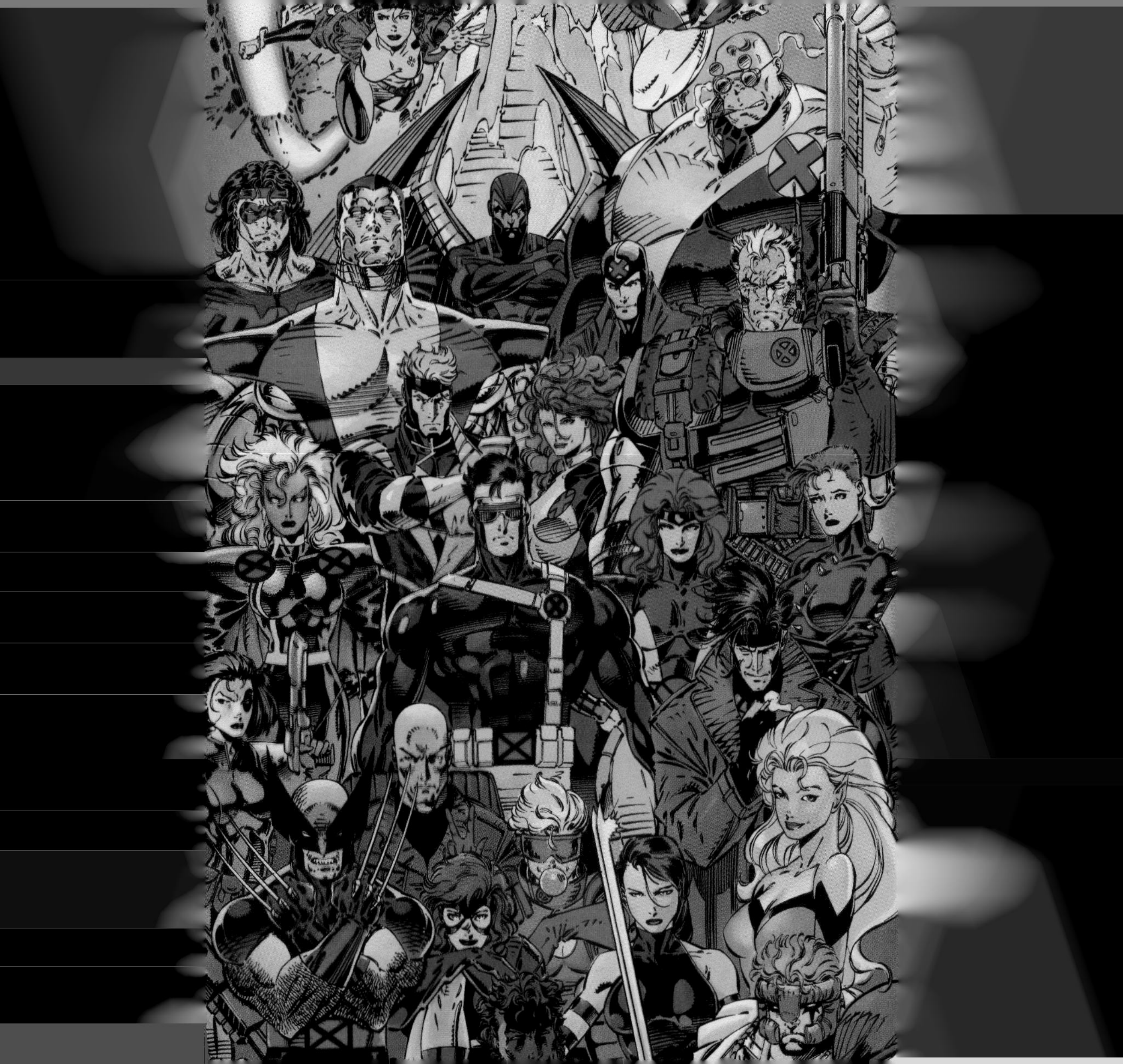

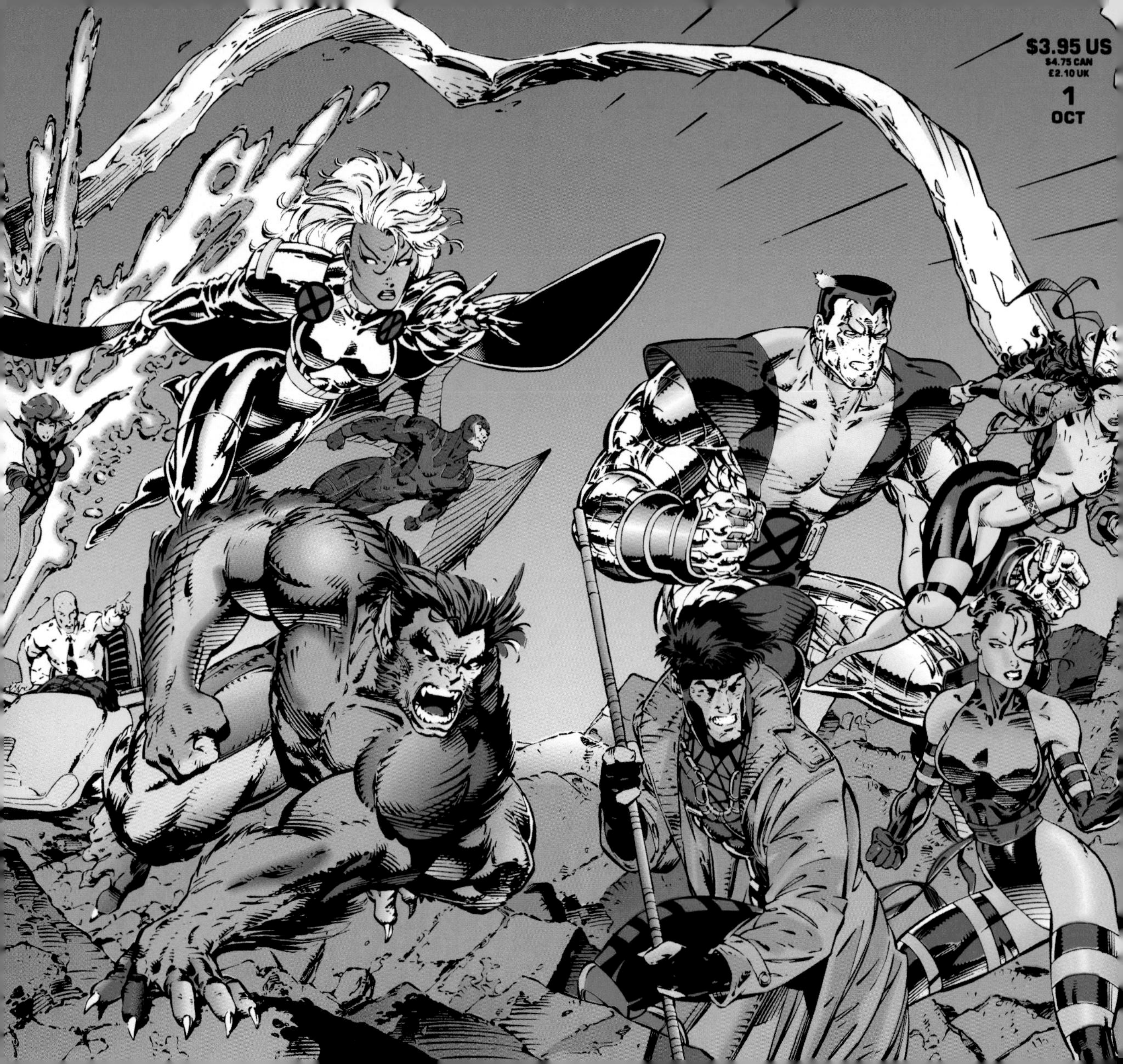
$3.95 US
$4.75 CAN
£2.10 UK
1
OCT

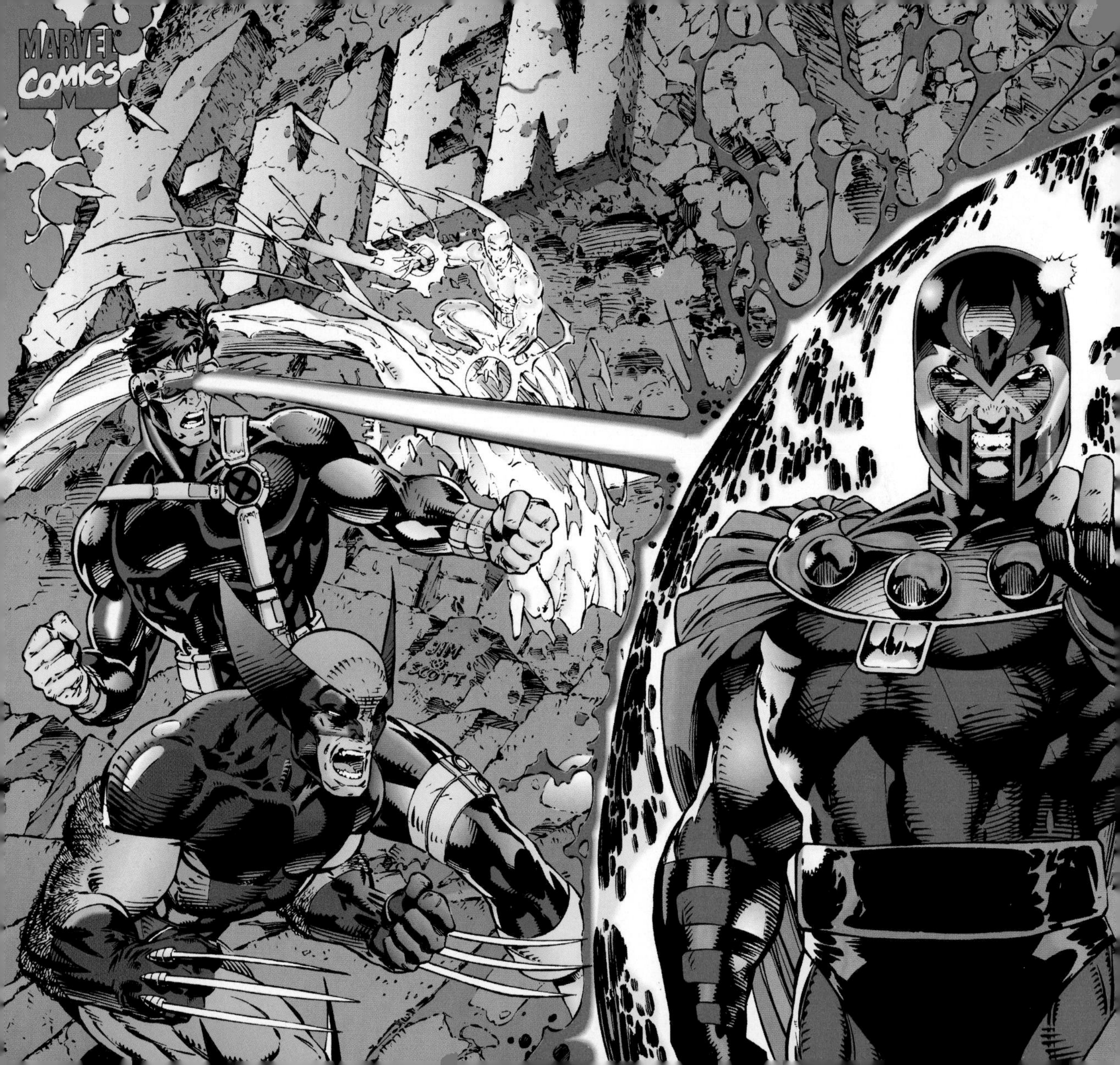
MARVEL COMICS
JIM
SCOTT

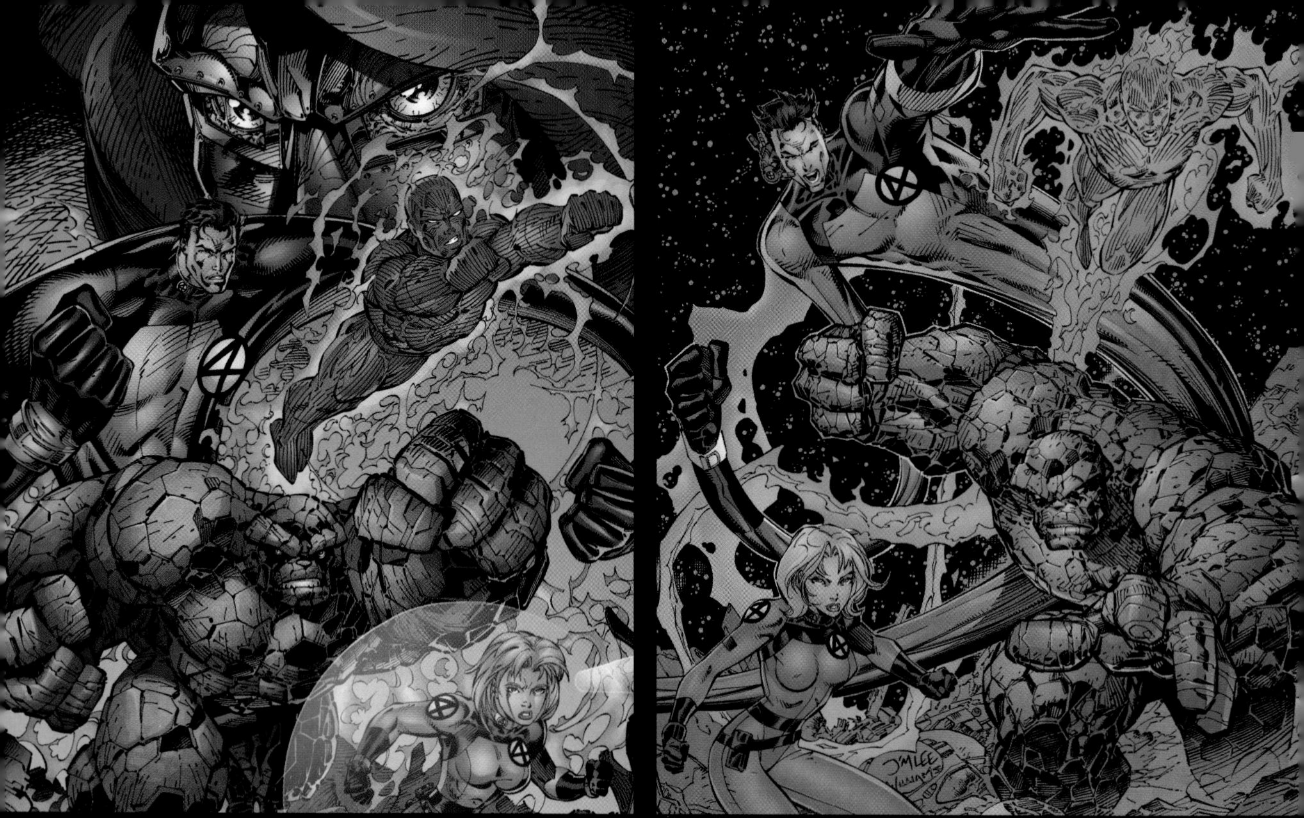

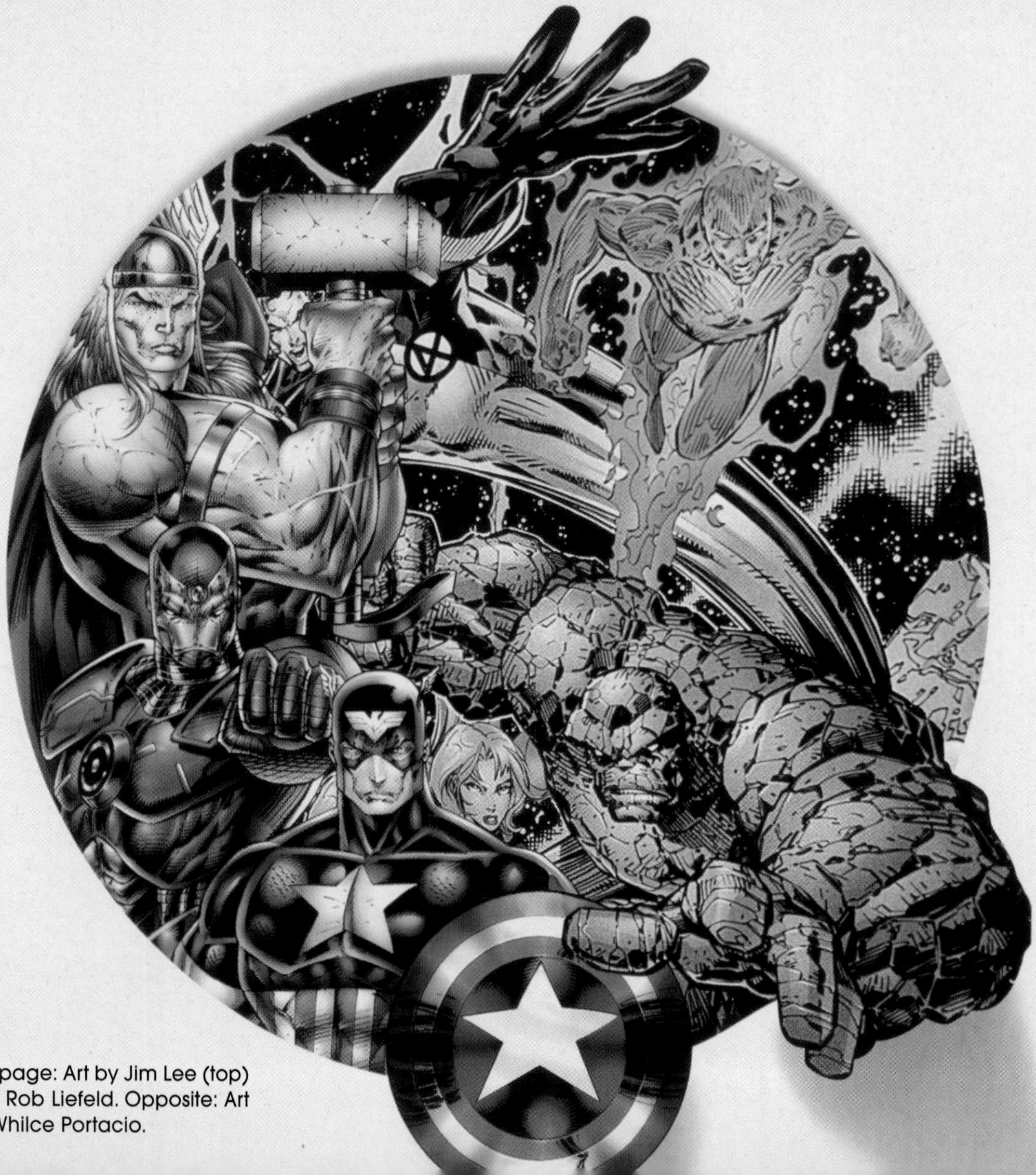

This page: Art by Jim Lee (top) and Rob Liefeld. Opposite: Art by Whilce Portacio.

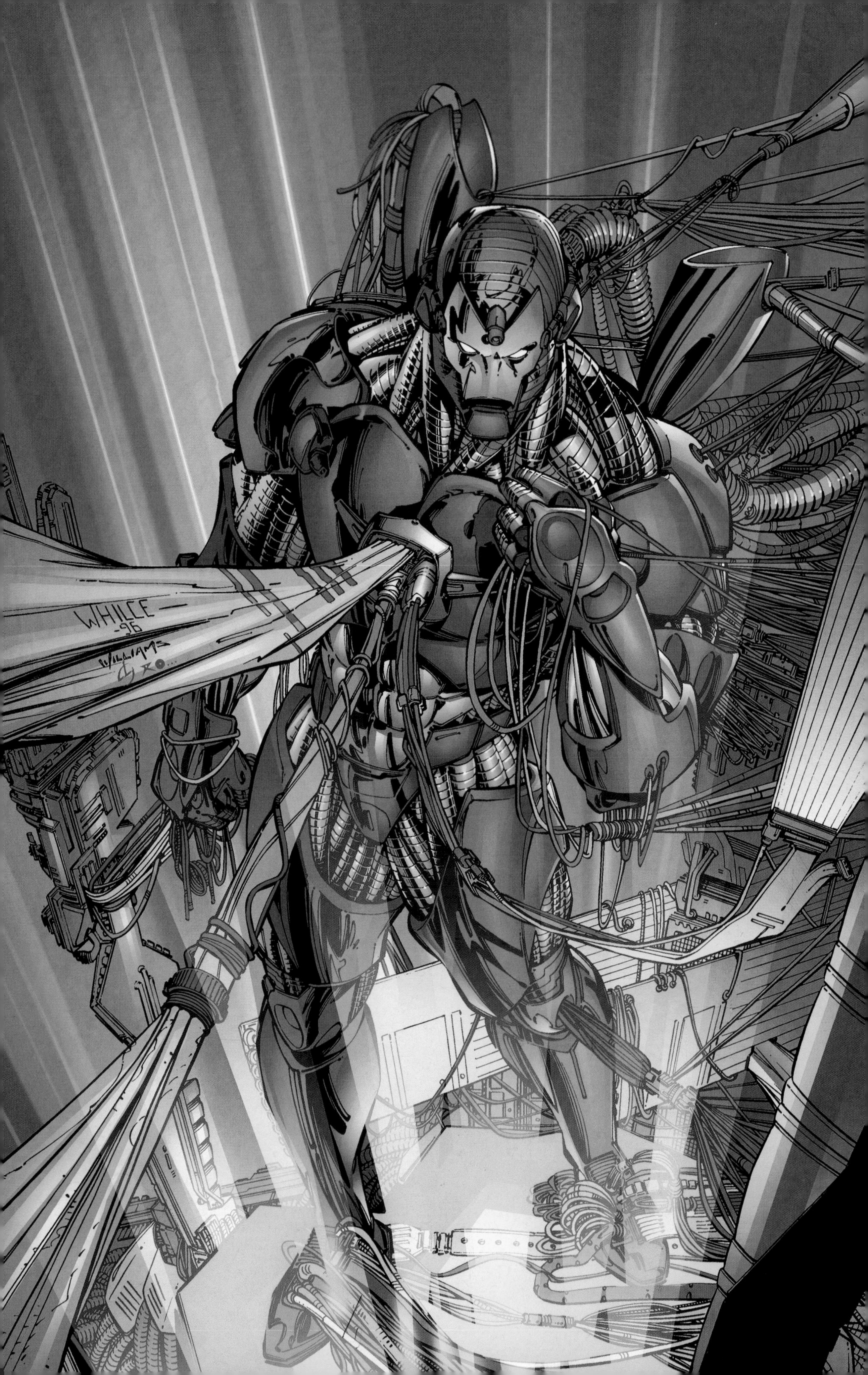
WHILCE
-96
WILLIAMS

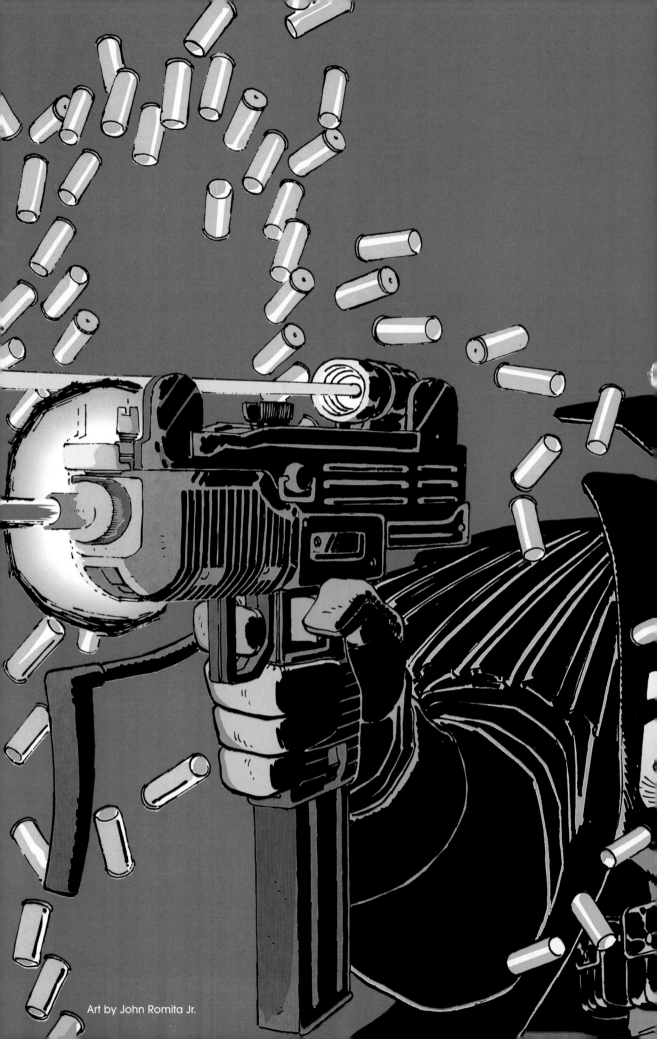

Art by John Romita Jr.

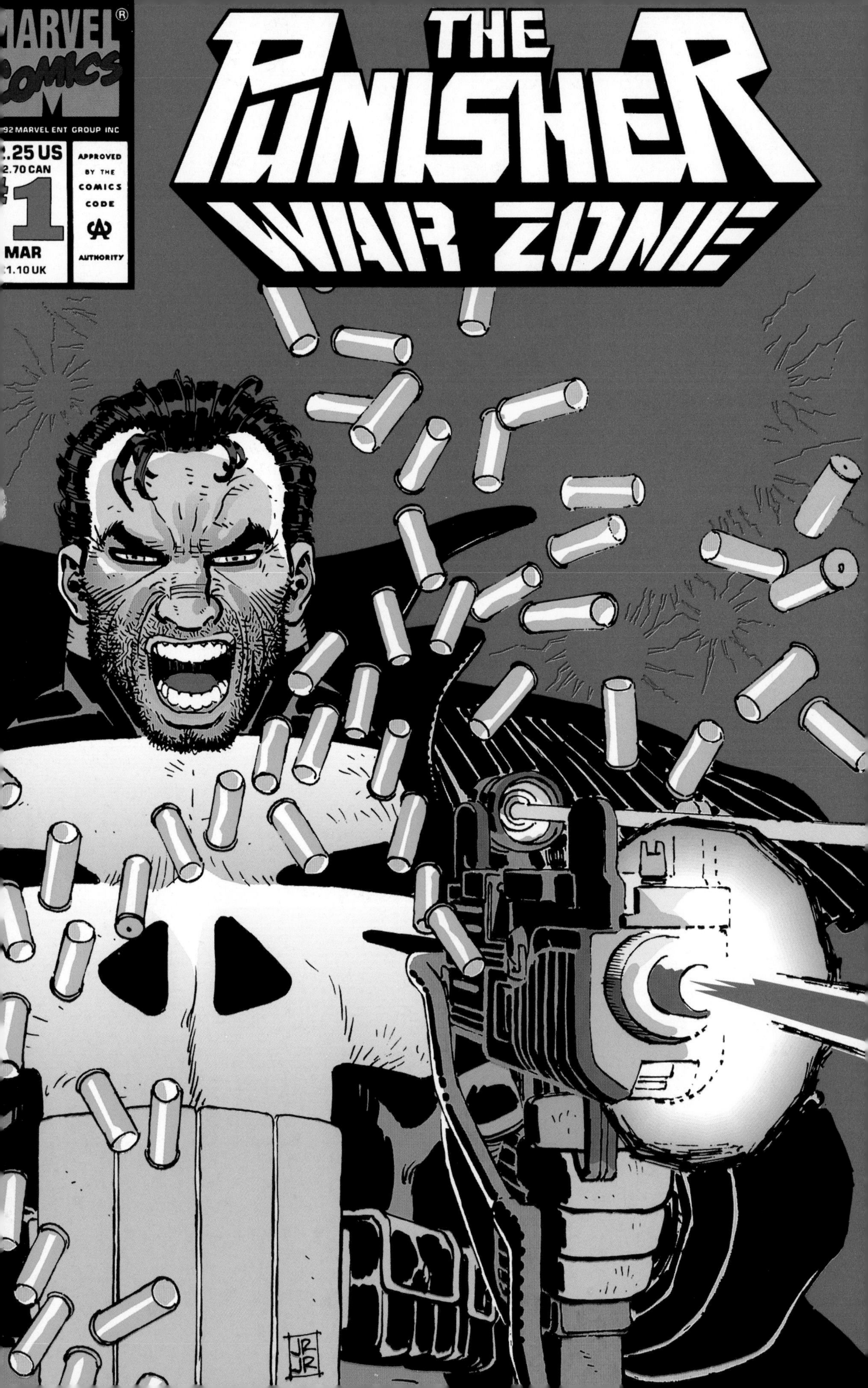
MARVEL COMICS
THE PUNISHER
WAR ZONE
92 MARVEL ENT GROUP INC
.25 US
2.70 CAN
1
MAR
1.10 UK
APPROVED BY THE COMICS CODE AUTHORITY
JR JR

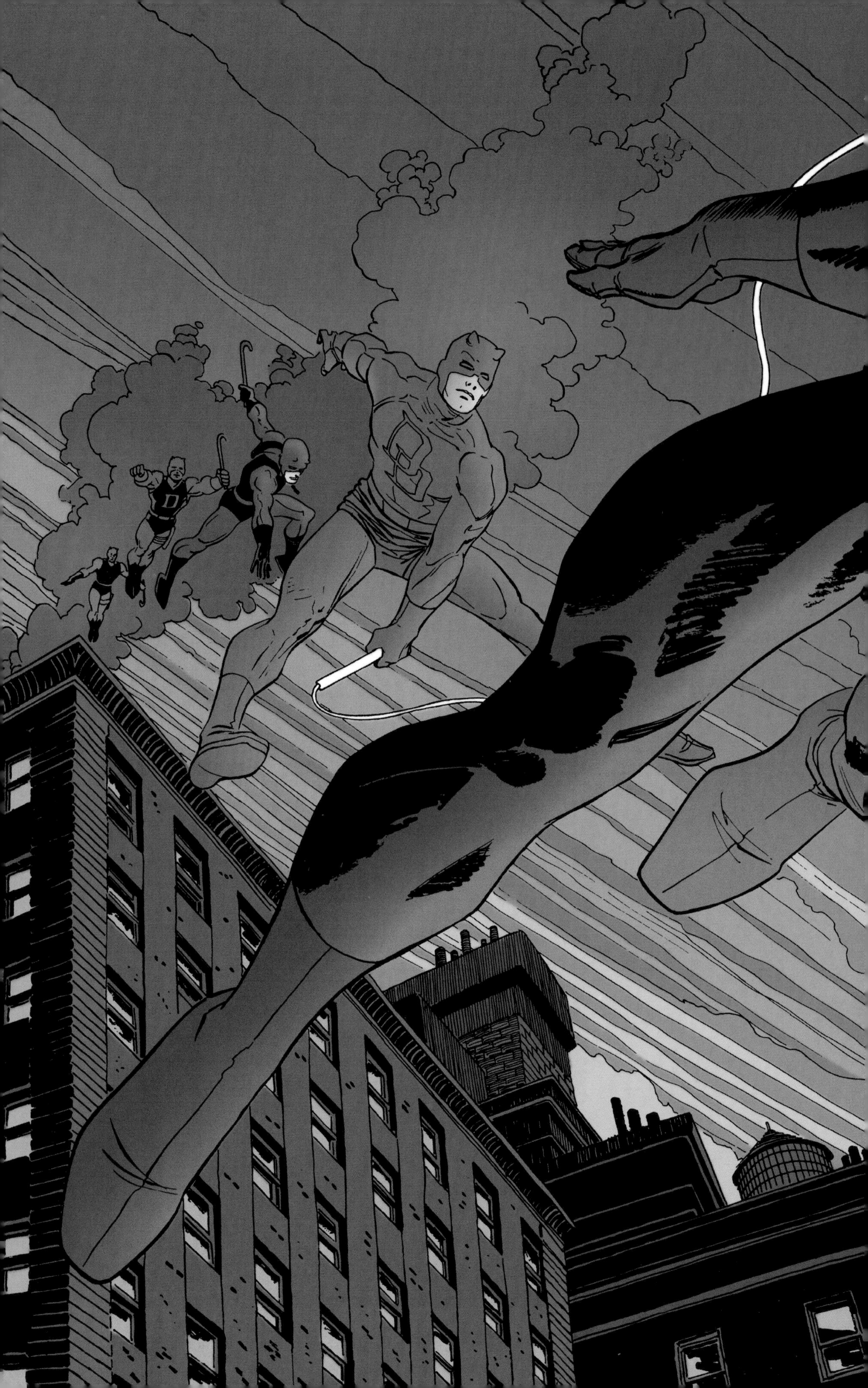

GOD ONLY KNOWS
WHAT IT LOOKS
LIKE.

BIG
APPLE
MOVERS
7233933
WE MOVE
ANYTHING

Art by John Romita Jr.

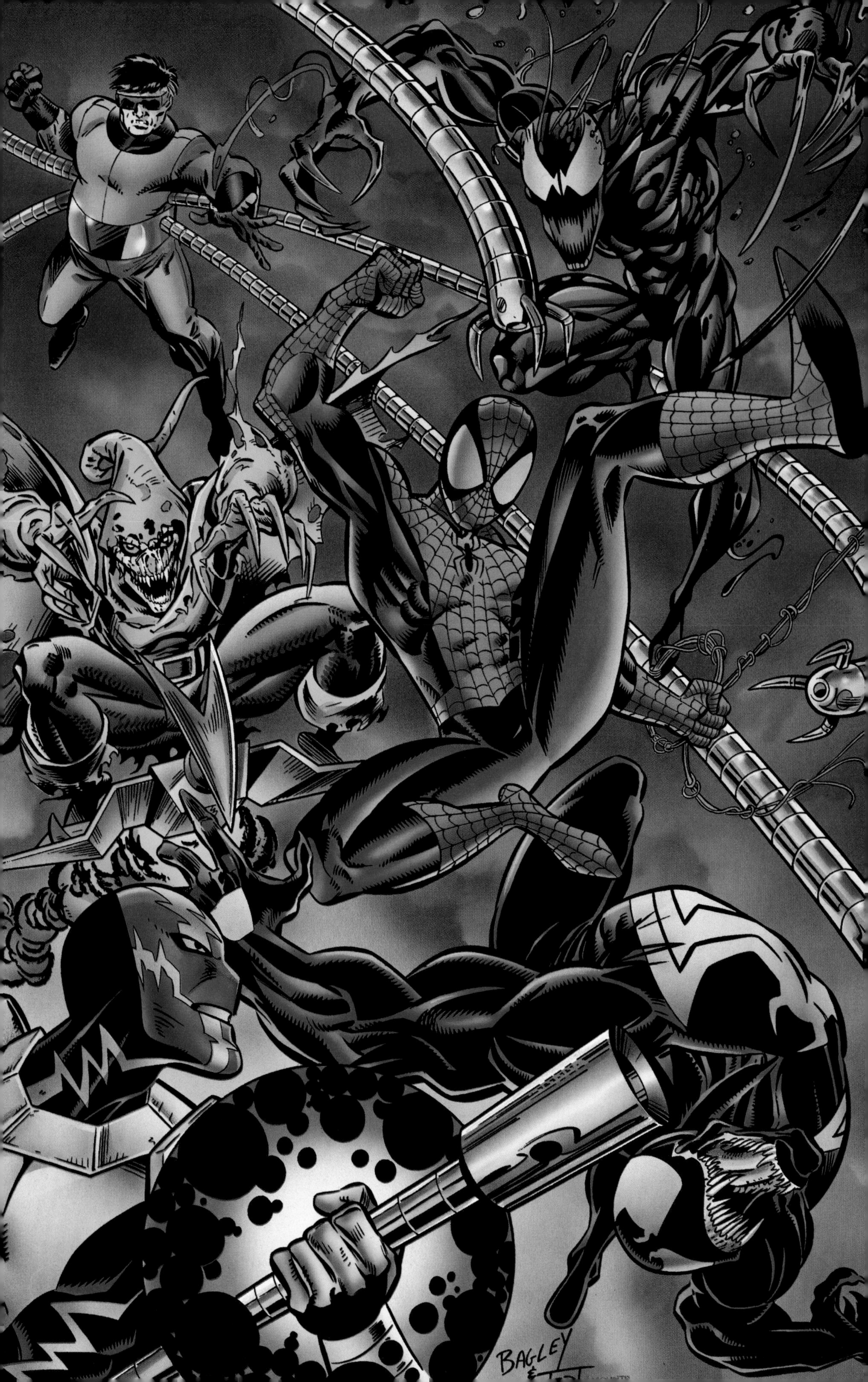
BAGLEY

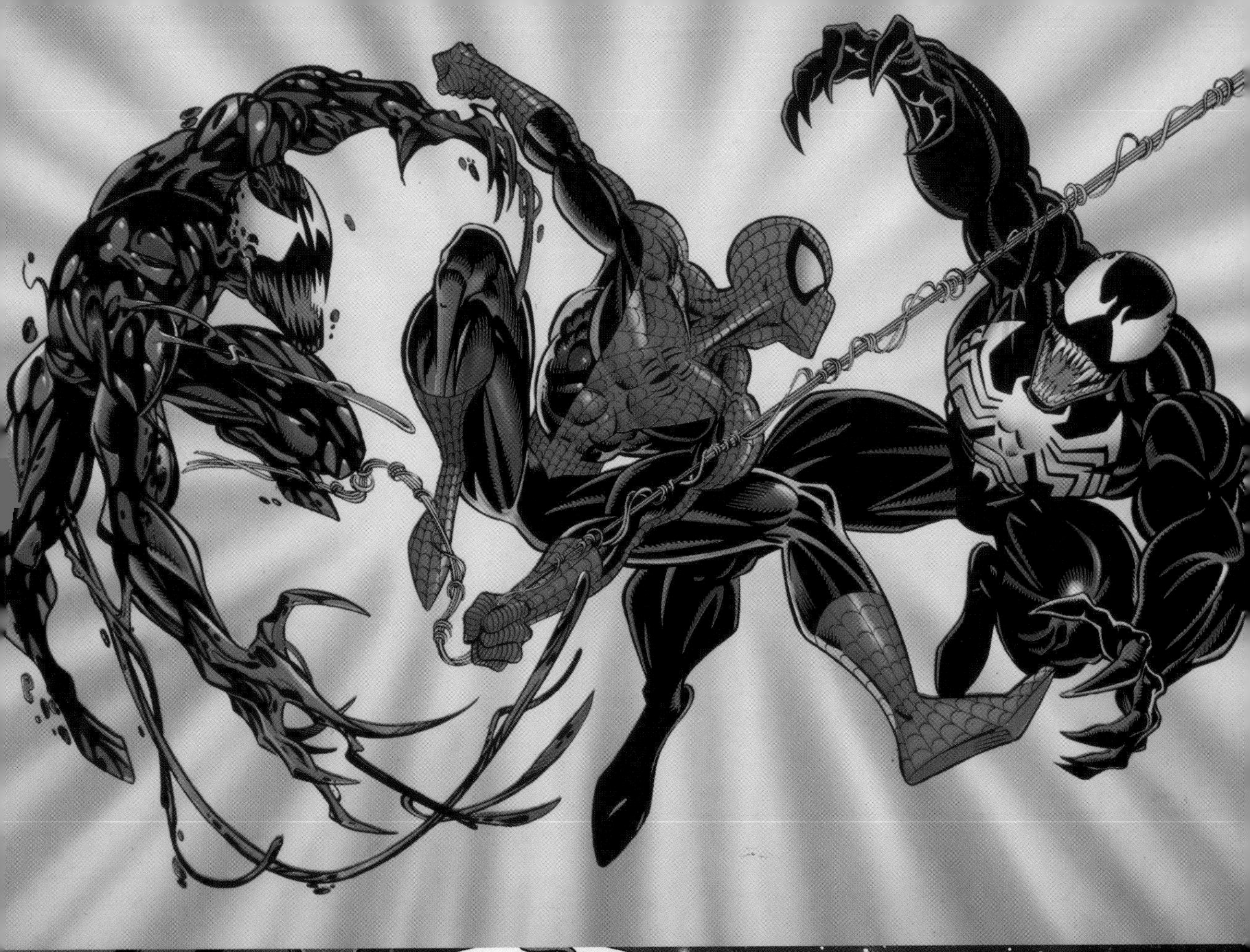

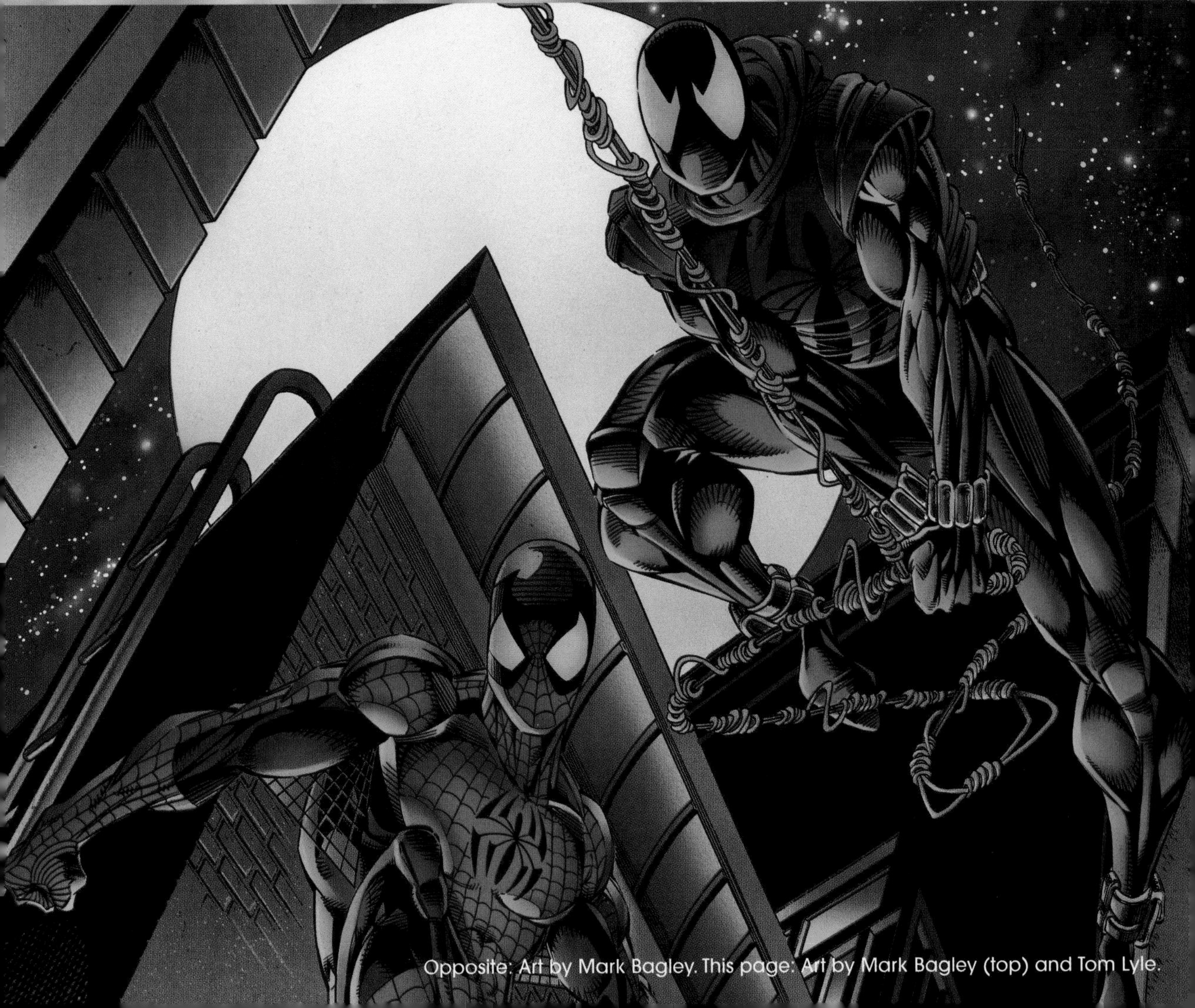

Opposite: Art by Mark Bagley. This page: Art by Mark Bagley (top) and Tom Lyle.

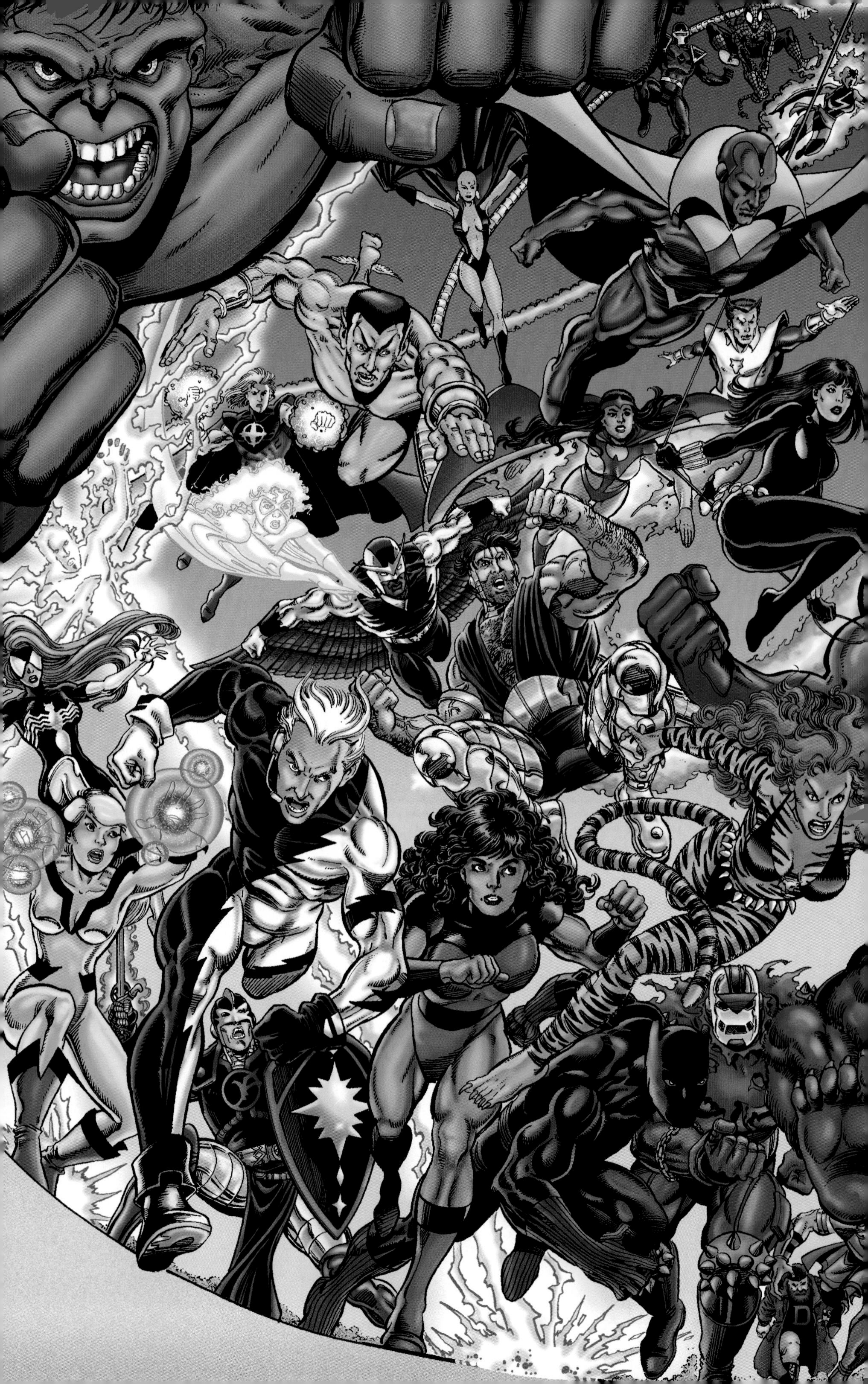

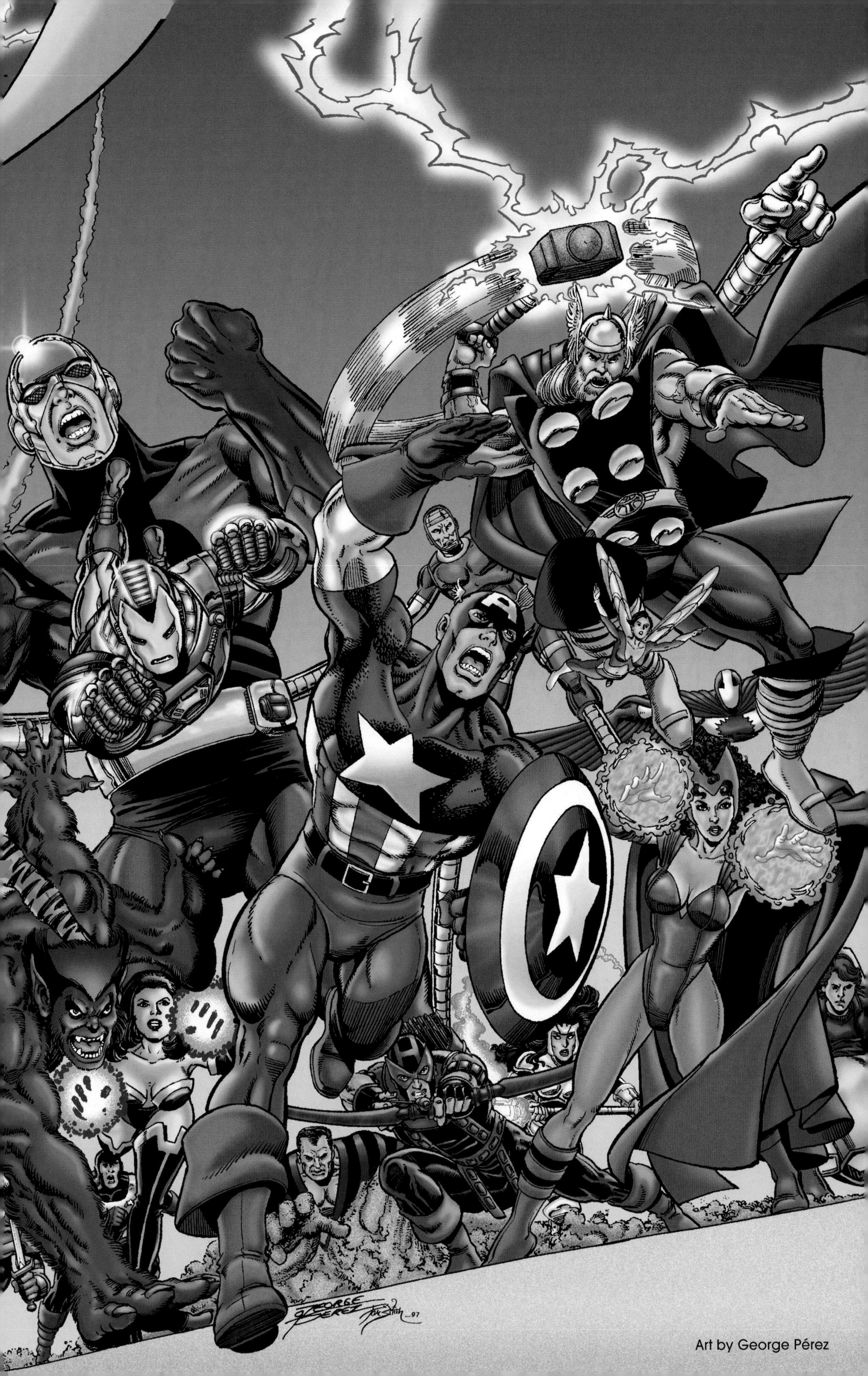

Art by George Pérez

# TODAY

With a feature film in the works and no fewer than four ongoing comic-book series on store shelves, the Fantastic Four stand poised on the brink of pop-culture superstardom. Following the lead of *Ultimate Spider-Man*, *Ultimate X-Men* and *The Ultimates*, the revisionist *Ultimate Fantastic Four* chronicles the early adventures of high-school genius Reed Richards, classmates Johnny and Susan Storm, and best friend Ben Grimm — reimagined as super-hero icons for the modern age. In the darker, edgier world of *Marvel Knights 4*, the members of comics' first family face their most personal and unpredictable crisis yet: bankruptcy. Along with *Marvel Age Spider-Man*, *Marvel Age Spider-Man Team-Up* and *Marvel Age Hulk*, *Marvel Age Fantastic Four* revisits the earliest Marvel tales — introducing new and young readers to some of the greatest stories of the legendary Marvel Universe with dynamic new art and a modern flair. And carrying on the classic storylines and proud tradition begun by Stan and Jack forty years earlier, the original *Fantastic Four* series recently celebrated its landmark 500th issue.

Marvel's mutant movie stars, the X-Men, have also returned to classic greatness. Lending a cinematic vitality to their comic-book adventures are artists John Cassaday on *Astonishing X-Men*, Alan Davis on *Uncanny X-Men*, Salvador Larroca on *X-Men* and John Romita Jr. on *Wolverine*.

As the Fantastic Four come together and the X-Men unite, Earth's Mightiest Heroes find themselves torn asunder — disassembled by writer Brian Michael Bendis and artist David Finch in an epic storyline setting the stage for the debut of the all-new, all-different team of *New Avengers*. Bendis, perhaps the most popular and acclaimed writer in comics, reveals the darkest chapter in Marvel Universe history in *Secret War* — featuring the American debut of stunning Italian painter Gabriele Dell'Otto. And in *The Pulse*, he and artist Mark Bagley present an inside look at Marvel's most notorious newspaper, The Daily Bugle.

In *Marvel Knights Spider-Man*, writer Mark Millar and artist Terry Dodson put comics' top-grossing box-office star through his paces. A mysterious villain has discovered the wall-crawler's secret identity and is using the information to slowly destroy everything and everyone Peter Parker cares about. In *Amazing Spider-Man*, two new villains have emerged — ripped, perhaps, from the worst defeat Peter ever endured, the death of Gwen Stacy — courtesy of writer J. Michael Straczynski and artist Mike Deodato Jr. Deodato's bold strokes have also graced the pages of *Incredible Hulk* and *Witches*; and the covers of *Identity Disc*, *Venom* and *Wolverine/Punisher*.

No more merely Daredevil's love interest, newly minted leading lady Elektra heads the charge as a host of the House's woman warriors take center stage — including Araña, Black Widow, Mystique, Rogue and She-Hulk in their own titles; X-23 in *NYX*; and Sif in *Thor: Son of Asgard* and *Loki*, the latter featuring the breathtaking painted artwork of Esad Ribic.

And writer Garth Ennis, whose stories inspired the *Punisher* motion picture, takes Marvel's one-man-army to the MAX — literally — in a no-holds-barred mature-readers series featuring digitally rendered covers by artist Tim Bradstreet.

Art by Alex Ross. Opposite: *Ultimate Fantastic Four #1* cover by Bryan Hitch.

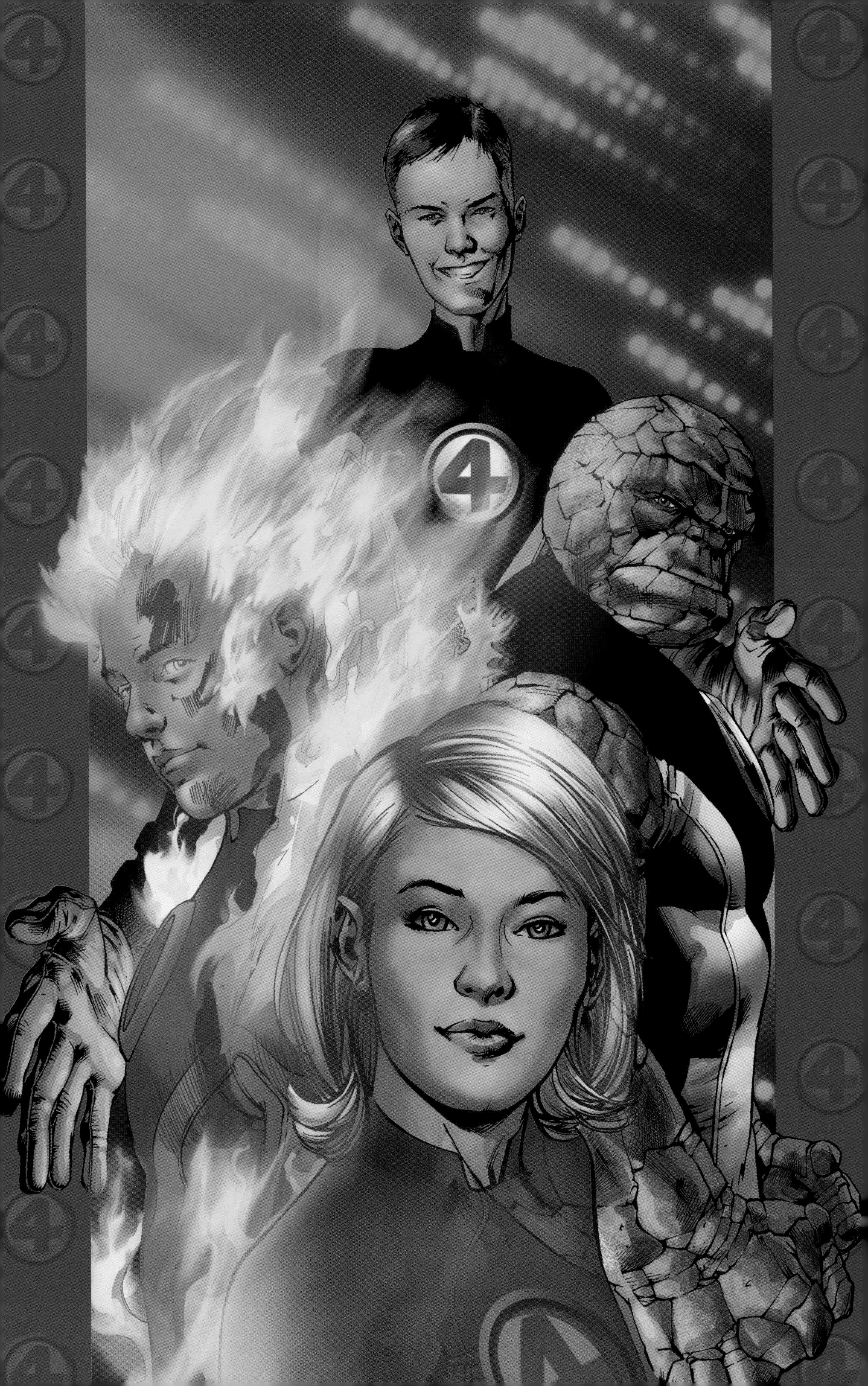

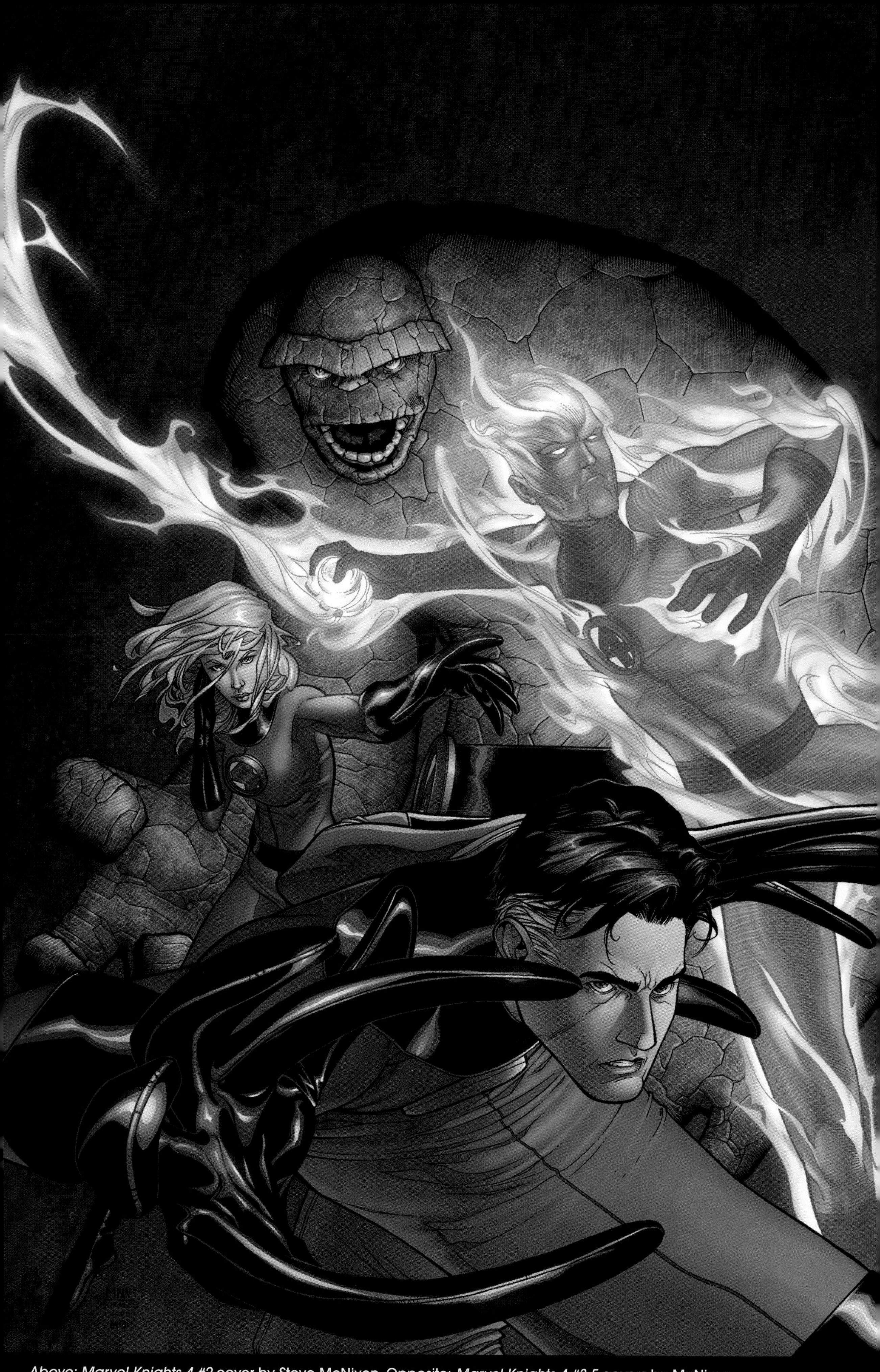

*Above: Marvel Knights 4 #2* cover by Steve McNiven. Opposite: *Marvel Knights 4 #3-5* covers by McNiven.

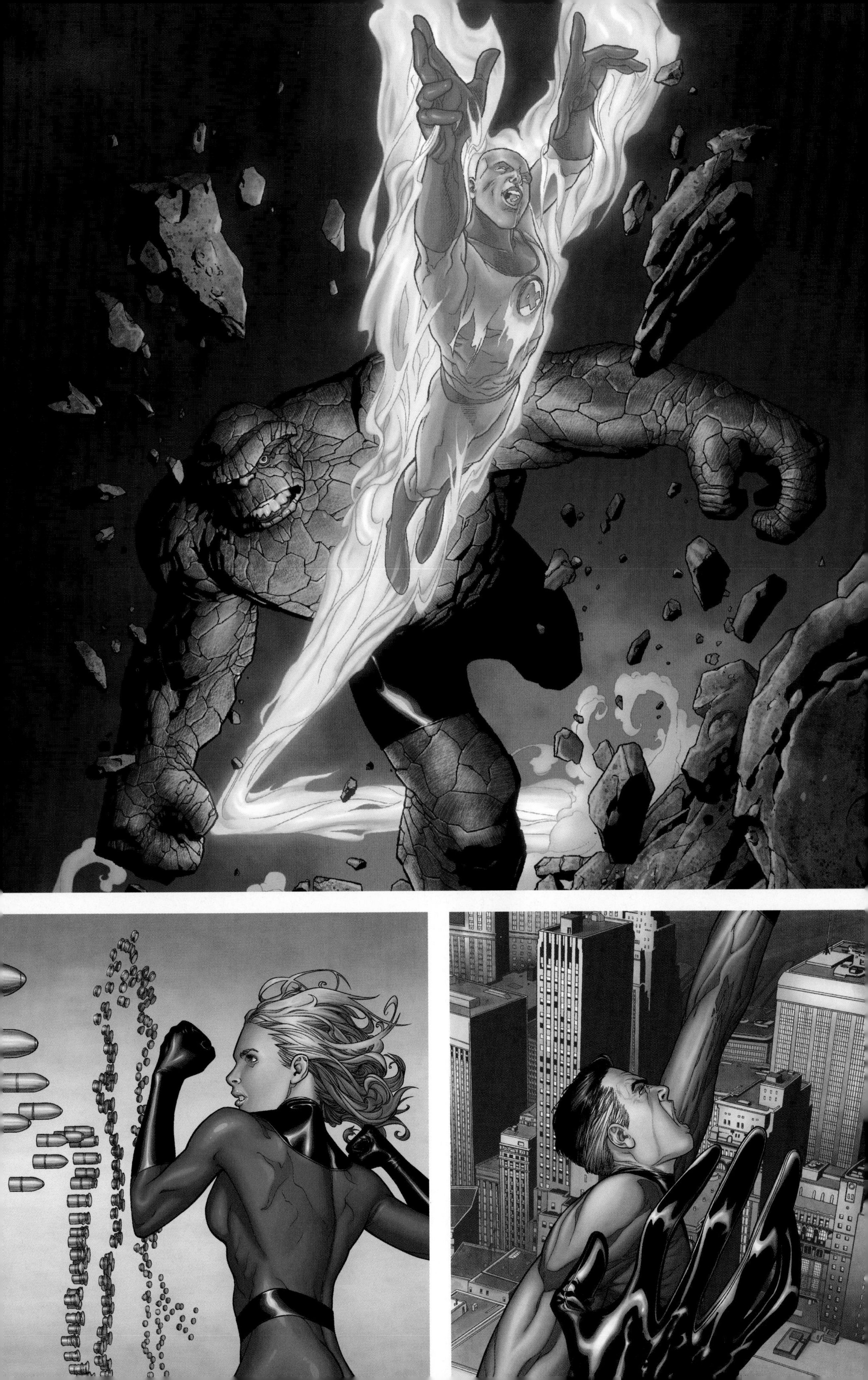

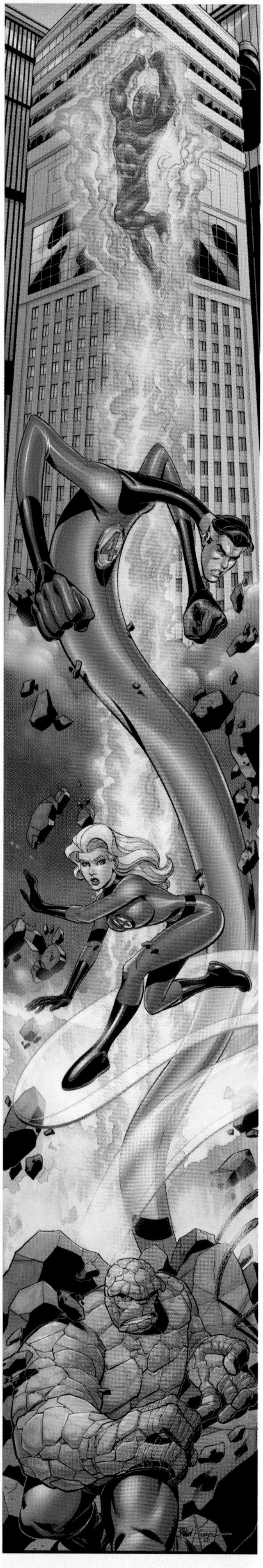

*"I go back to Stan and Jack. I certainly go other places — I look to friends, I look to relationships I've had — but mostly I just go straight back to Stan and Jack."*

Mark Waid
Writer, *Fantastic Four*

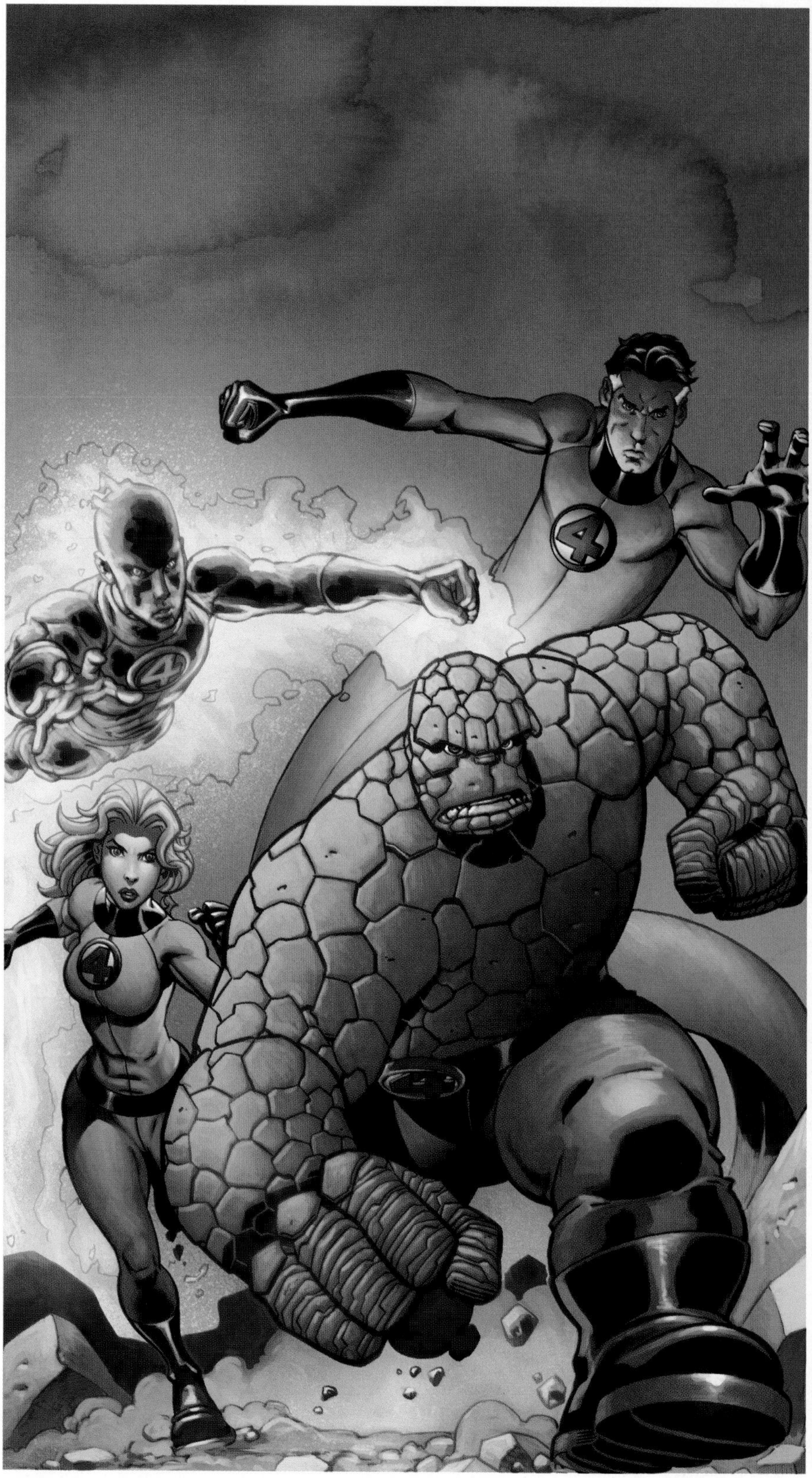

Left: *Fantastic Four #51-54* covers by Mike Wieringo. Above: *Fantastic Four #509* cover by Wieringo. Opposite: *Ultimate Fantastic Four #11* cover by Stuart Immonen.

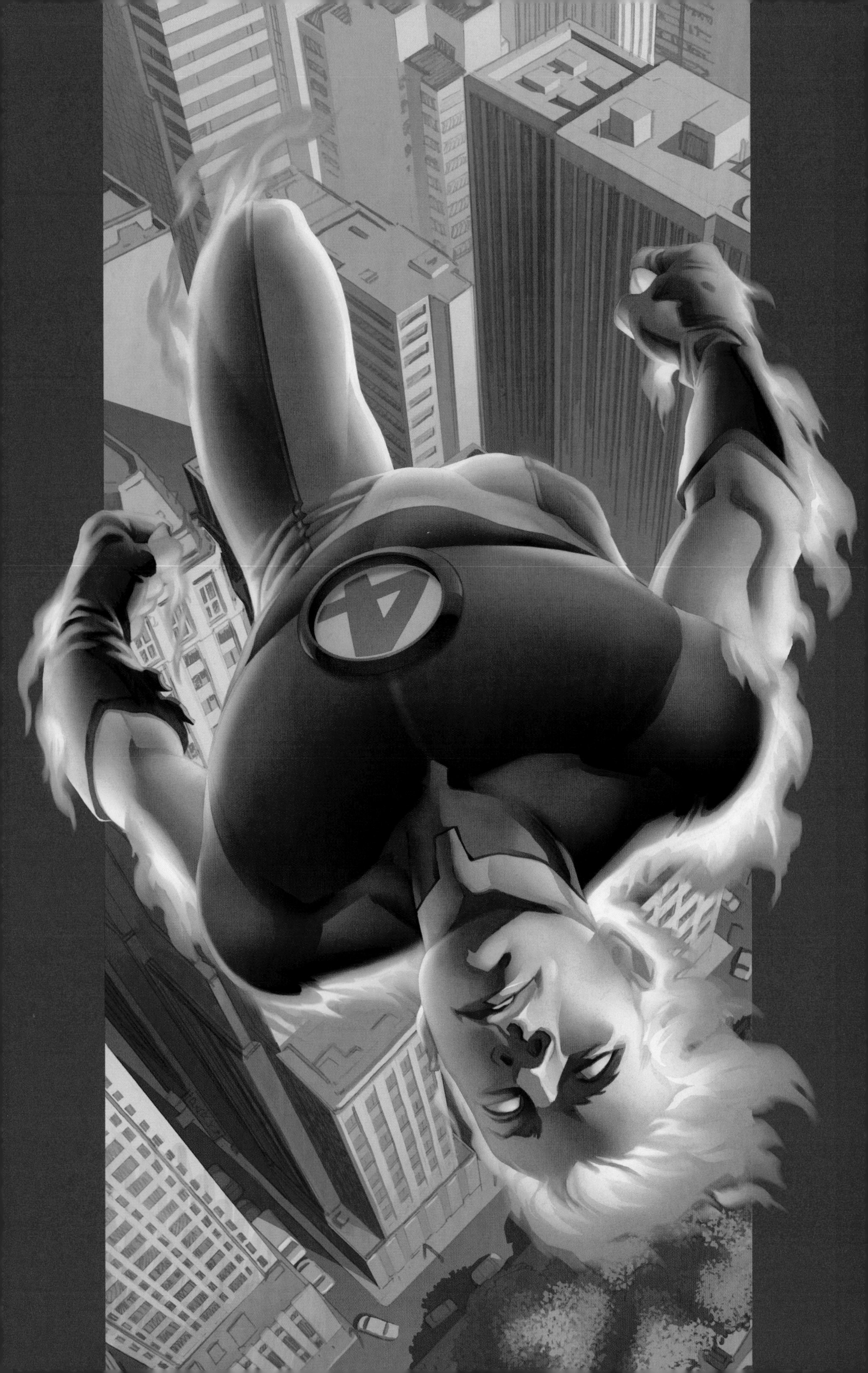

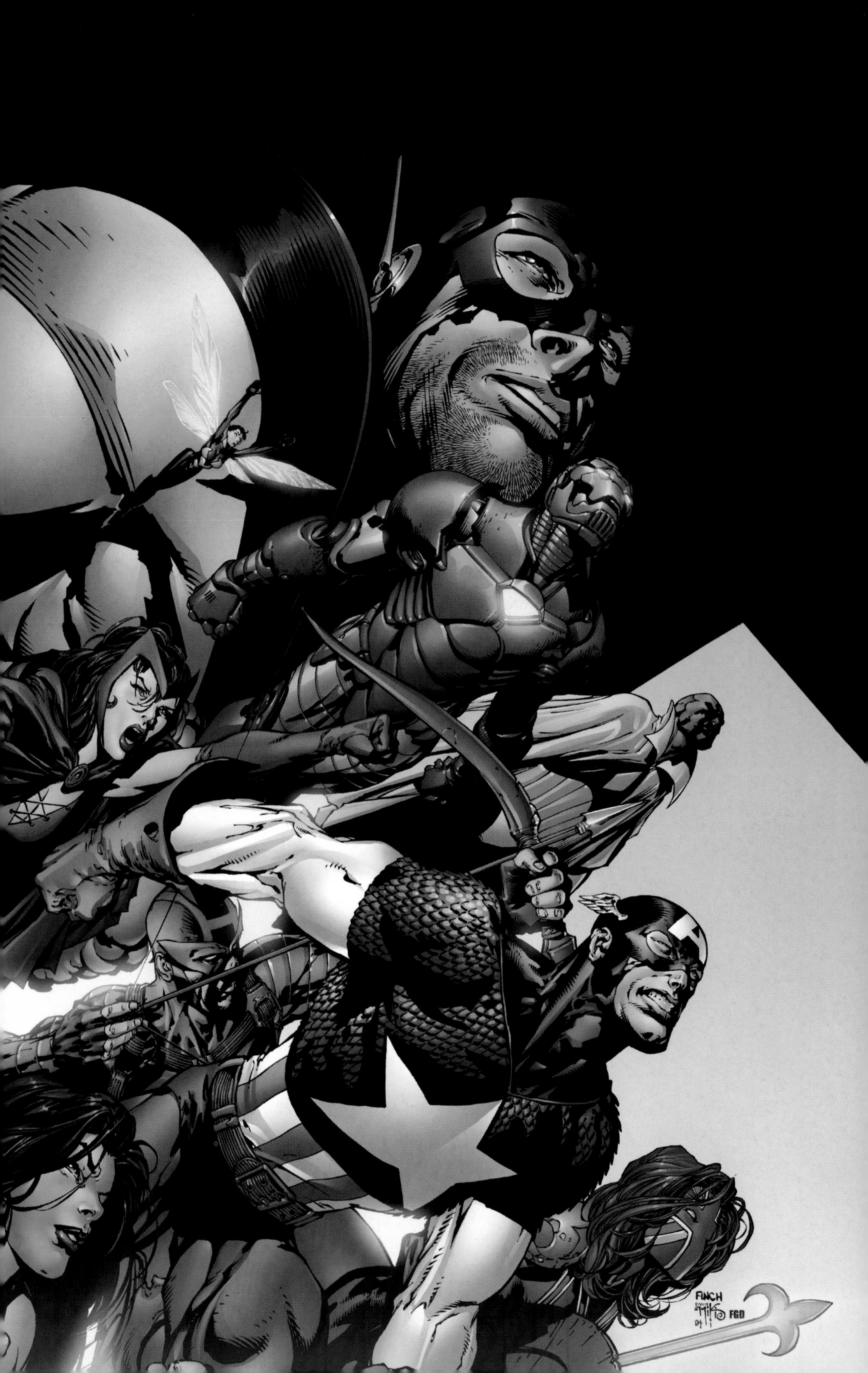
FINCH
FGD

Opposite: *Avengers #500* cover by David Finch. This page: *Avengers #500 Director's Cut* cover by John Cassaday.

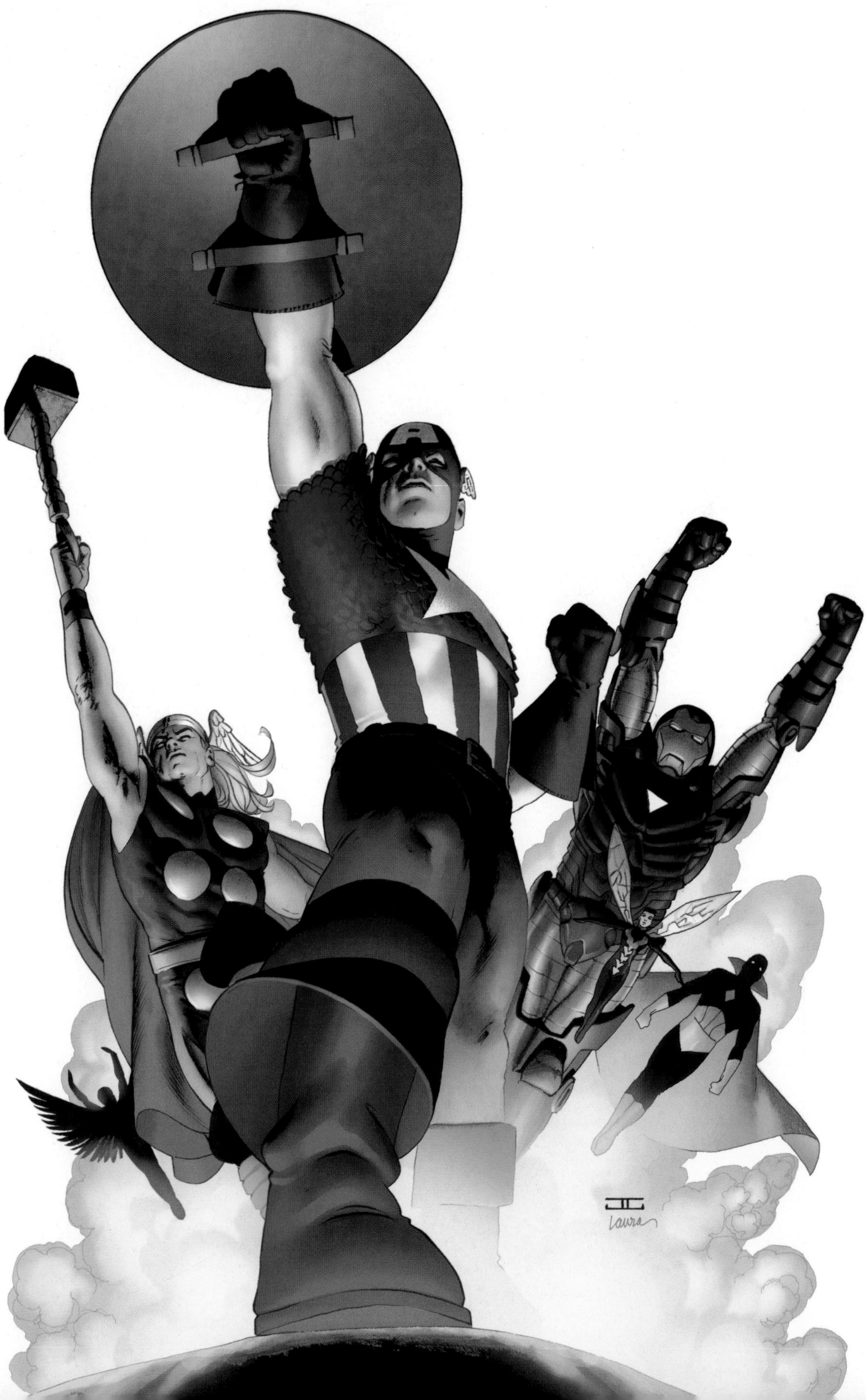

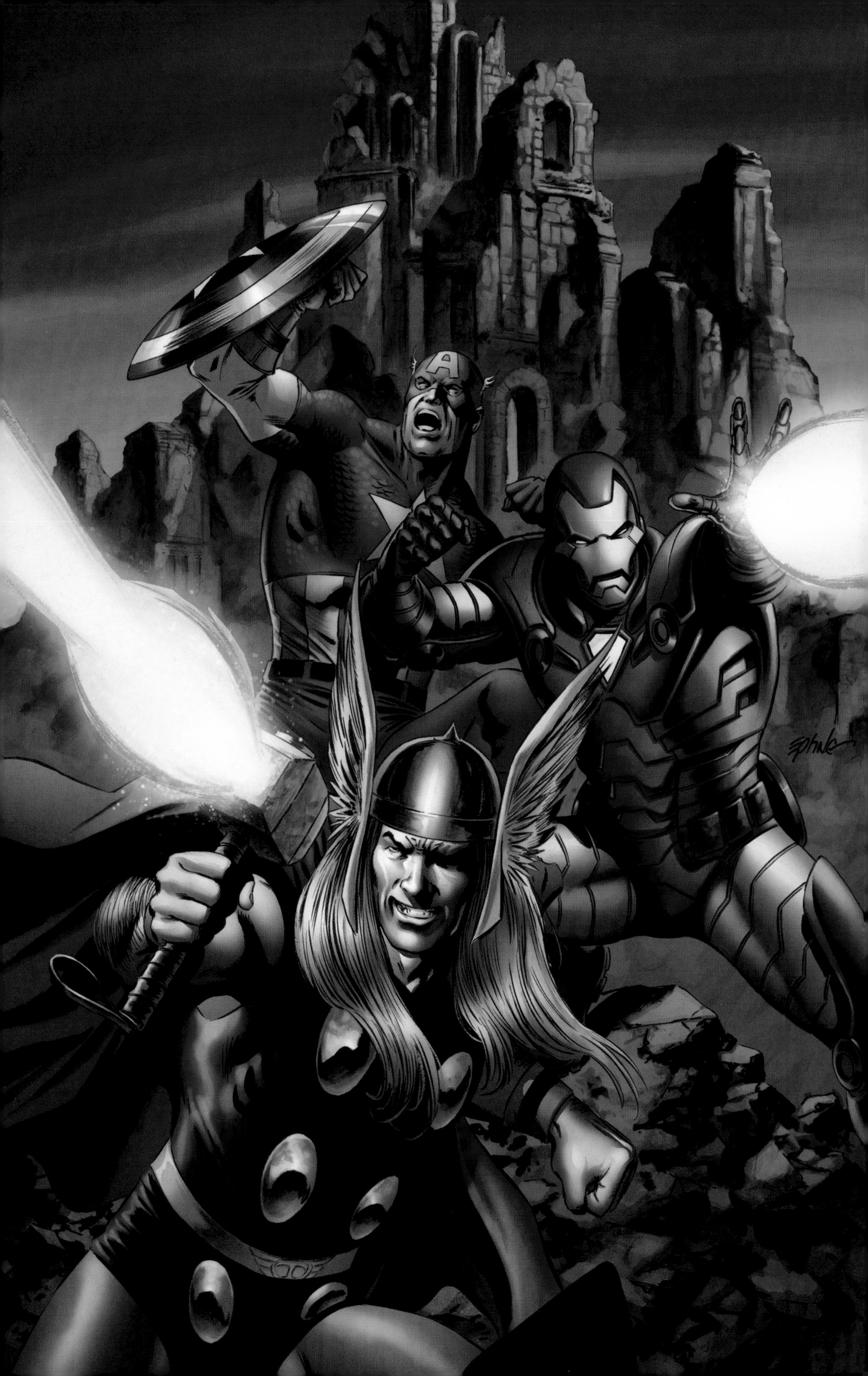

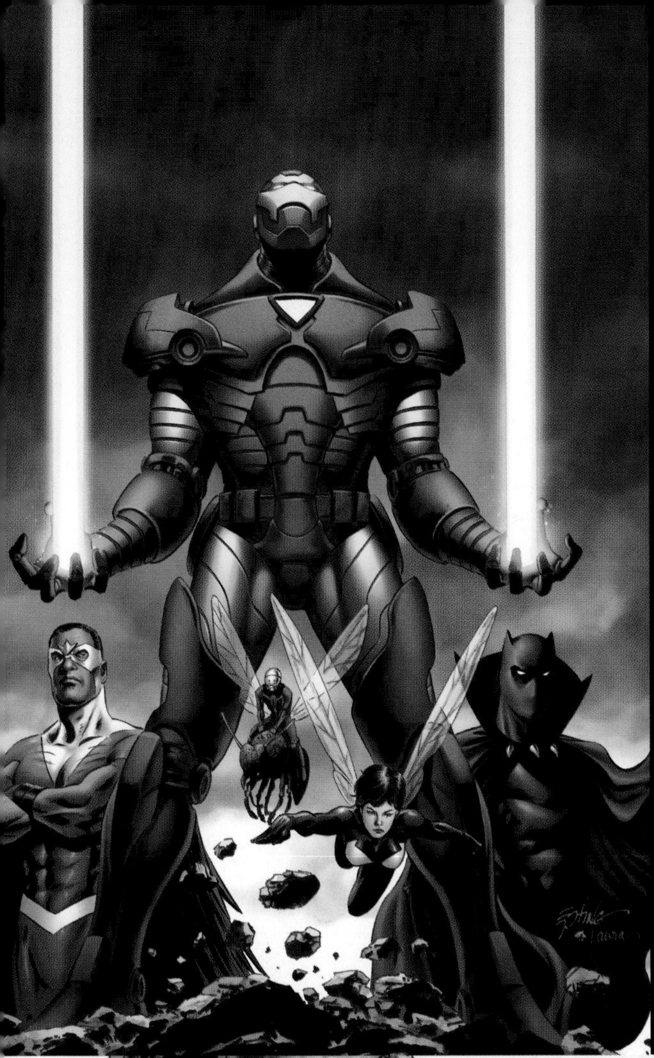

*"There are certain clichés of the team book genre that we have accepted over the years as good stories, and I thought if Spider-Man, Daredevil, the X-Men, and all these other books can grow as the sophistication of the audience has grown, why not the Avengers. If all these books can turn and twist with modern society and storytelling, why can't the Avengers? Why can't the Avengers be the best super hero comic on the stands?"*

Brian Michael Bendis
Writer, *Avengers*

Opposite: *Thor #81* cover by Steve Epting. This page, clockwise from top left: *Iron Man #84*, *Captain America and the Falcon #5* and *Spectacular Spider-Man #15* covers by Epting.

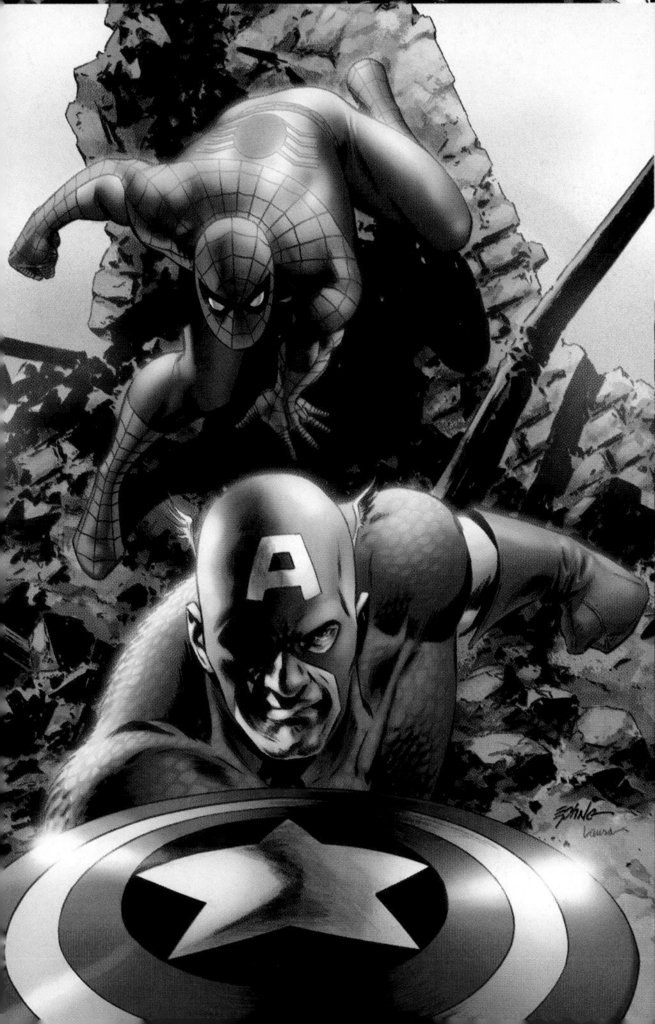

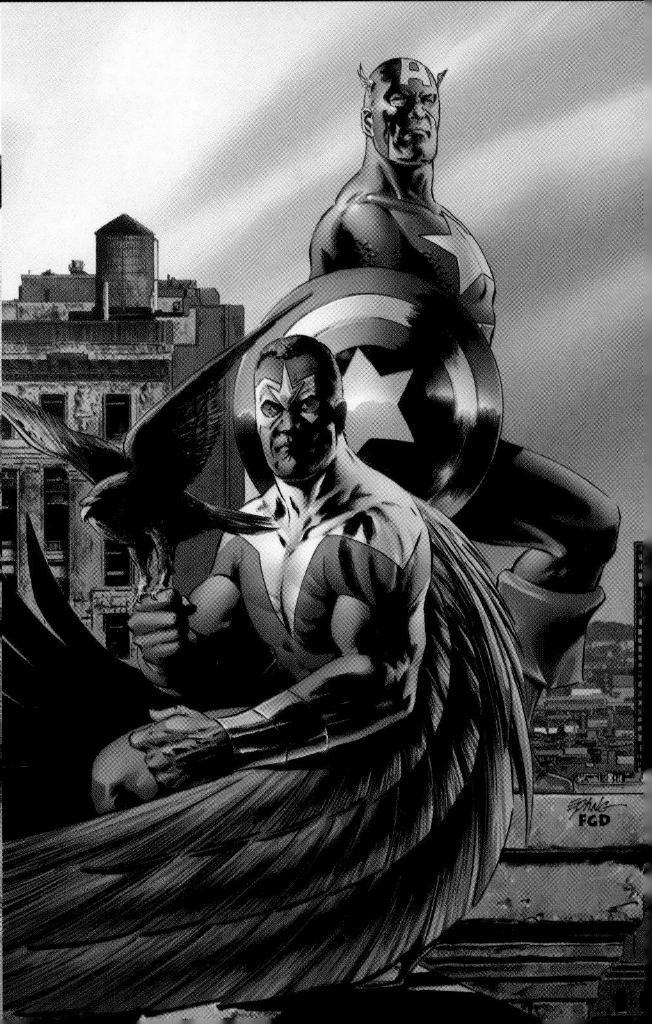

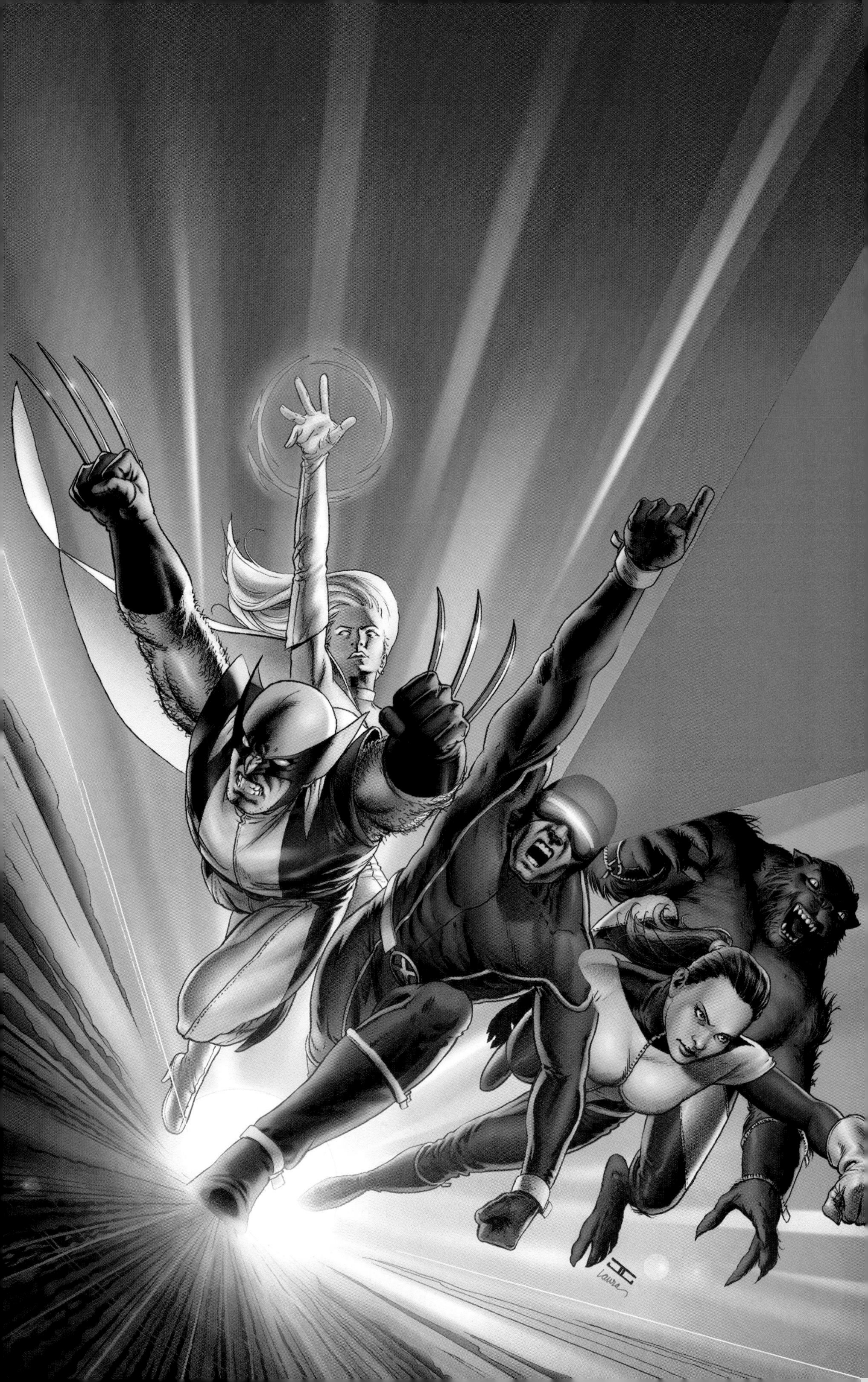

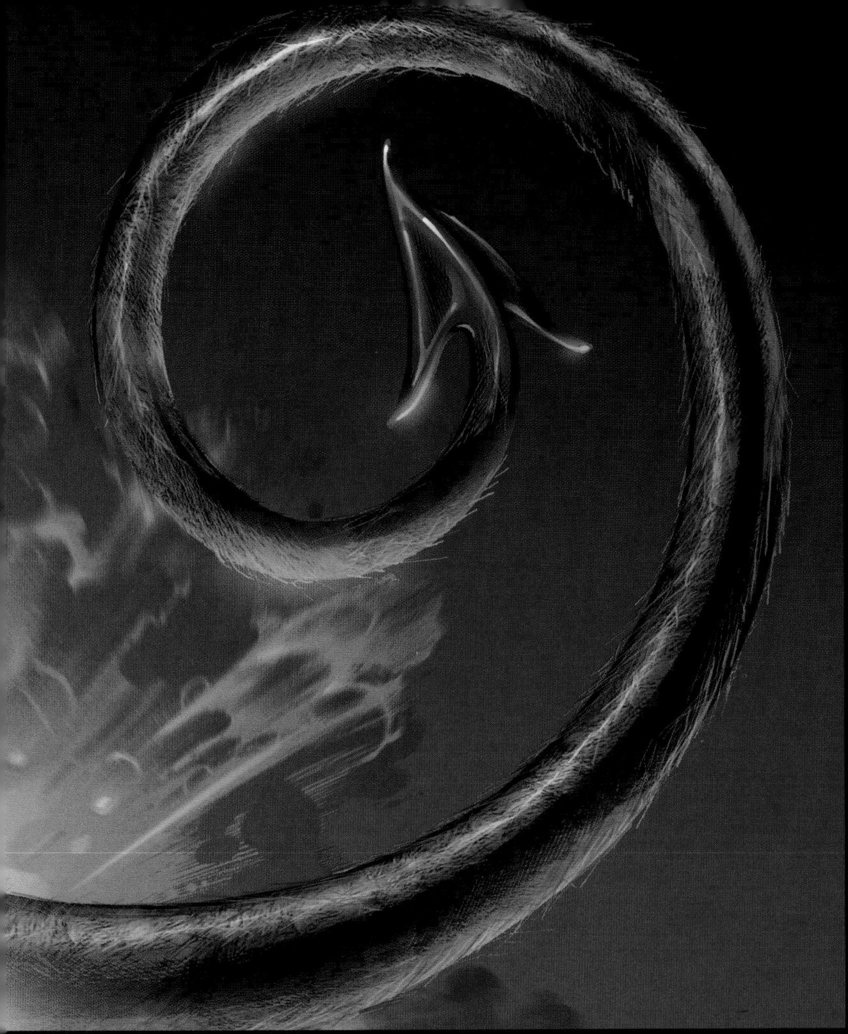

*"Fact is, (the X-Men) shouldn't be friends. It's like watching the 'Real World' or 'Survivor.' They all have such differences and wouldn't be caught dead in the same circles. These heroes are together only because they must be. The rest of the world doesn't want them."*

John Cassaday

Artist, *Astonishing X-Men*

Opposite: *Astonishing X-Men #1* variant cover by John Cassaday. This page, top left: *Uncanny X-Men #444* cover by Alan Davis. Bottom left: *X-Men #157* cover by Salvador Larroca. Bottom right: *Astonishing X-Men #1* cover by Cassaday.

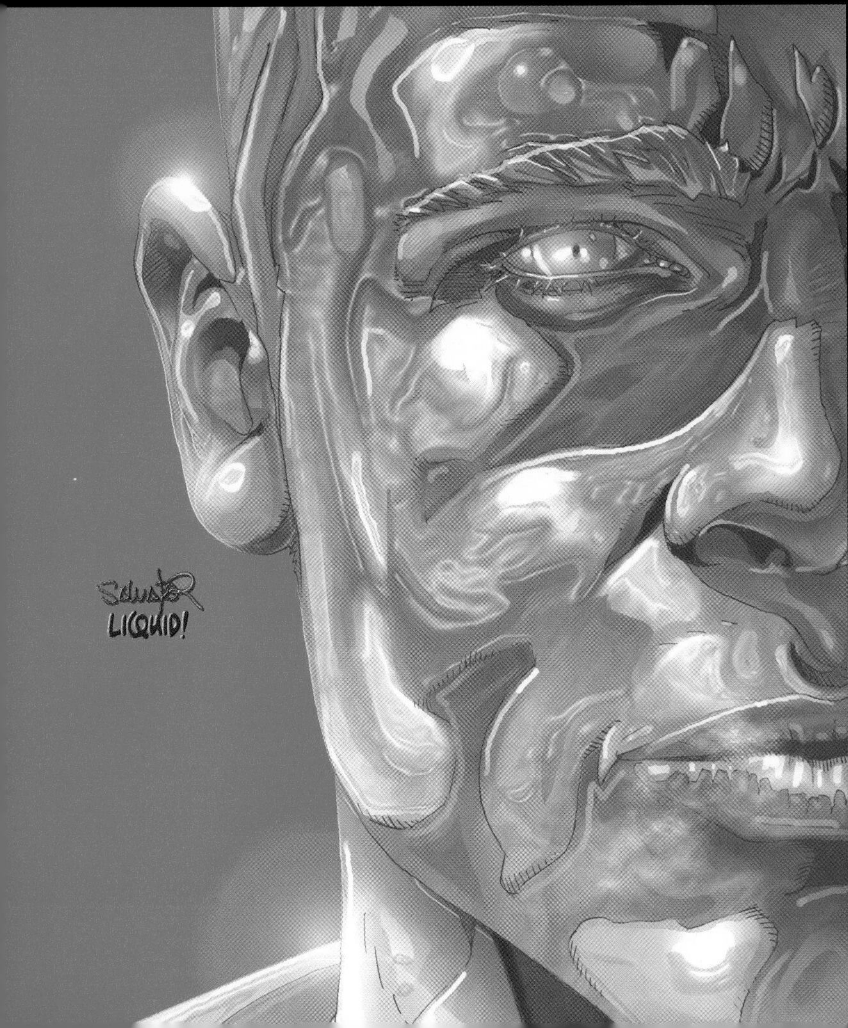
LIQUID!

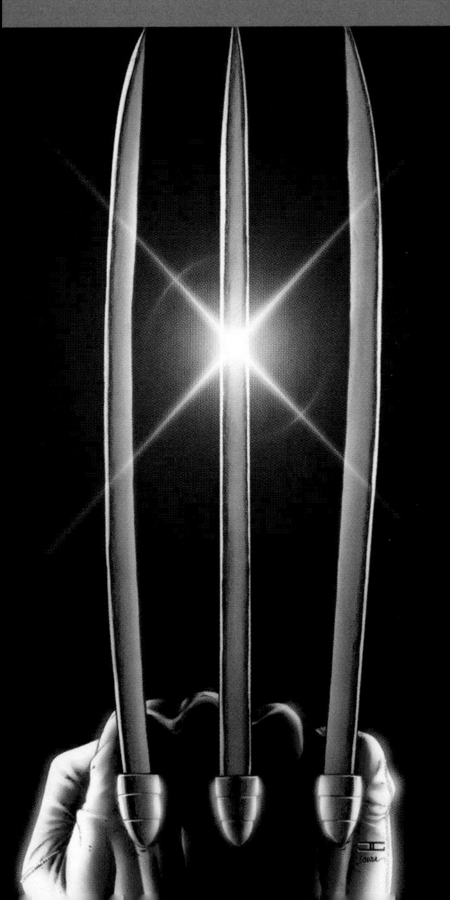

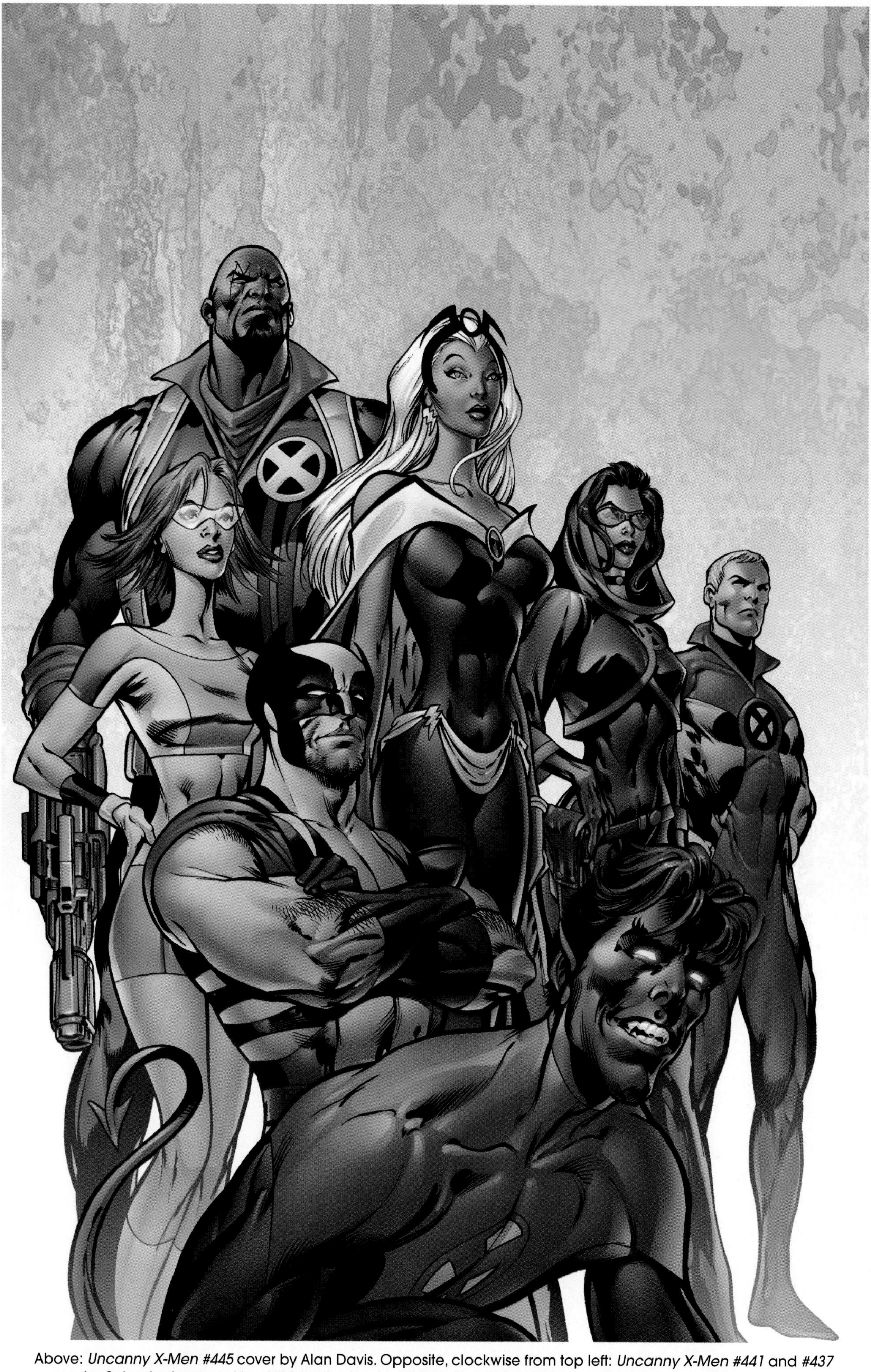

Above: *Uncanny X-Men #445* cover by Alan Davis. Opposite, clockwise from top left: *Uncanny X-Men #441* and *#437* covers by Salvador Larroca, *New X-Men #1* cover by Randy Green, and *X-Treme X-Men #39* cover by Larroca.

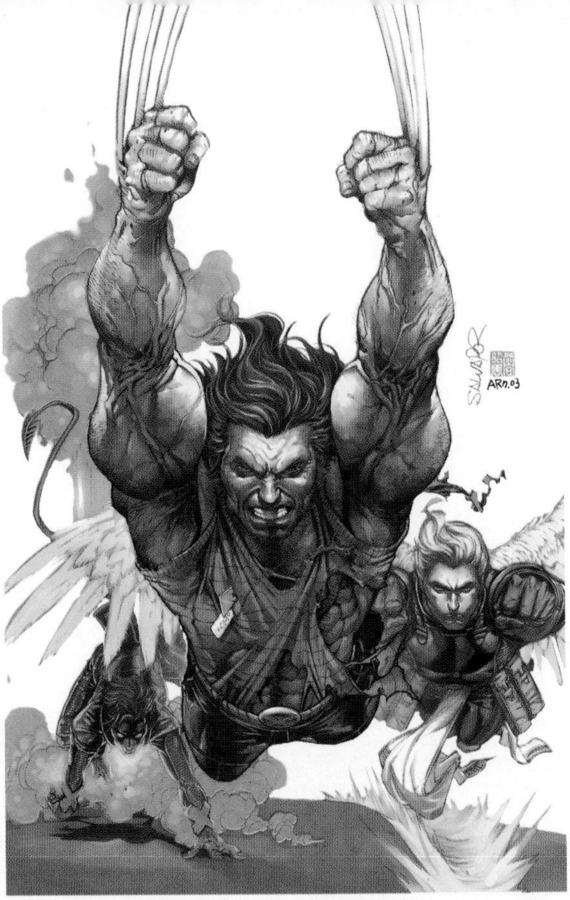
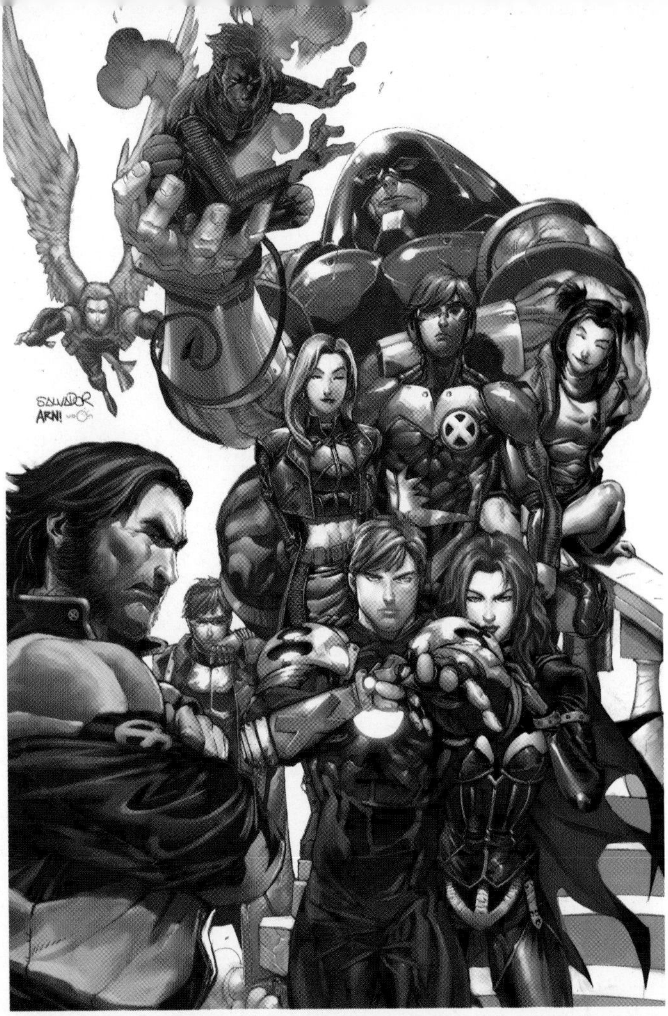
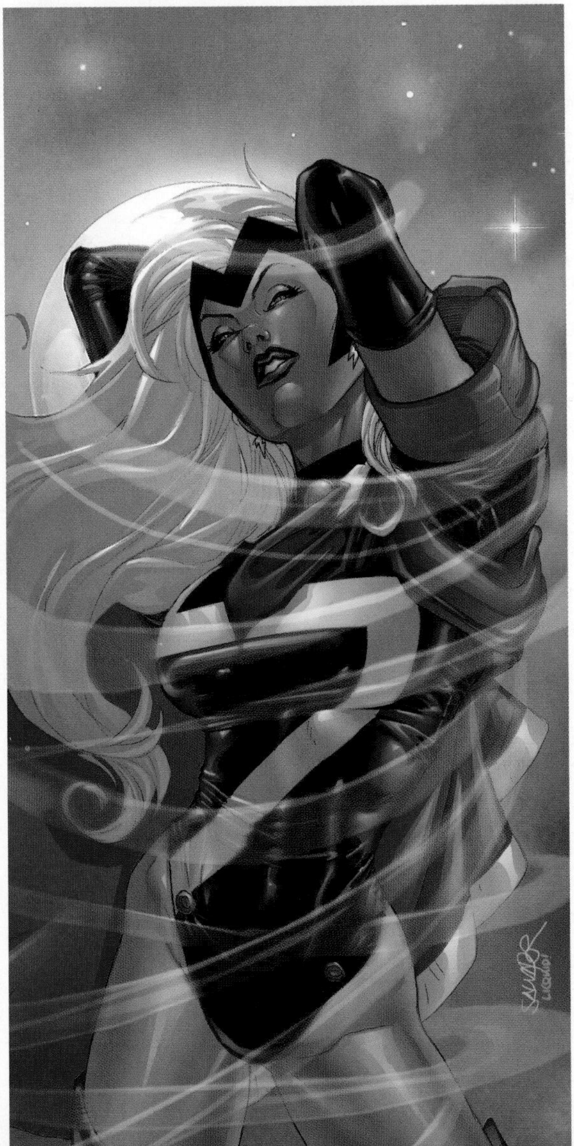
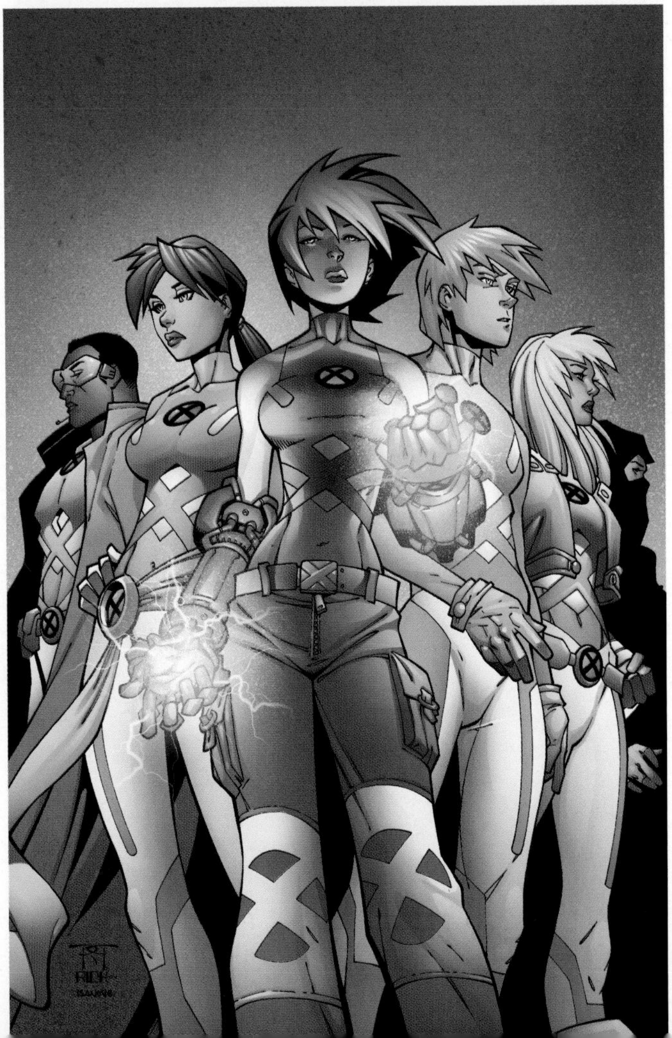

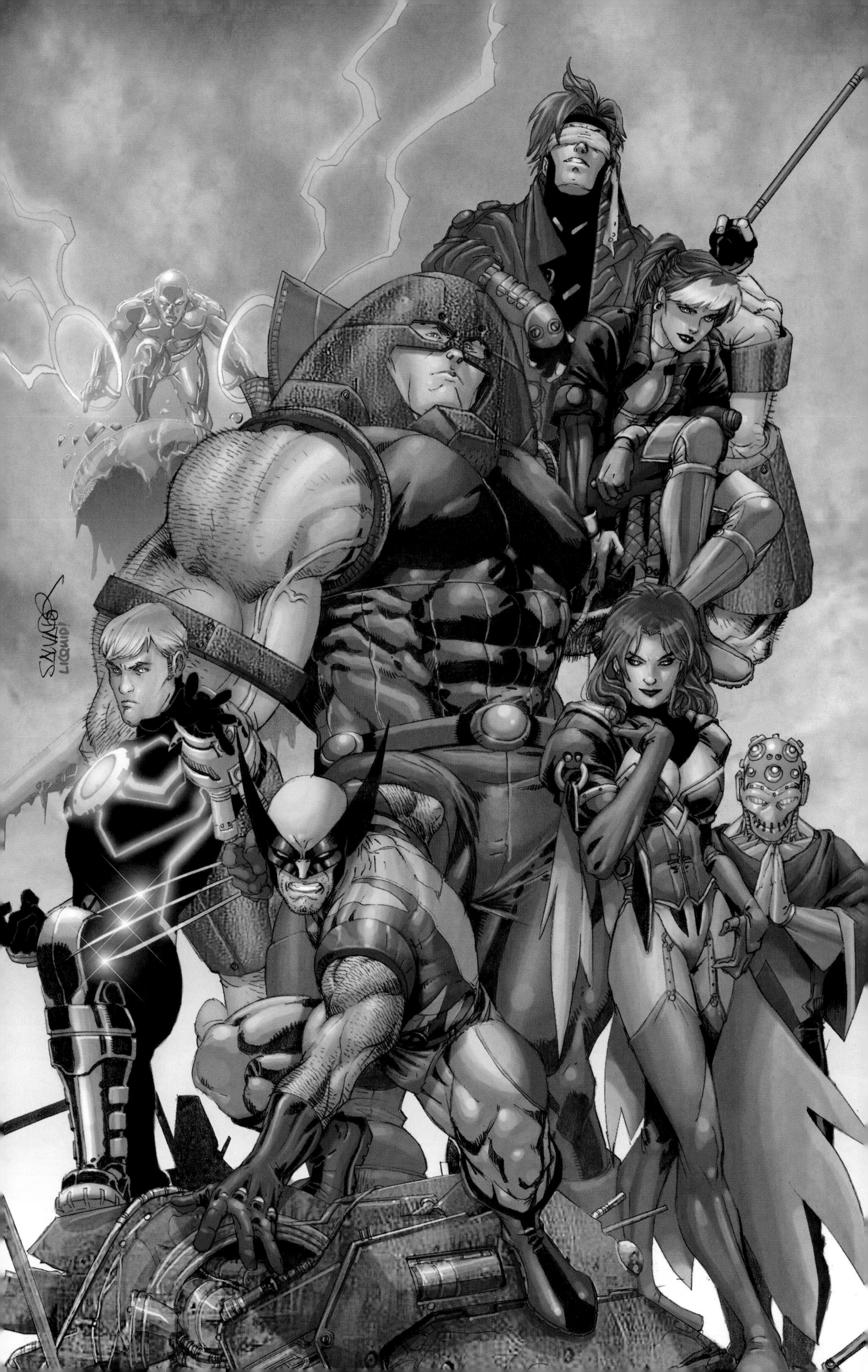

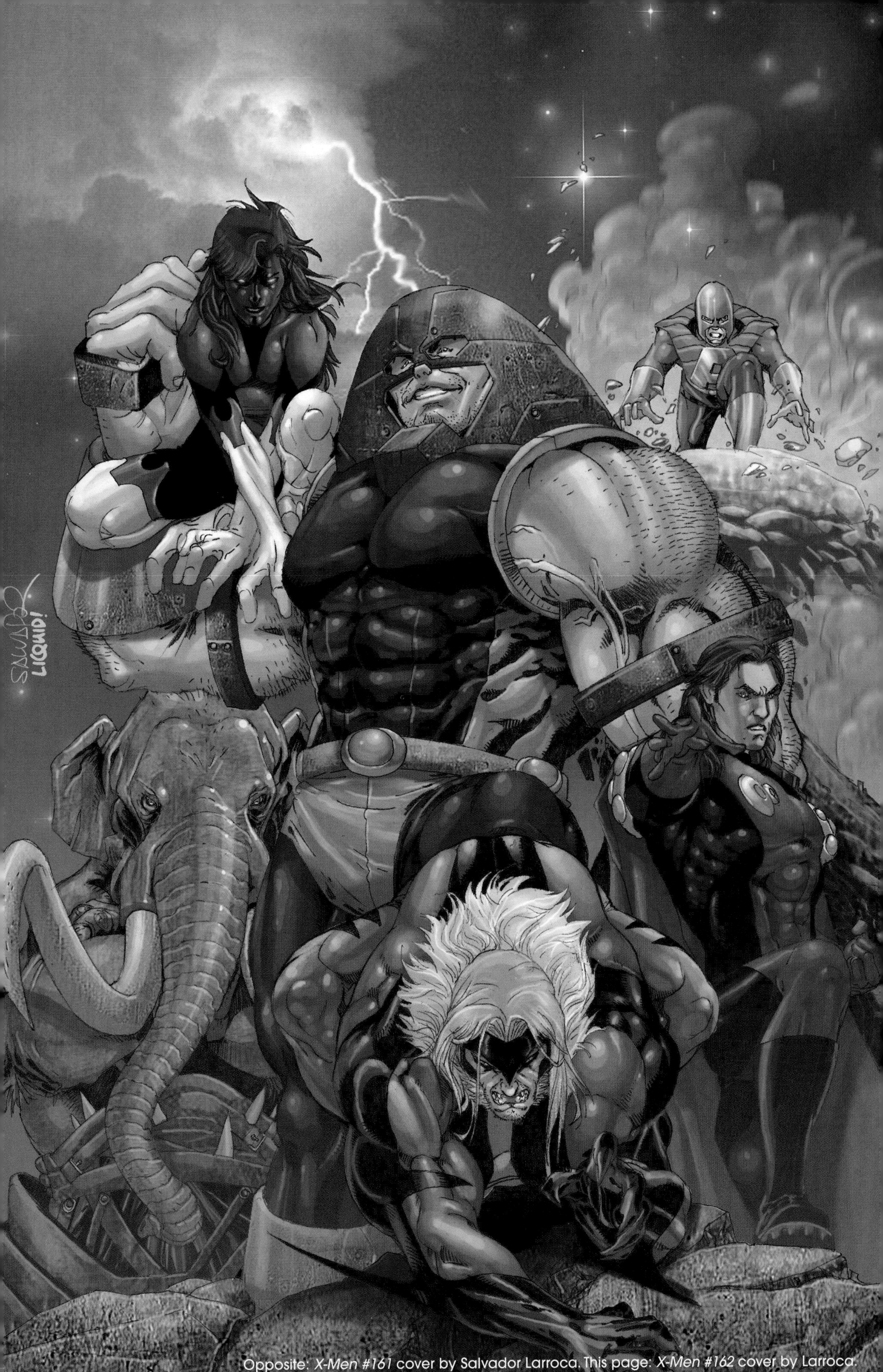
SALVADOR
LIQUID!

Opposite: *X-Men #161* cover by Salvador Larroca. This page: *X-Men #162* cover by Larroca.

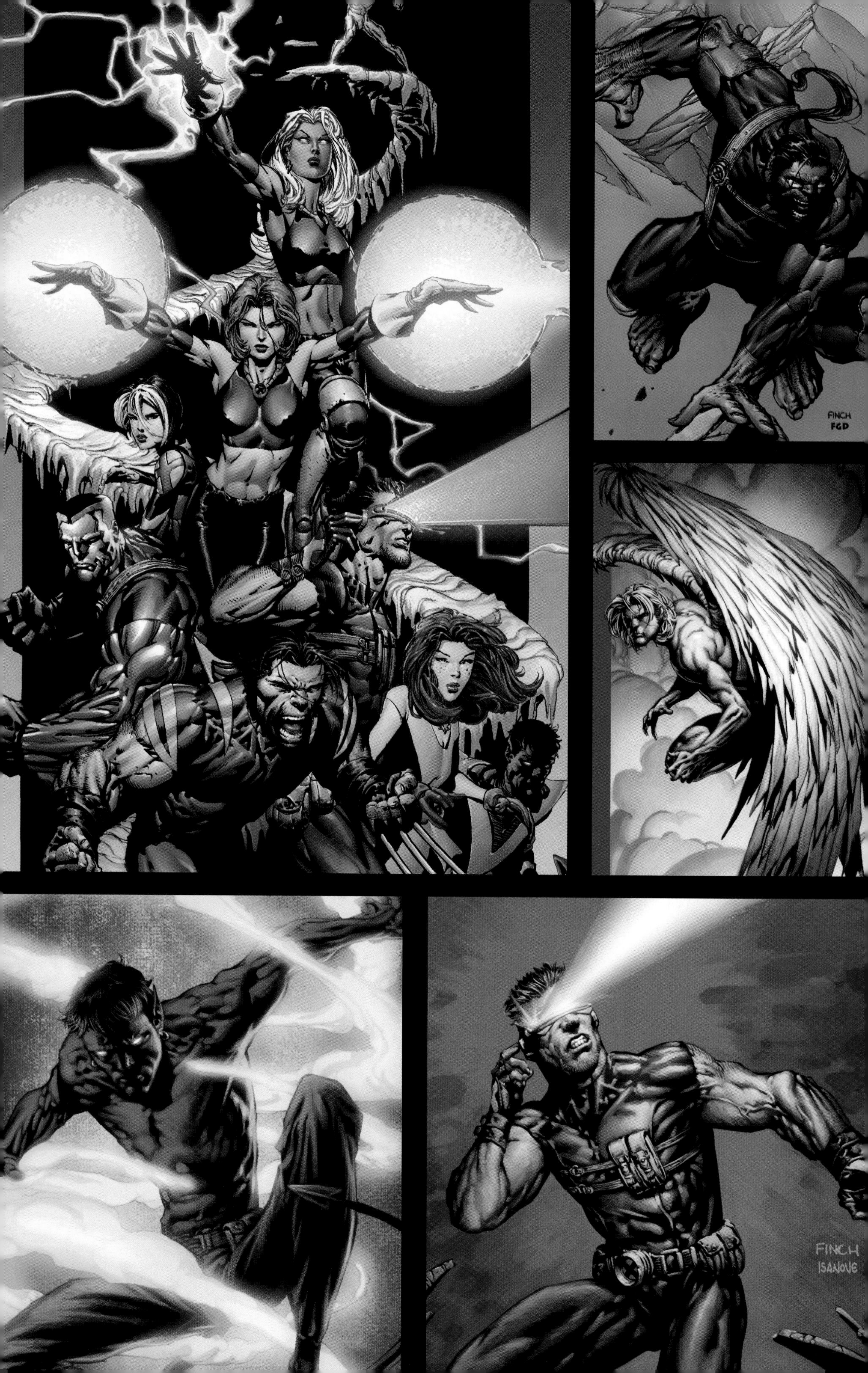
FINCH
FGD
FINCH
ISANOVE

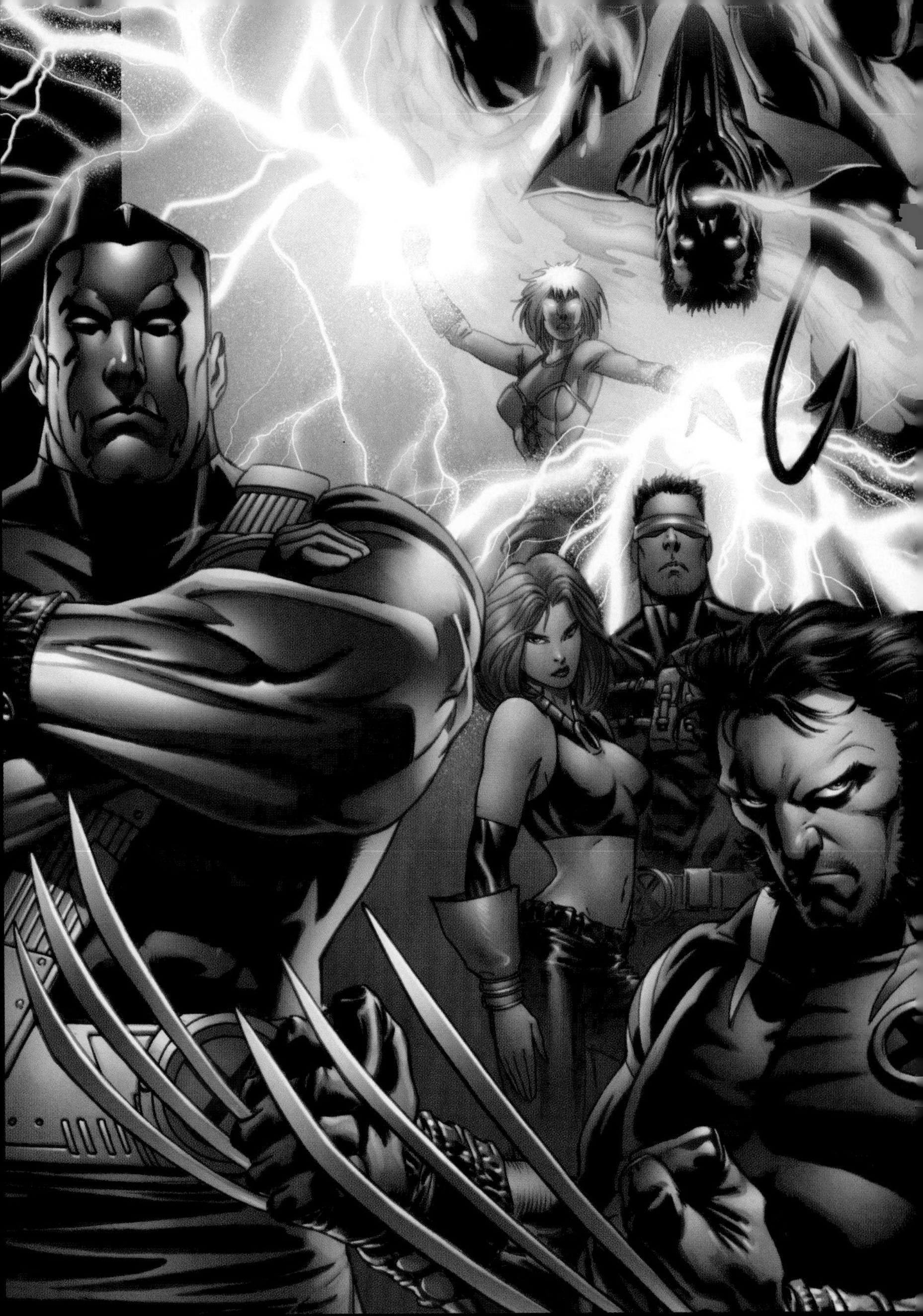

Opposite, clockwise from top right: *Ultimate X-Men #39, #40* and *#43-45* covers by David Finch. Below: *Ultimate X-Men #26* and *#33* covers by Adam Kubert. Right: *Ultimate X-Men #50* cover by Andy Kubert.

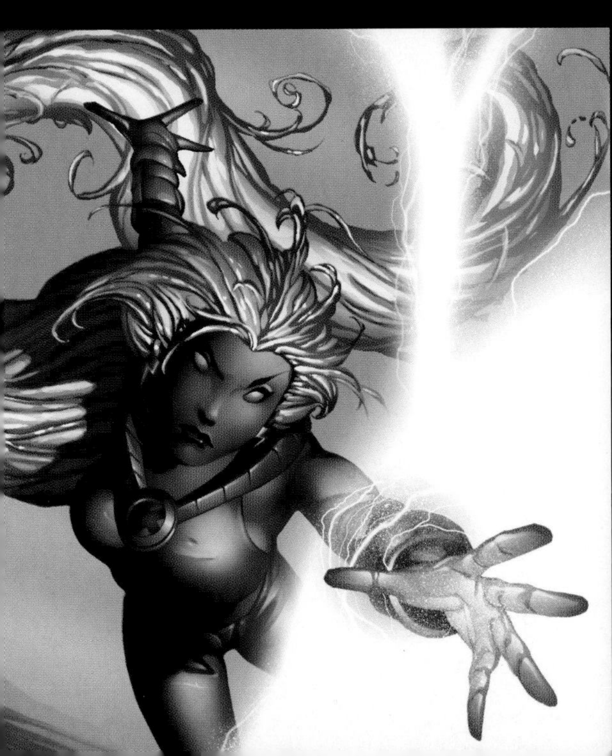

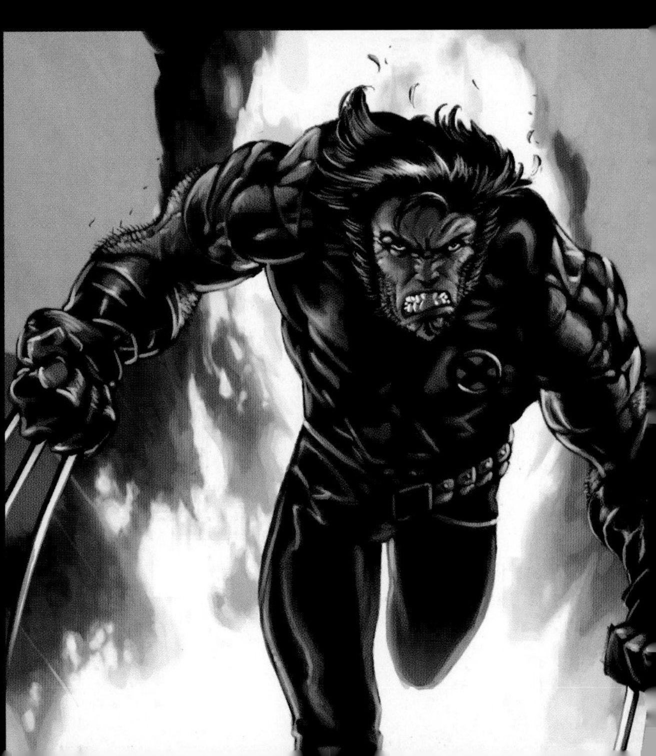

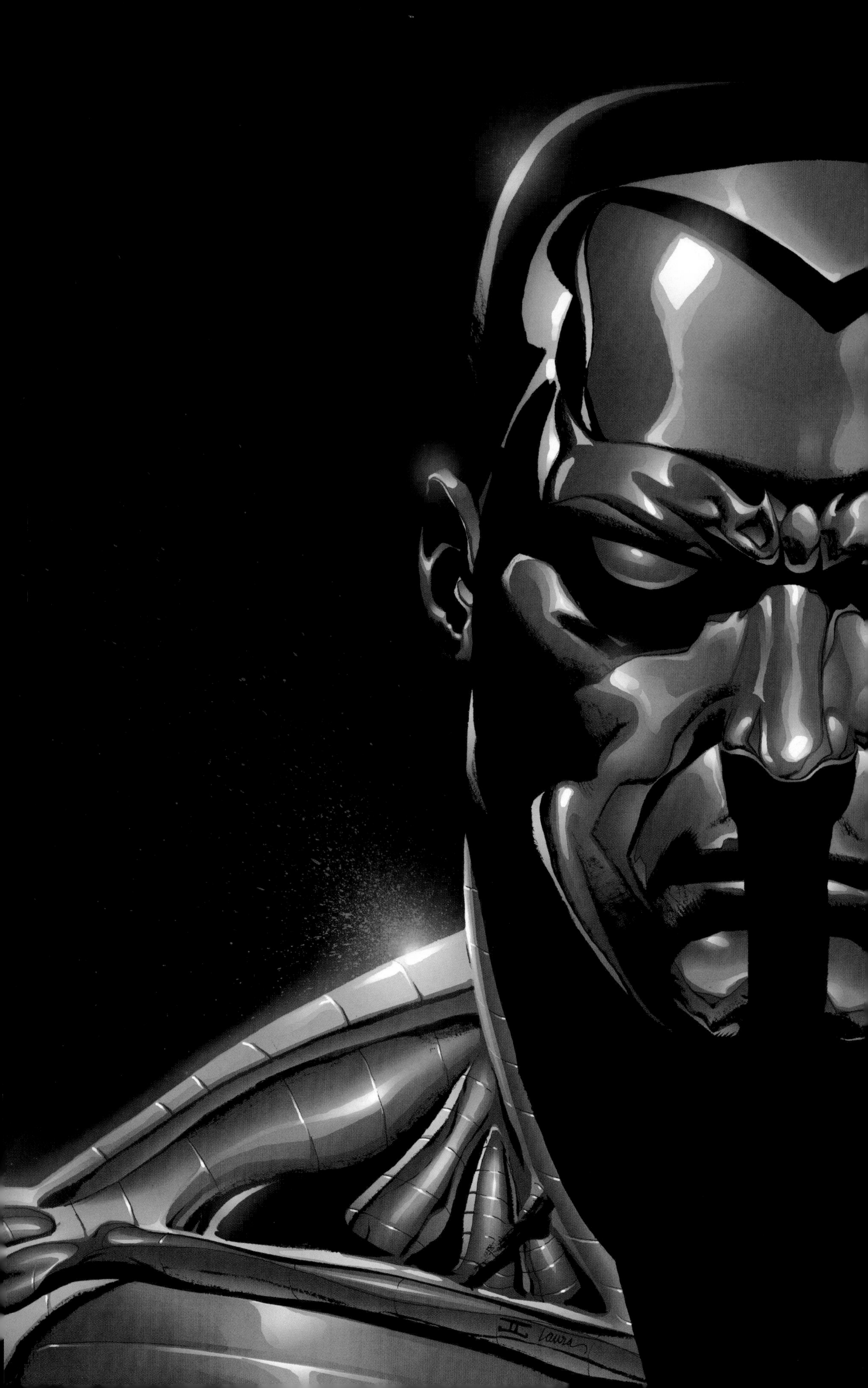

Opposite: *Astonishing X-Men #4* variant cover by John Cassaday.
This page: *Astonishing X-Men #1* variant cover by Gabriele Dell'Otto.

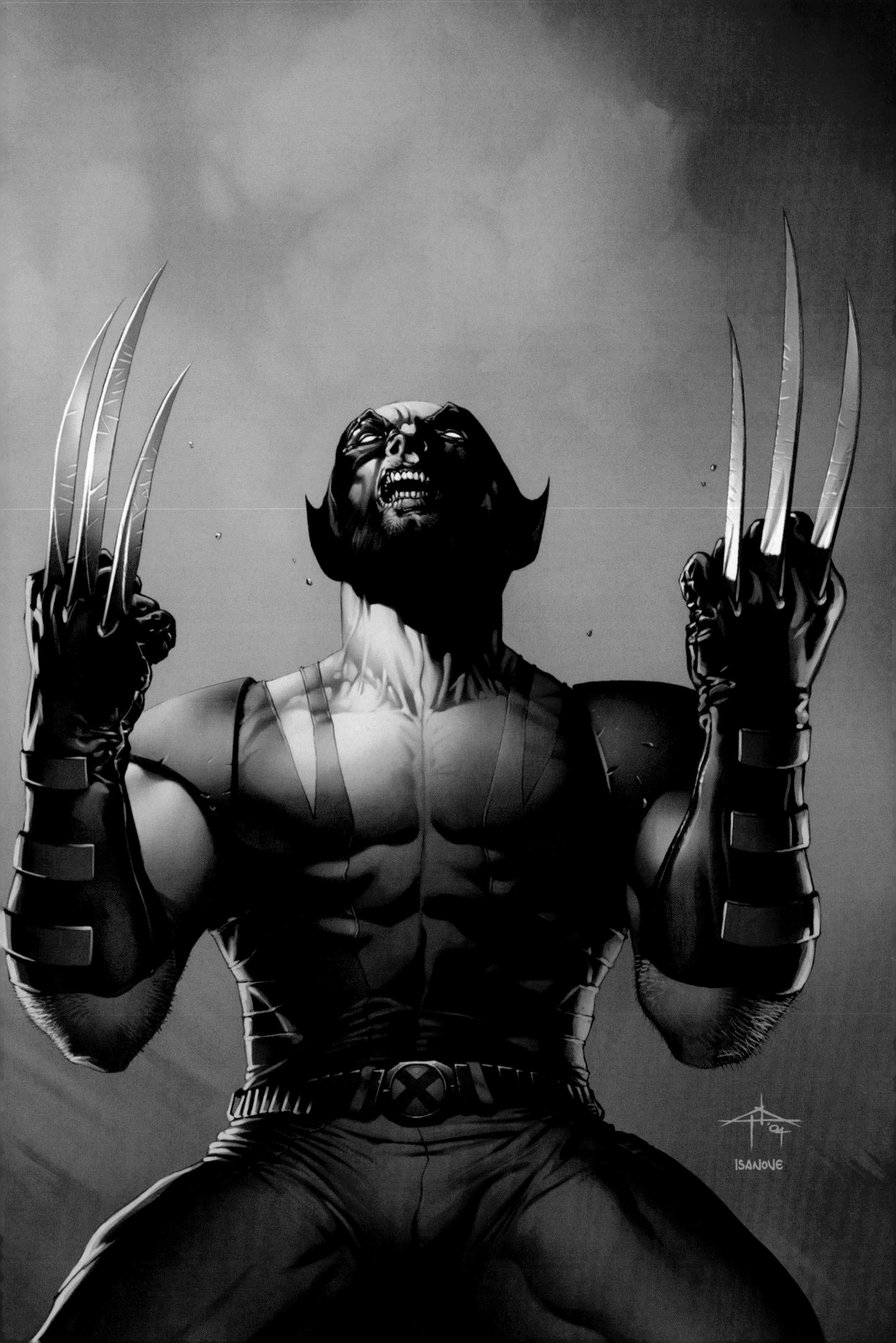
ISANOVE

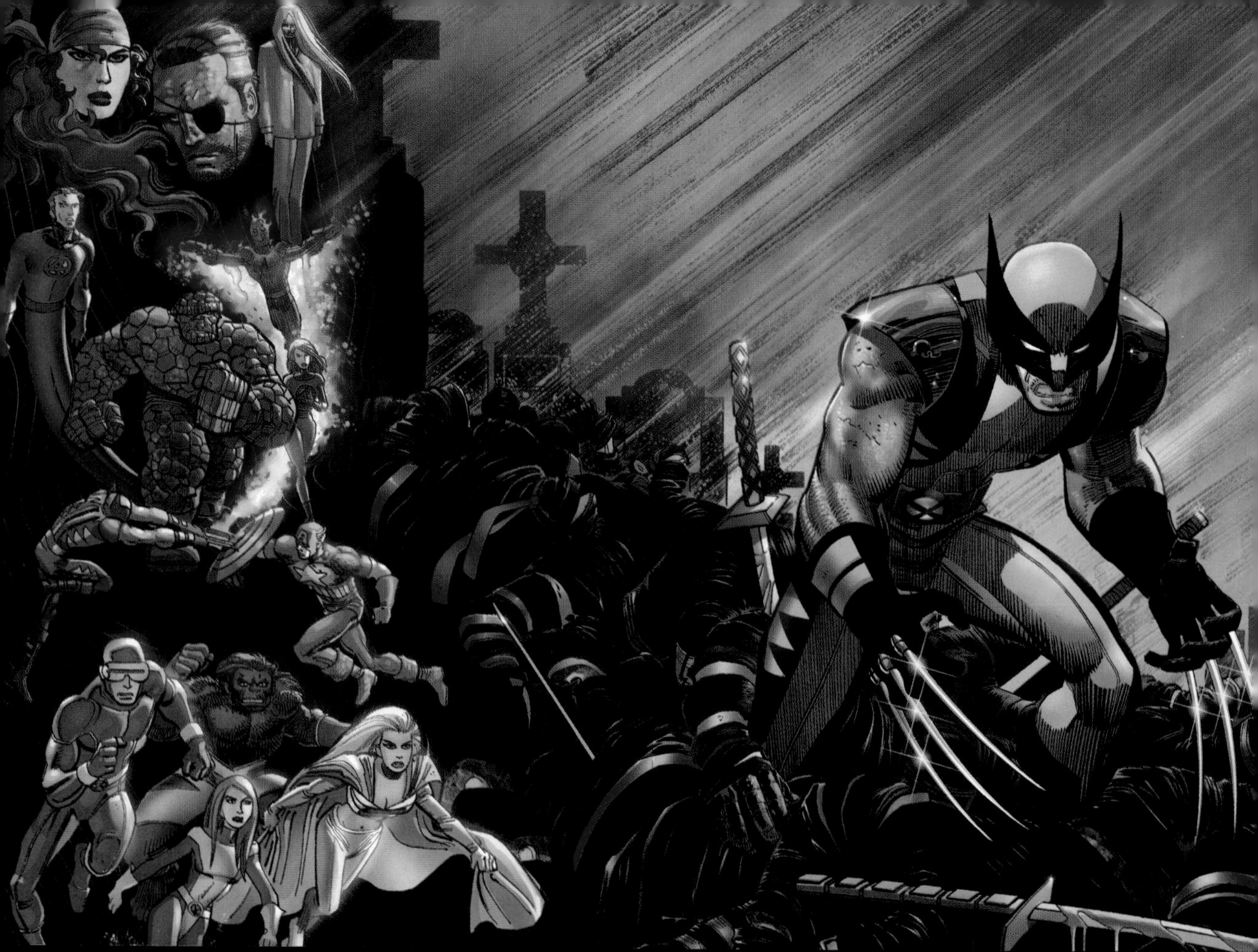

Above: *Wolverine #20* cover by John Romita Jr. Below: *Marvel Knights Spider-Man #1* cover by Terry Dodson. Opposite: *Amazing Spider-Man #509* cover by Mike Deodato Jr.

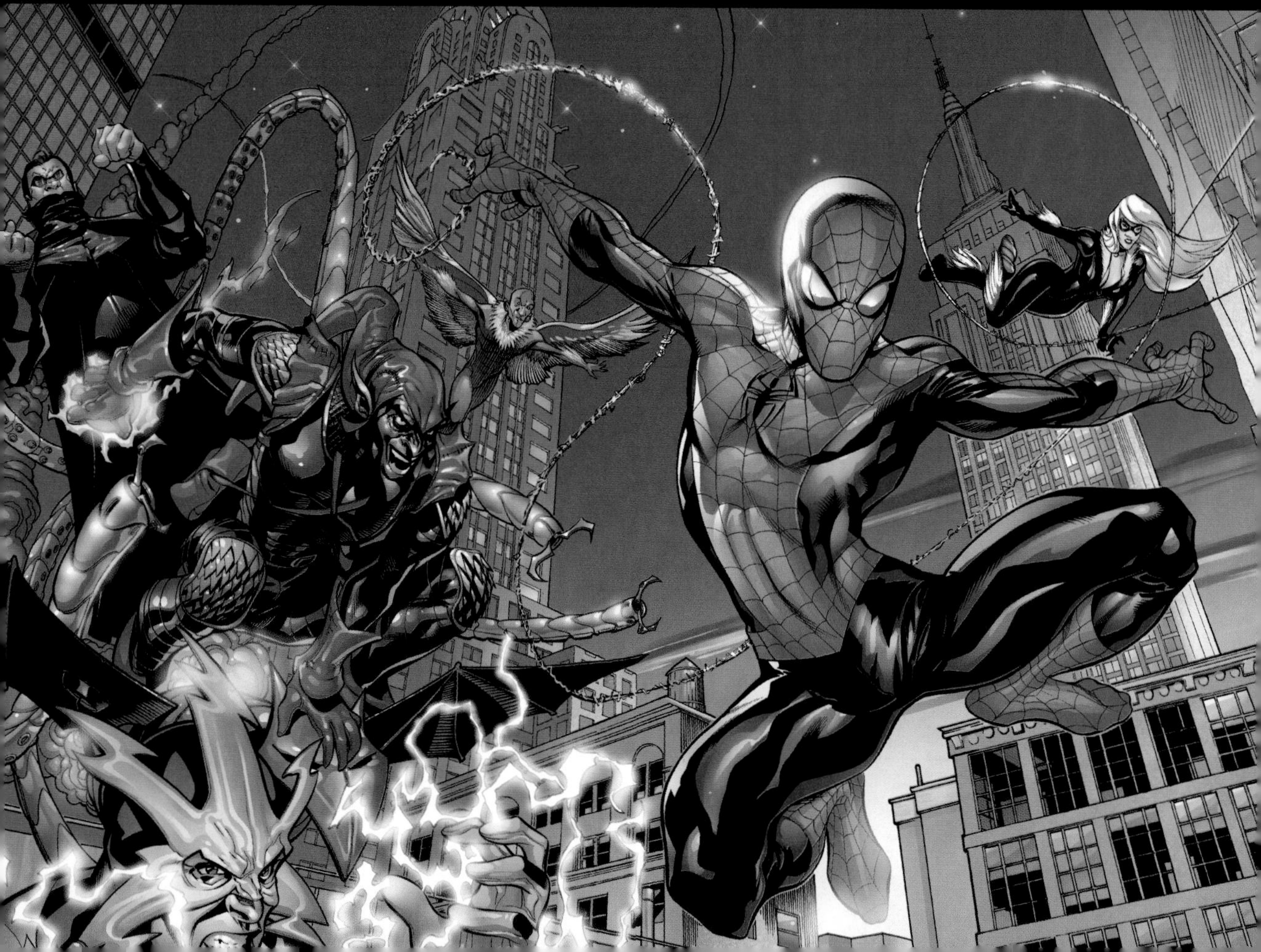

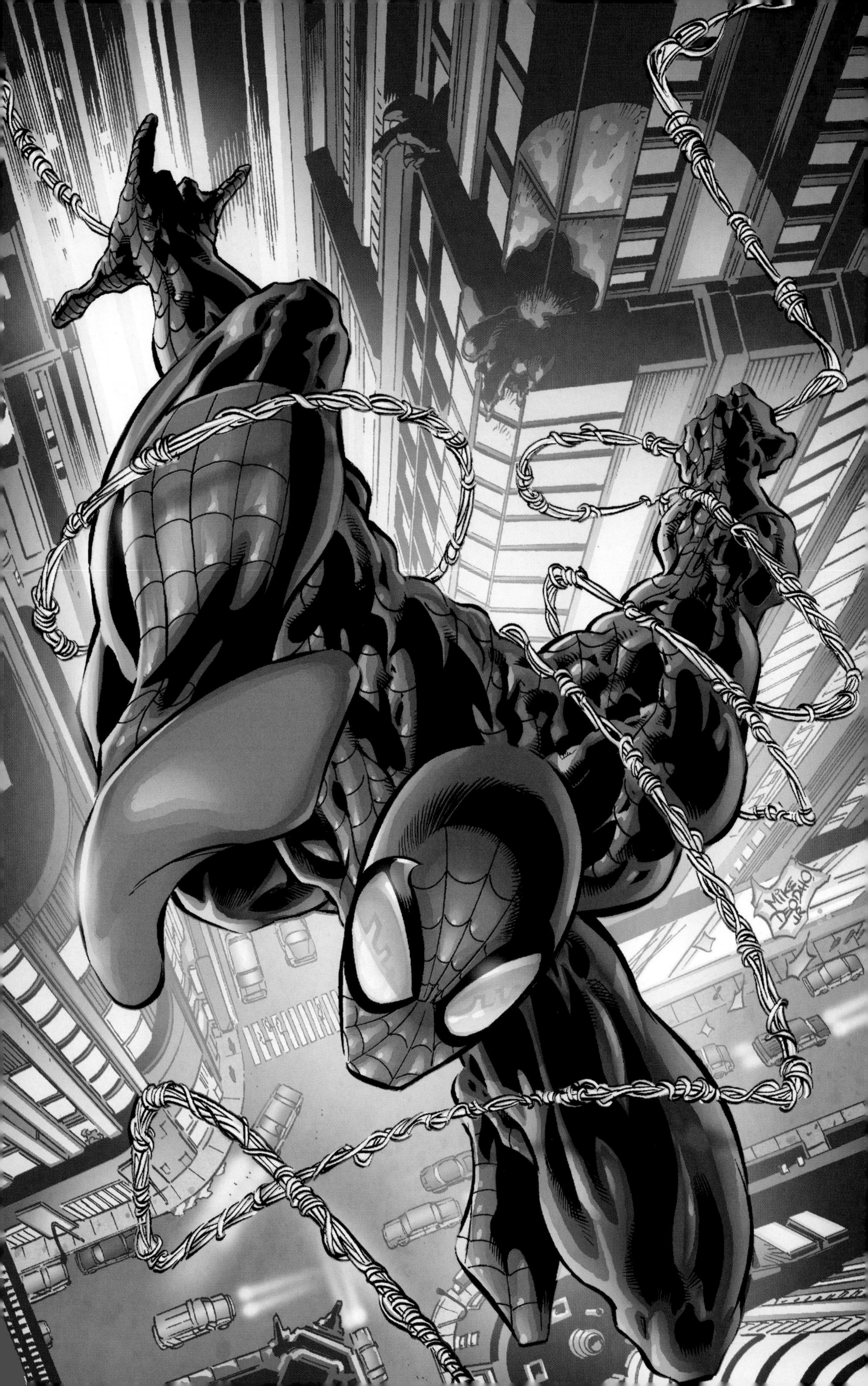

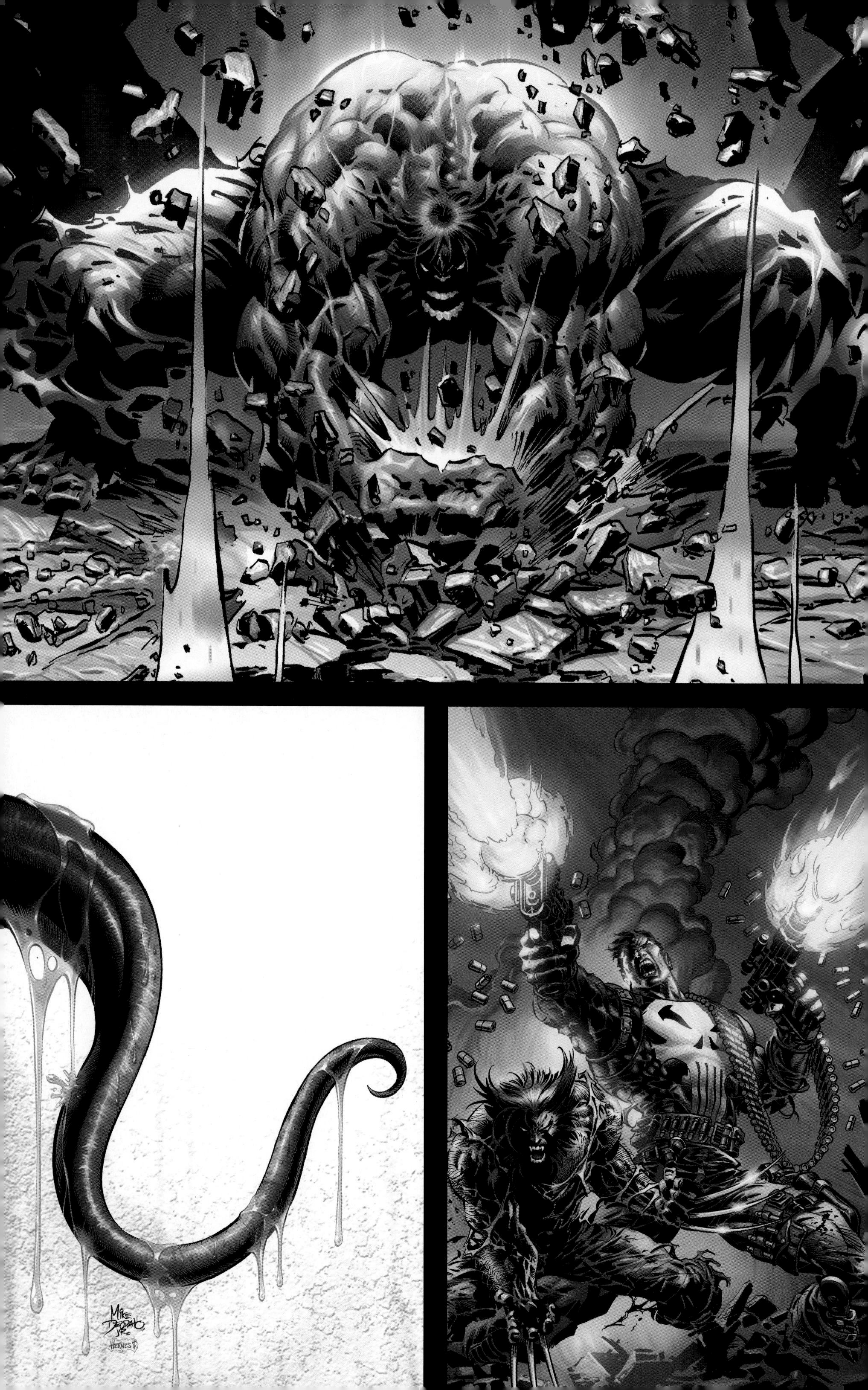
MIKE DEODATO, JR.
HERMES

*"Mike Deodato's assets are obvious — dynamic figures in motion and a talent for the still moment, stormy blacks and crackling whites."*

Warren Ellis
Writer, *Iron Man*

Opposite, clockwise from top: *Incredible Hulk #64*, *Wolverine/Punisher #1* and *Venom #11* covers by Mike Deodato Jr. This page: *Identity Disc #2* (top) and *Venom #12* (bottom) covers by Deodato.

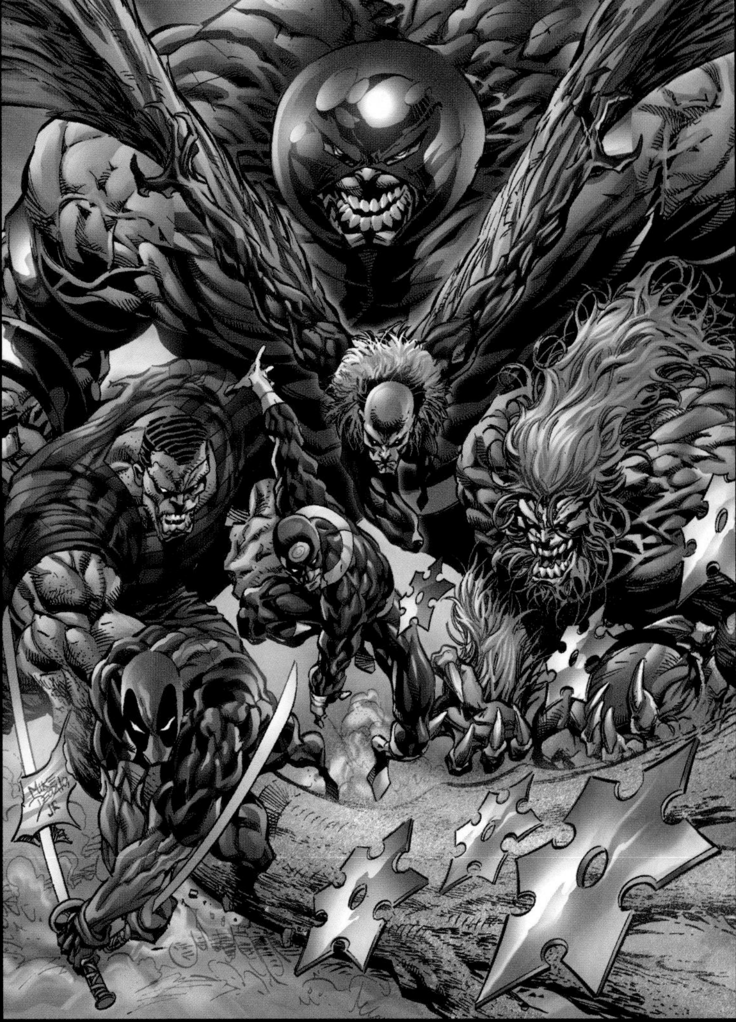

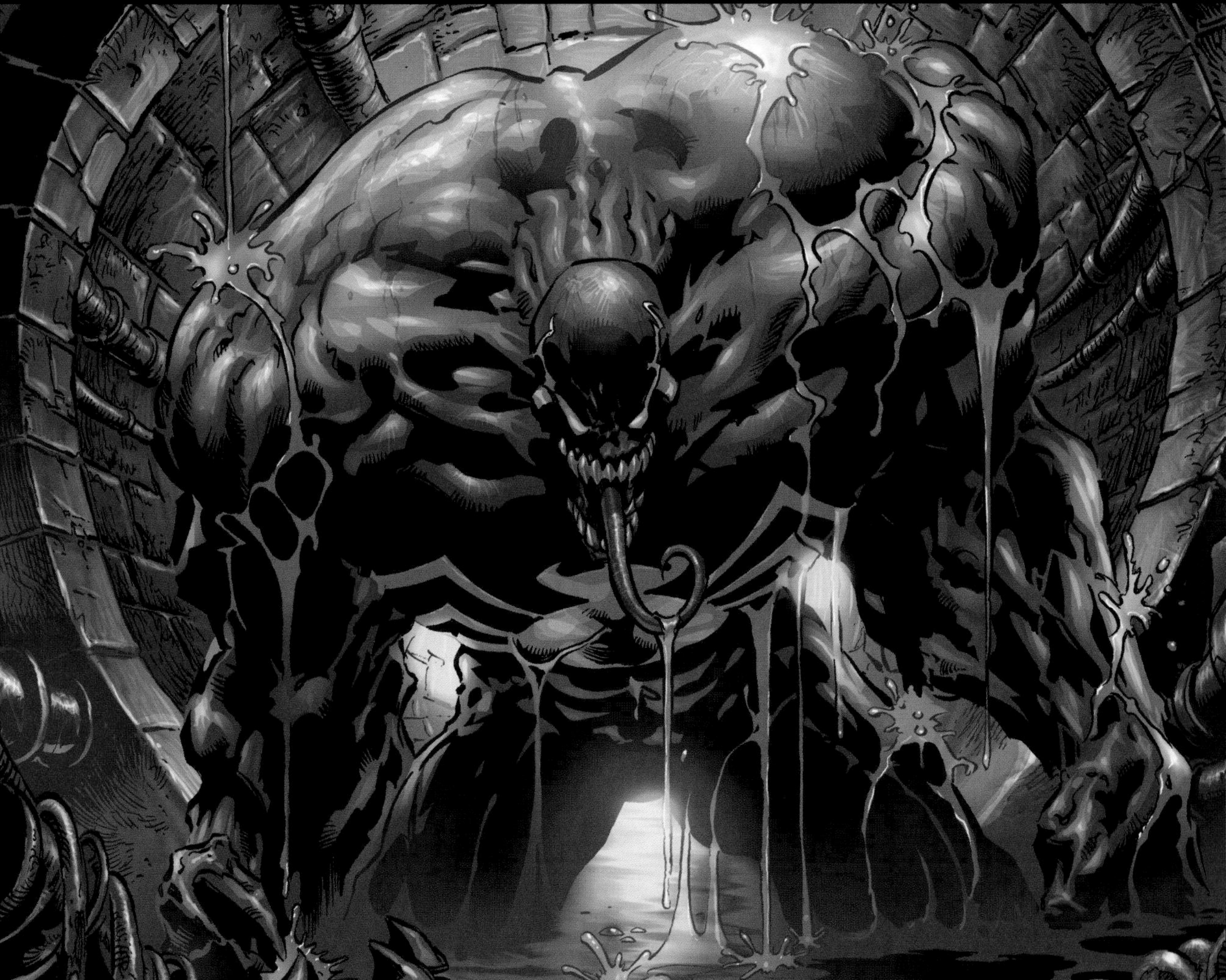

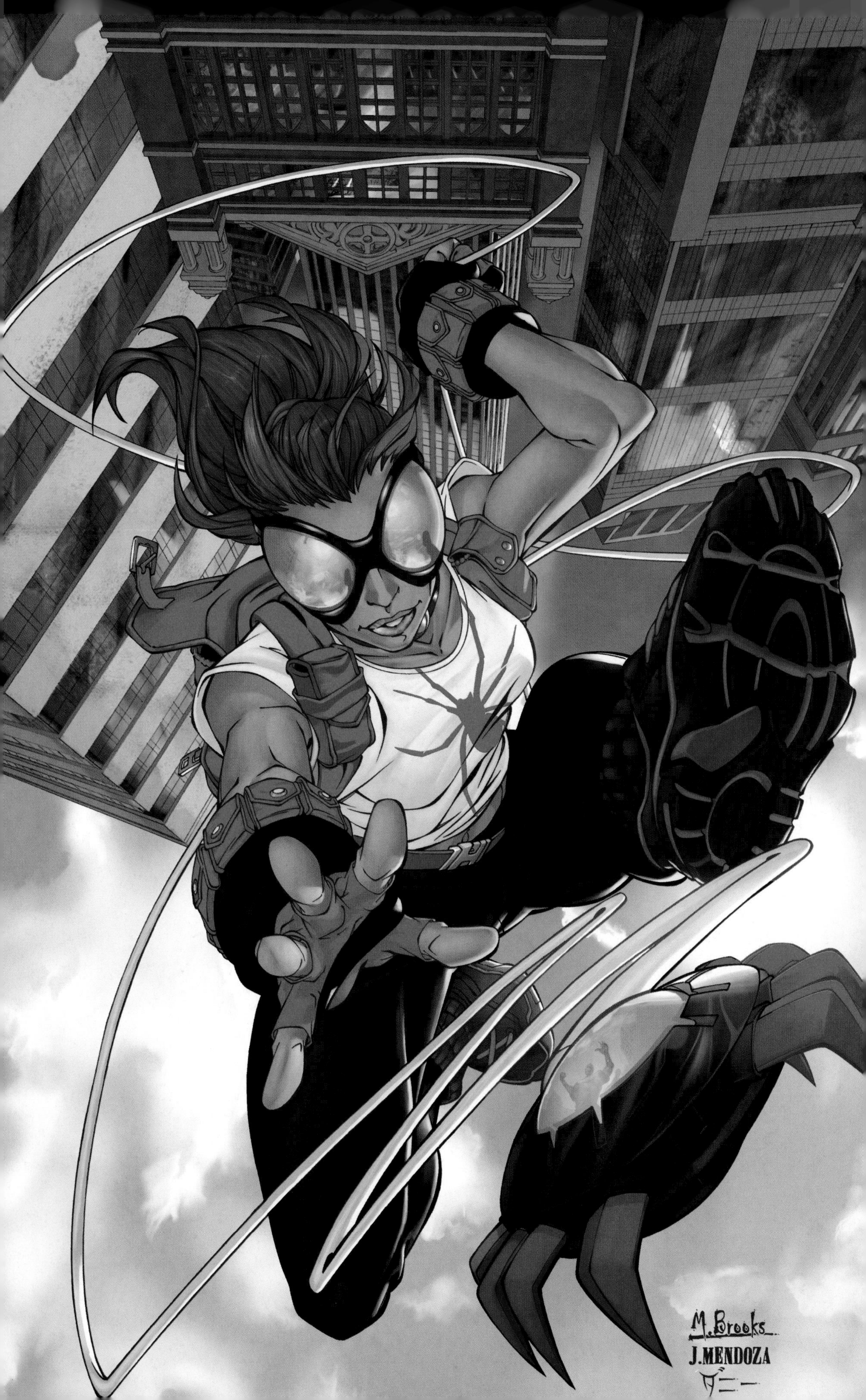
M.Brooks
J.MENDOZA

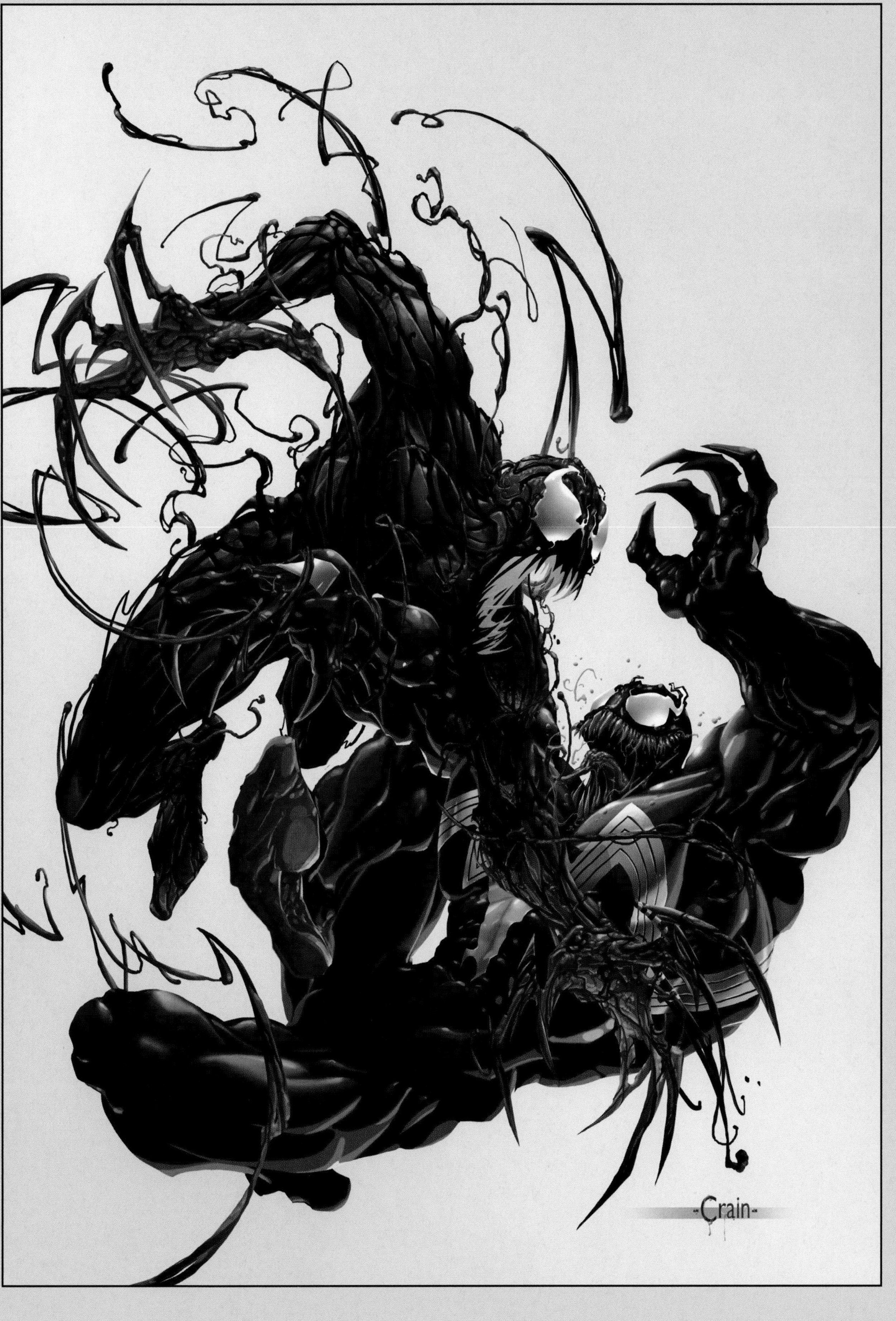
-Crain-

Opposite: *Amazing Fantasy #1* cover by Mark Brooks. Above: *Venom Vs. Carnage #1* cover by Clayton Crain.

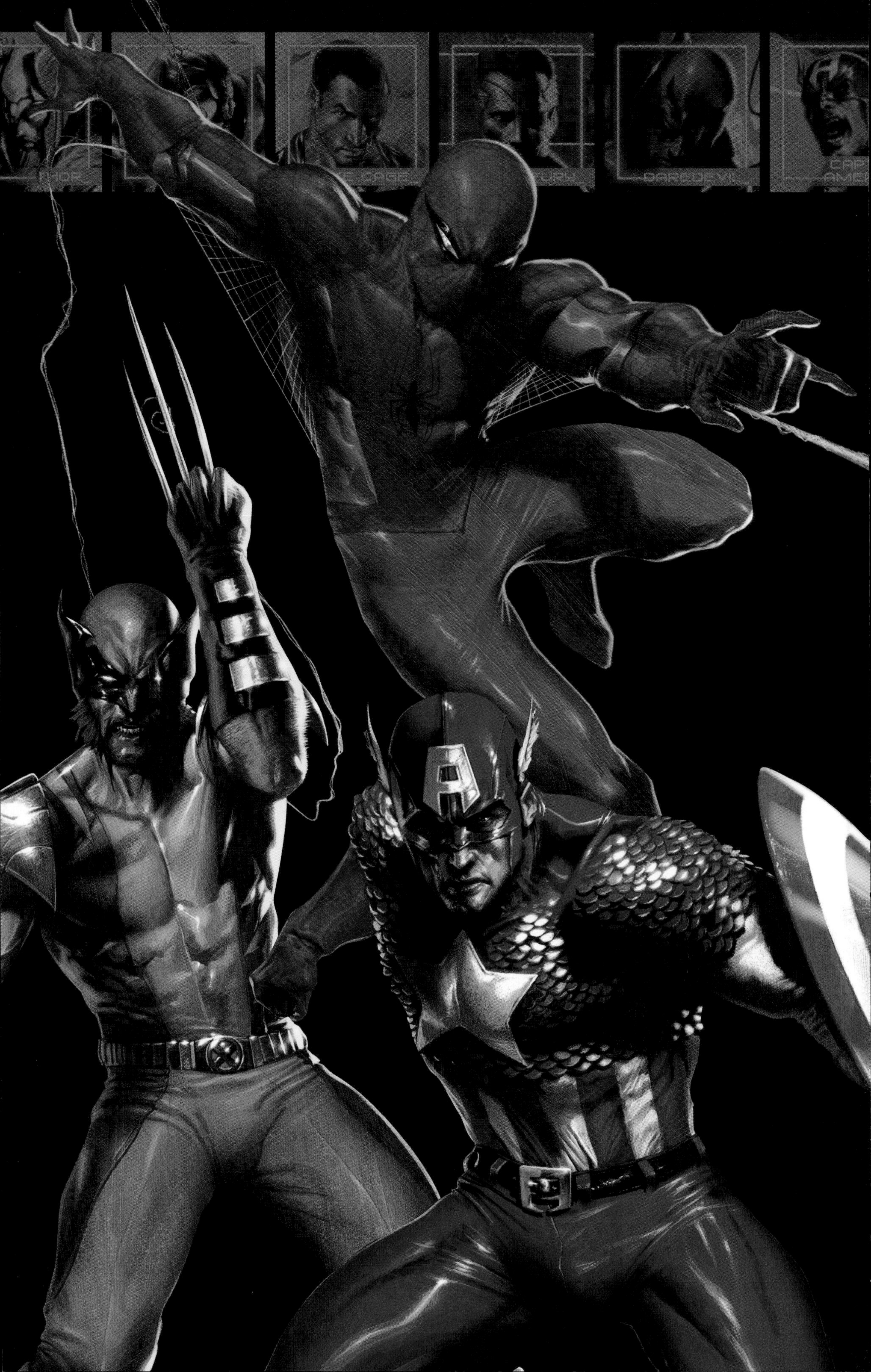
THOR
DAREDEVIL

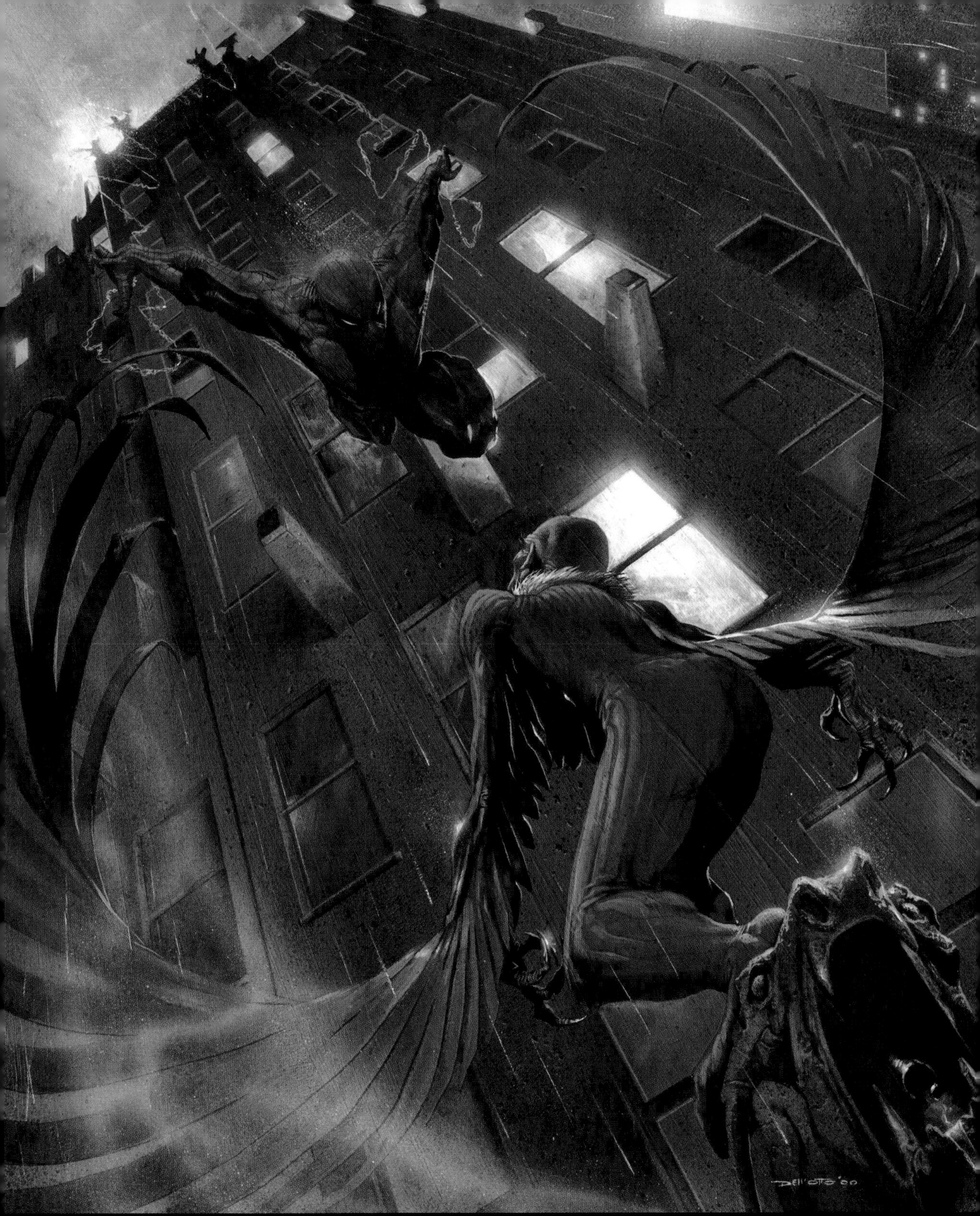

*"Gabriele was discovered by both (Marvel editor-in-chief) Joe Quesada and (writer/artist) David Mack. And when I say they both discovered him, I mean they both take credit. Mack and Gabriele were at one point going to do something together, but through skillful back-stabbing and deceit I was able to grab him for this project."*

Brian Michael Bendis

Writer, *Secret War*

Opposite: *Secret War* #1-3 covers by Gabriele Dell'Otto. Above: *The Pulse* #2 cover by Dell'Otto.

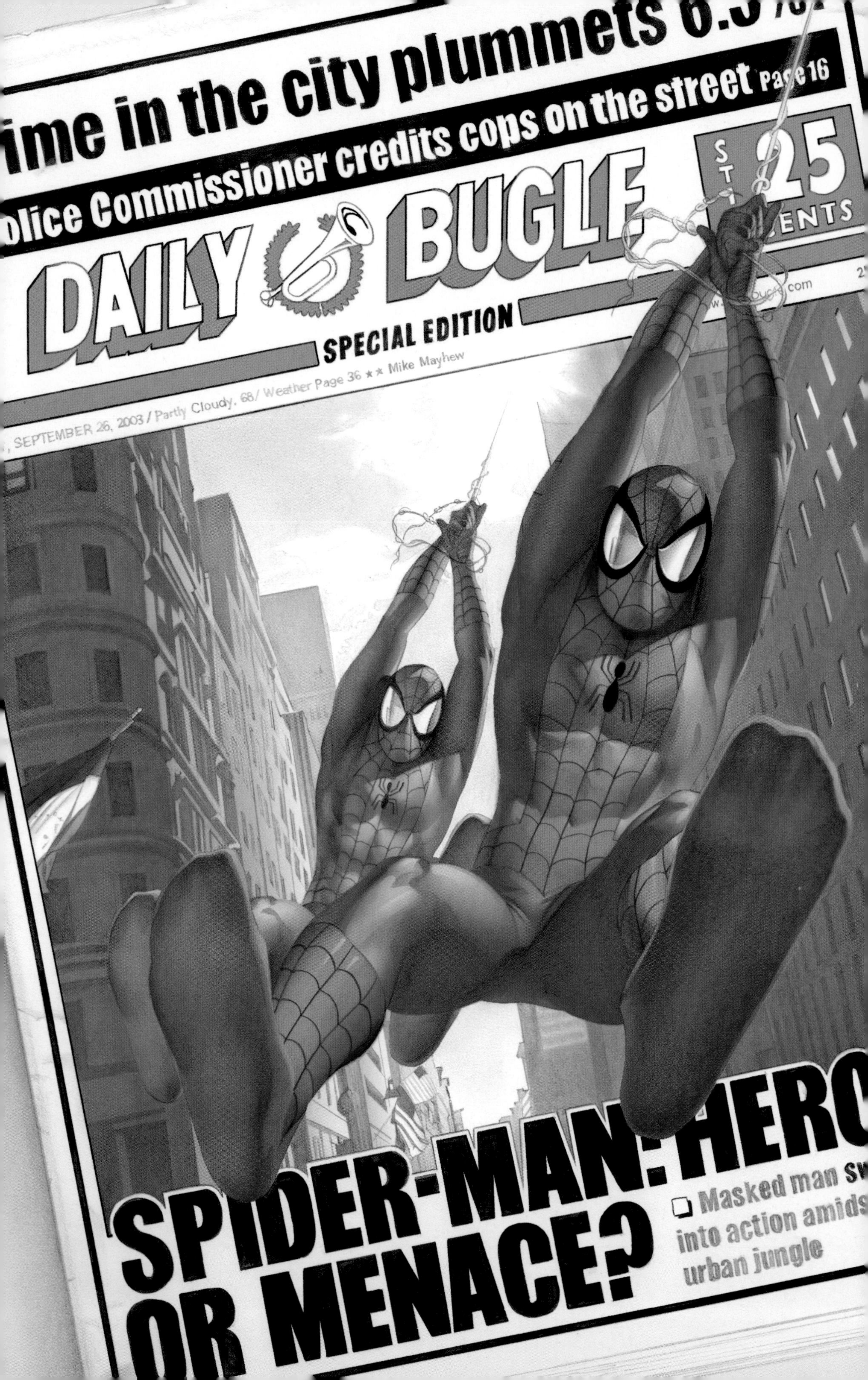

ime in the city plummets 6.5%!
olice Commissioner credits cops on the street Page 16
DAILY BUGLE
25 CENTS
SPECIAL EDITION
, SEPTEMBER 26, 2003 / Partly Cloudy, 68/ Weather Page 36 ★★ Mike Mayhew
SPIDER-MAN: HERO OR MENACE?
Masked man sw into action amids urban jungle

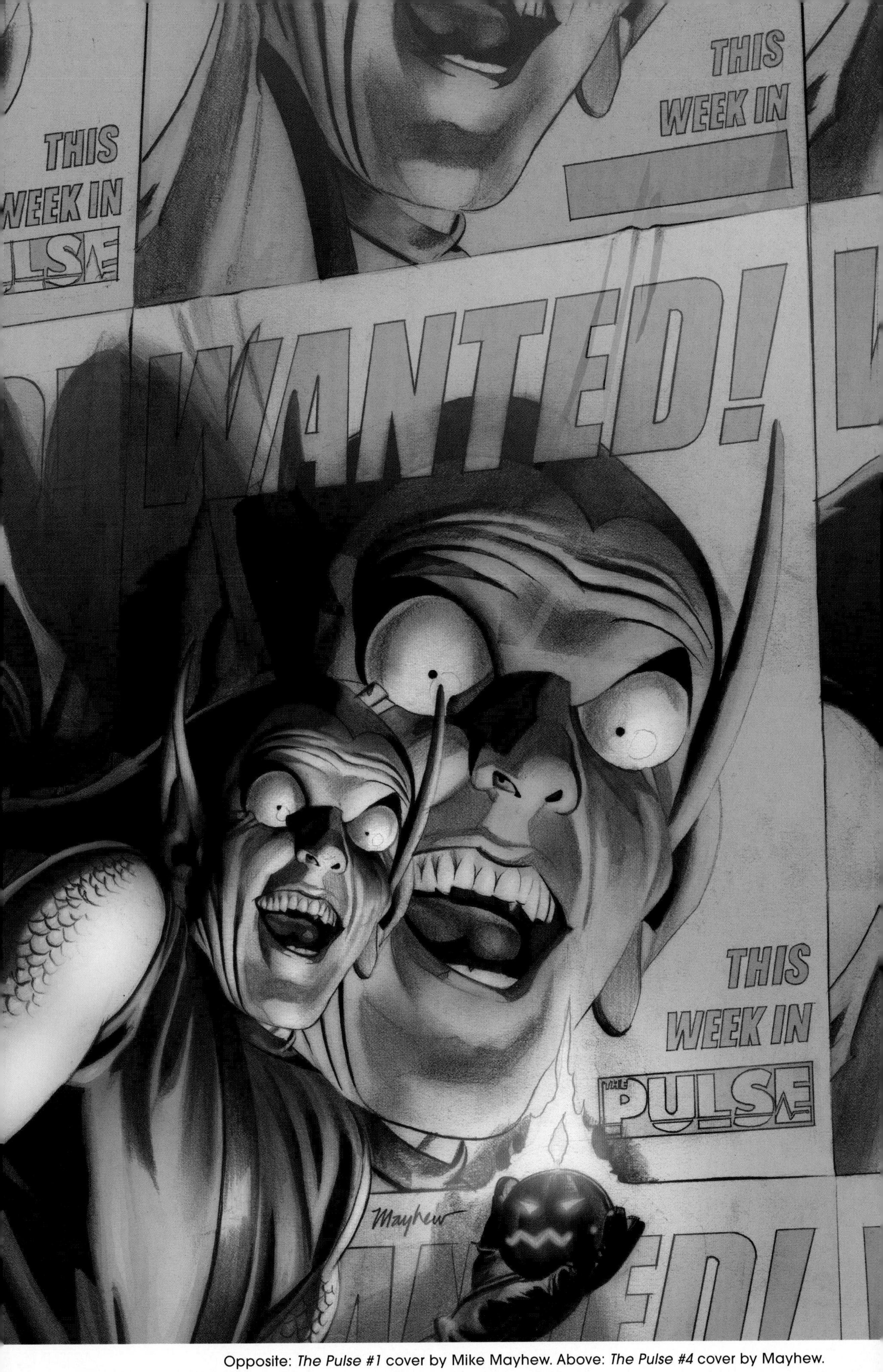
THIS
WEEK IN
THIS
WANTED!
THIS
WEEK IN
THE PULSE
Mayhew

Opposite: *The Pulse #1* cover by Mike Mayhew. Above: *The Pulse #4* cover by Mayhew.

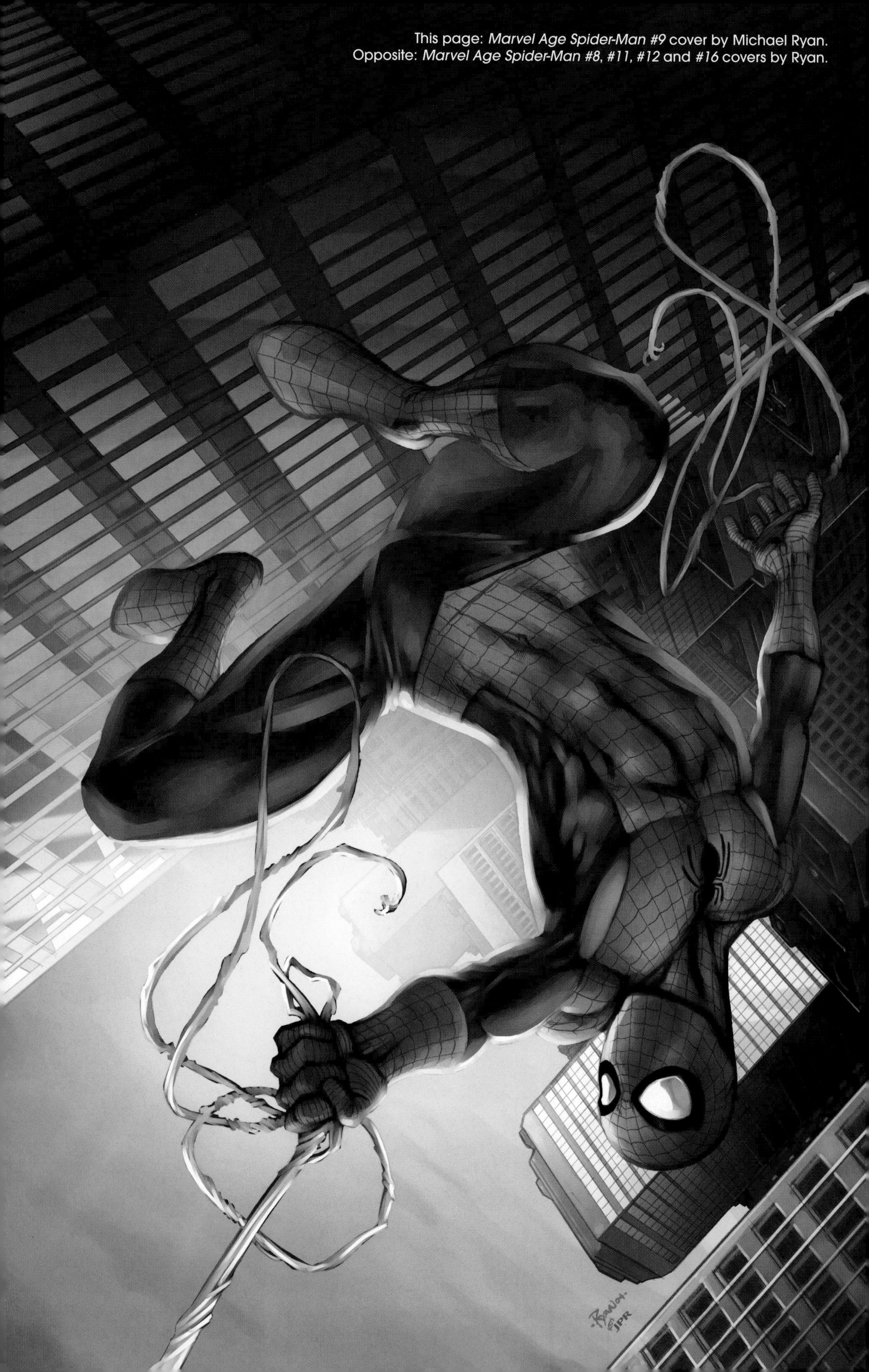

This page: *Marvel Age Spider-Man #9* cover by Michael Ryan.
Opposite: *Marvel Age Spider-Man #8*, *#11*, *#12* and *#16* covers by Ryan.

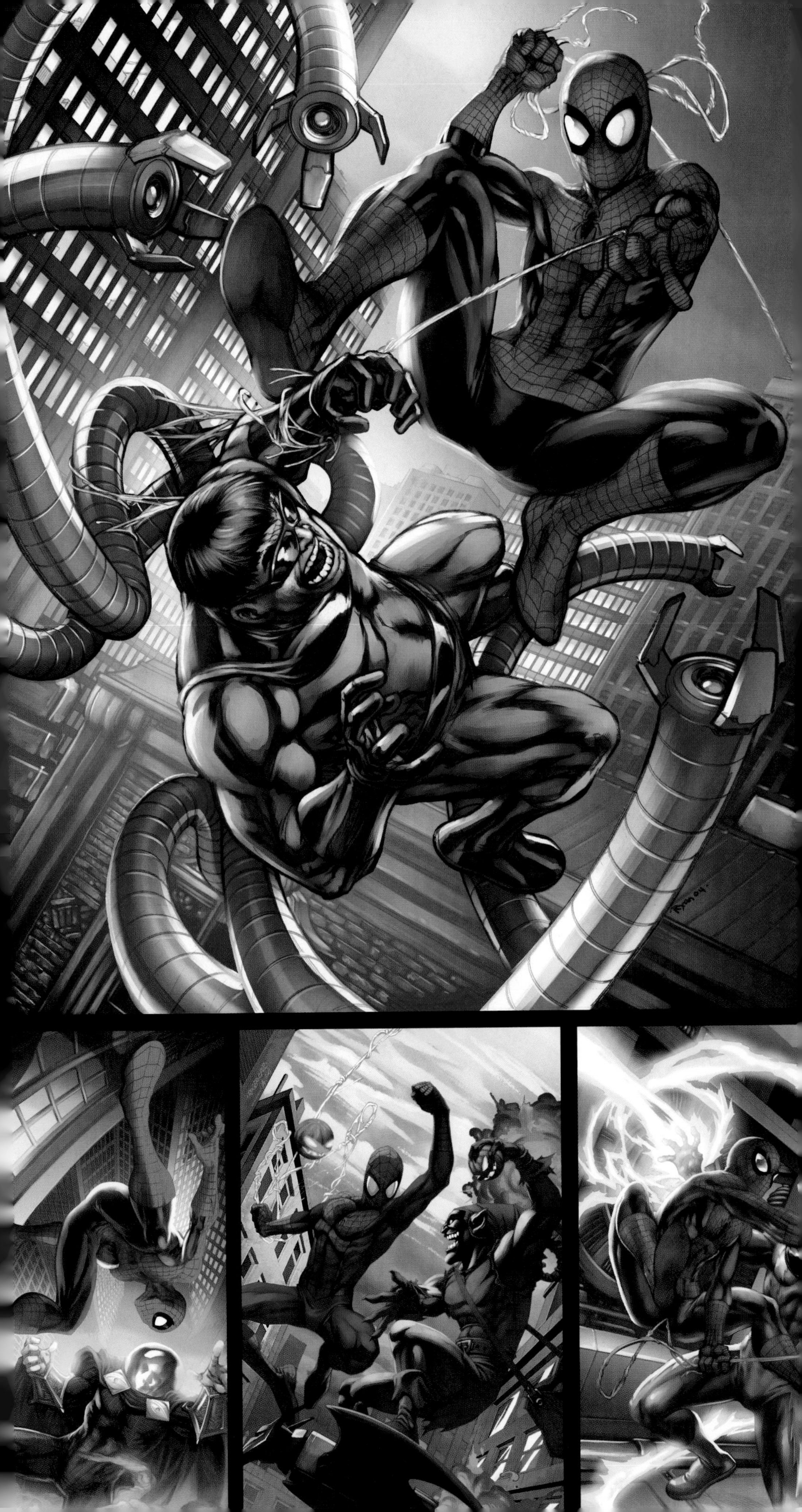

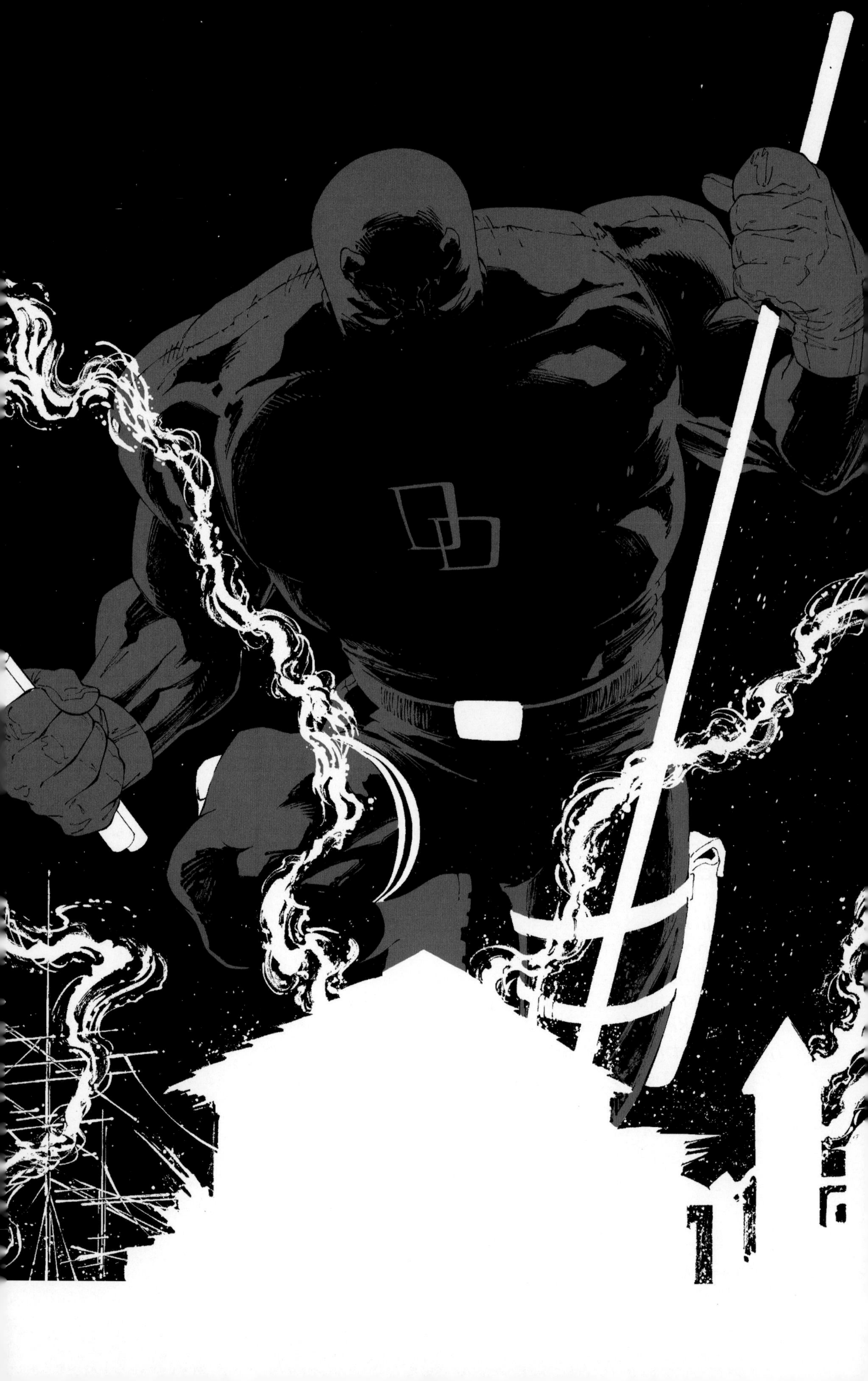

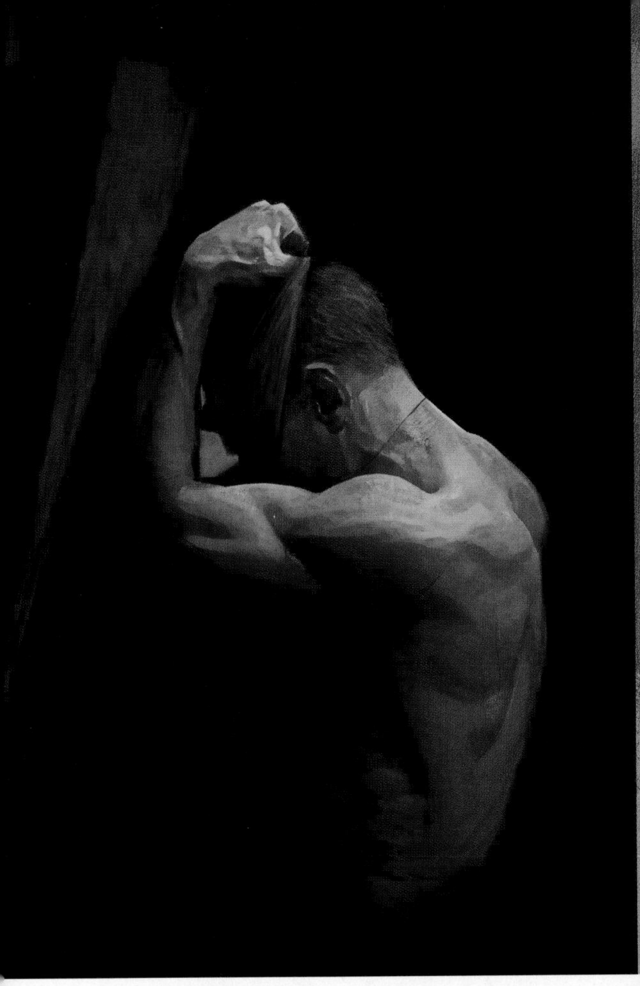

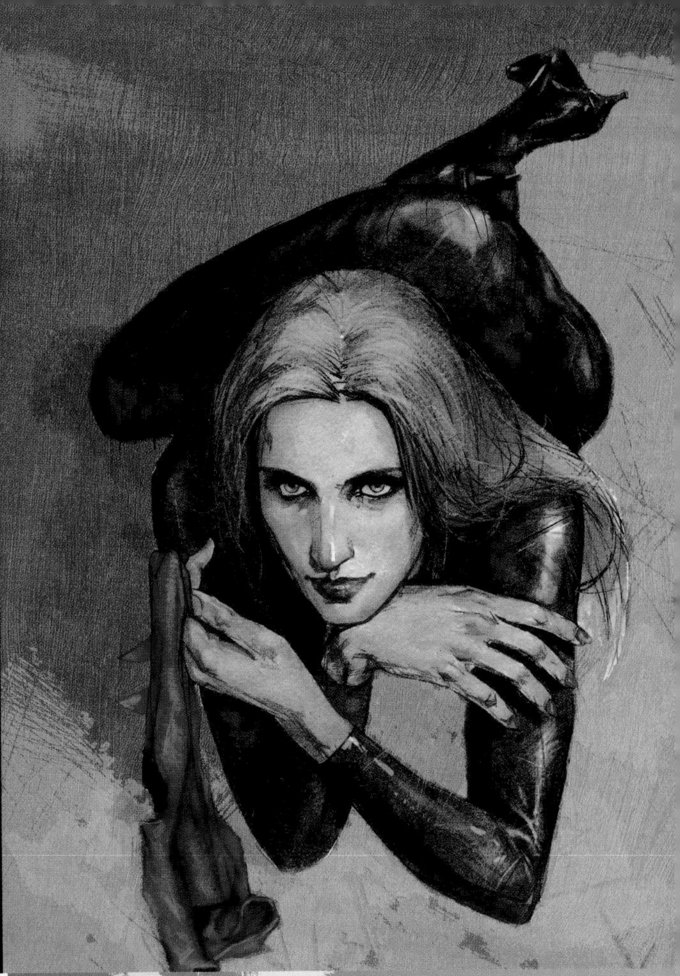

*"Right now I'm envisioning a different type of Daredevil, a different type of world he lives in. Let's face it, Daredevil has been interpreted in many ways, that's what makes him so cool. He's been drawn like a svelte dancer, and he's been drawn beefier as well by guys like Kirby and Romita, Sr. I'm just doing my current take on him and the Kitchen. In this current incarnation Daredevil is the new Kingpin of Hell's Kitchen, he's bigger than life and taking names."*

Joe Quesada

Writer/Artist, *Daredevil: Father*

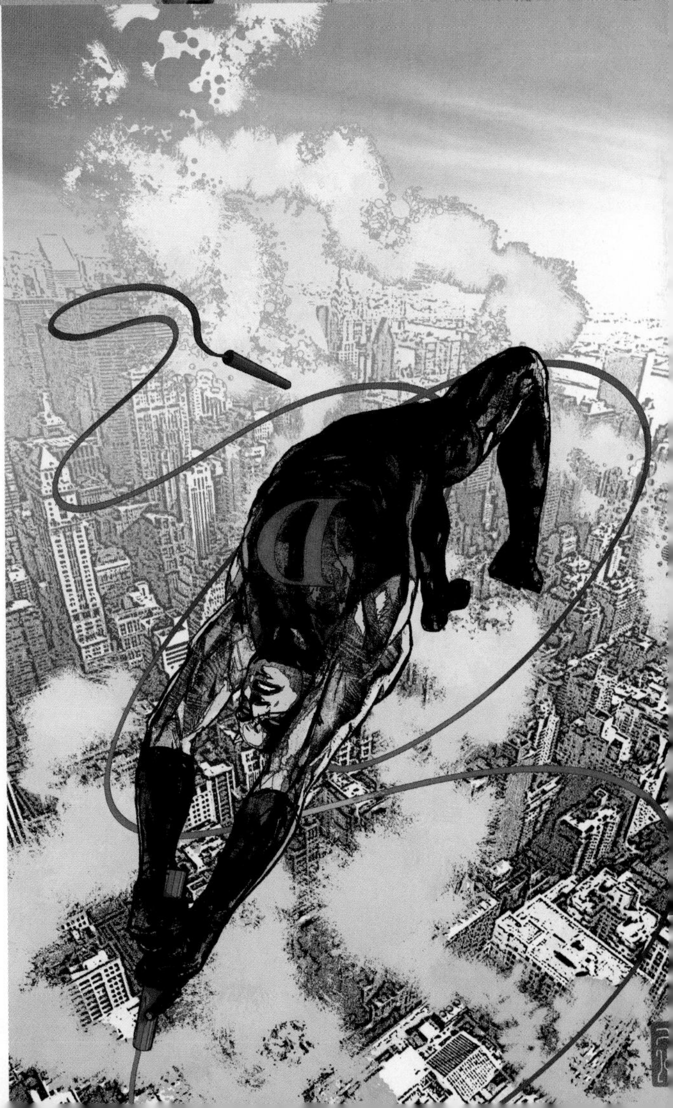

Opposite: *Daredevil: Father #1* cover by Joe Quesada. This page, clockwise from top left: *Daredevil #59*, *#61* and *#66* covers by Alex Maleev.

Below: *Ultimate Elektra #1* cover by Salvador Larroca. Opposite: *Ultimate Elektra #2-4* covers by Larroca.

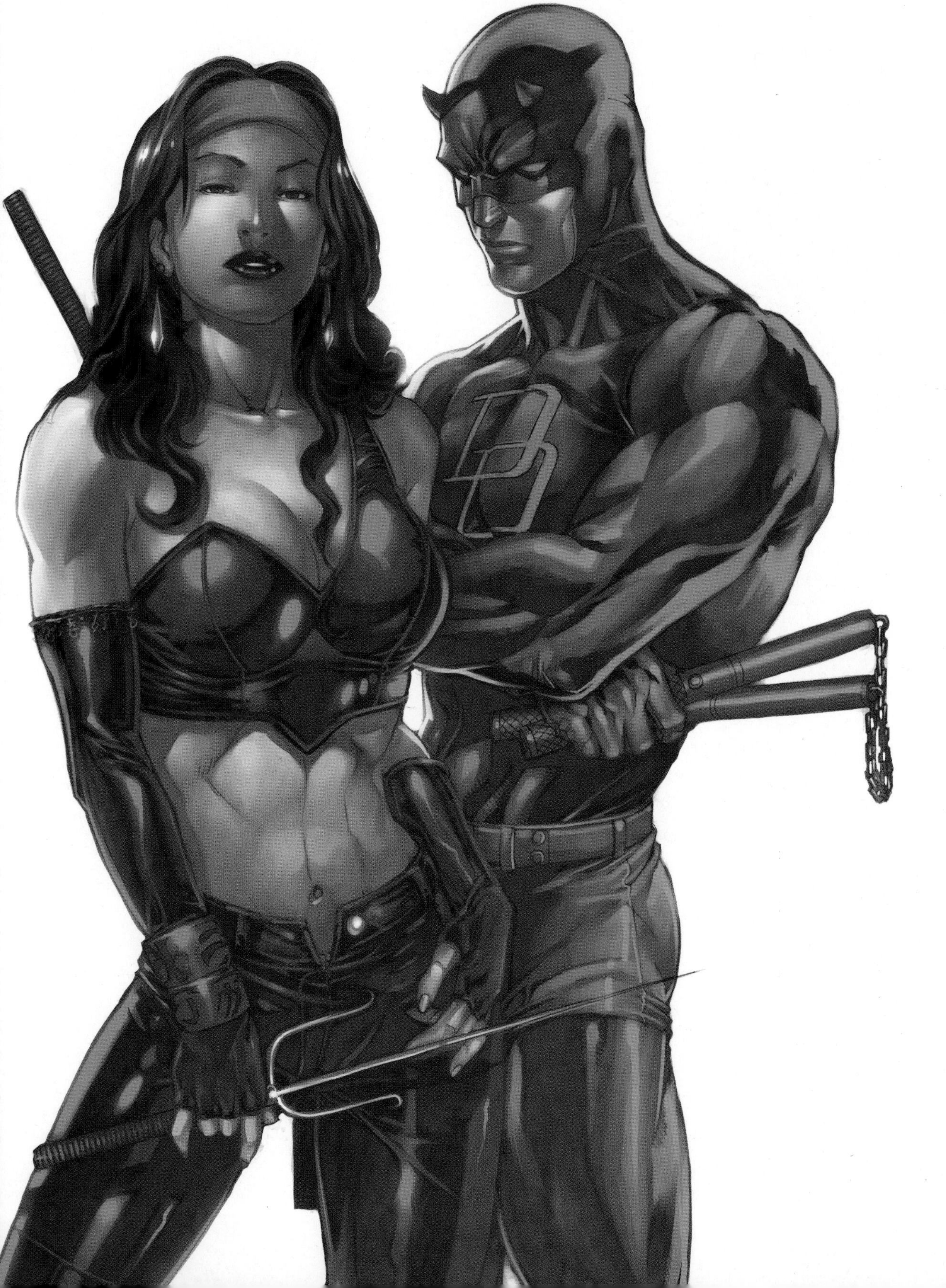

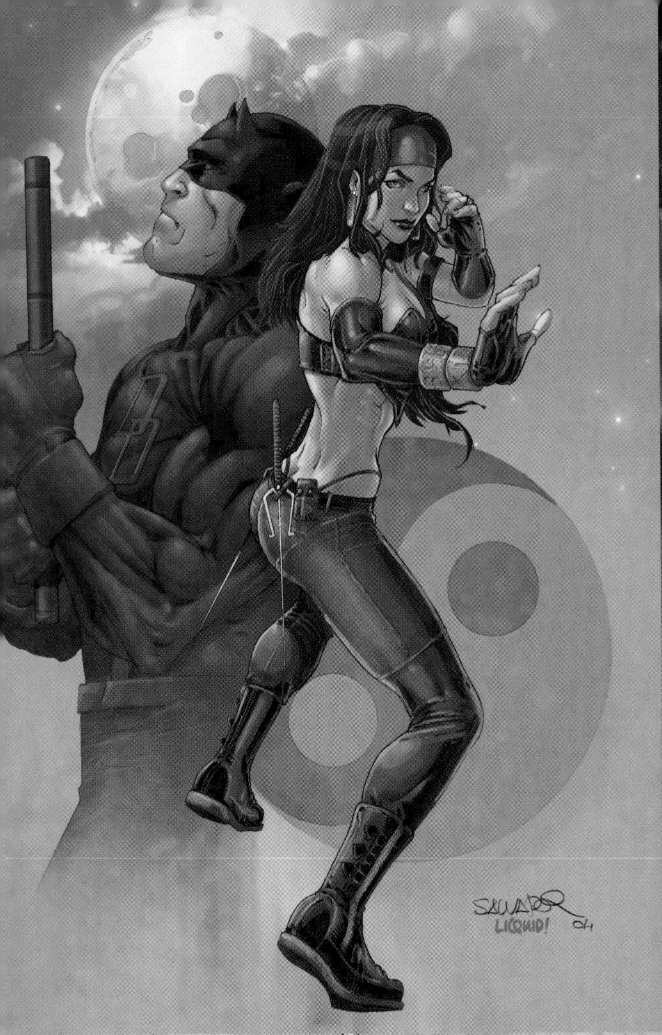
SALVADOR
LIQUID! 04

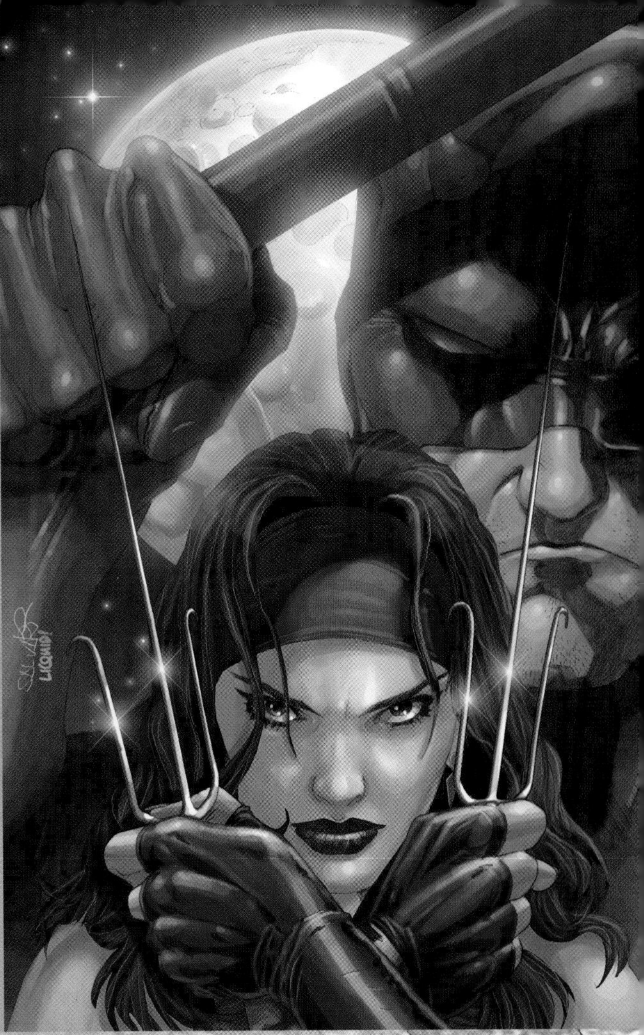
LIQUID!

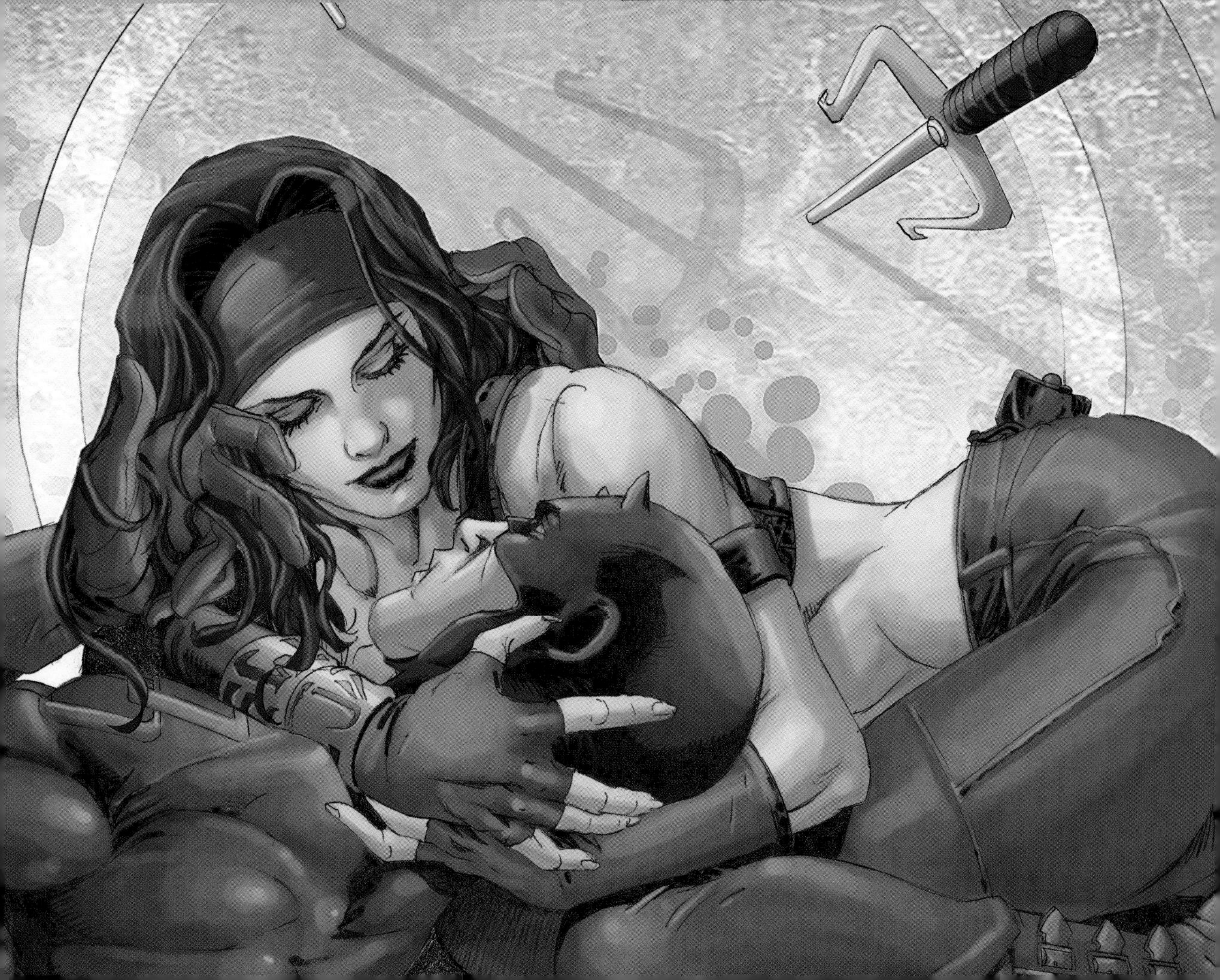

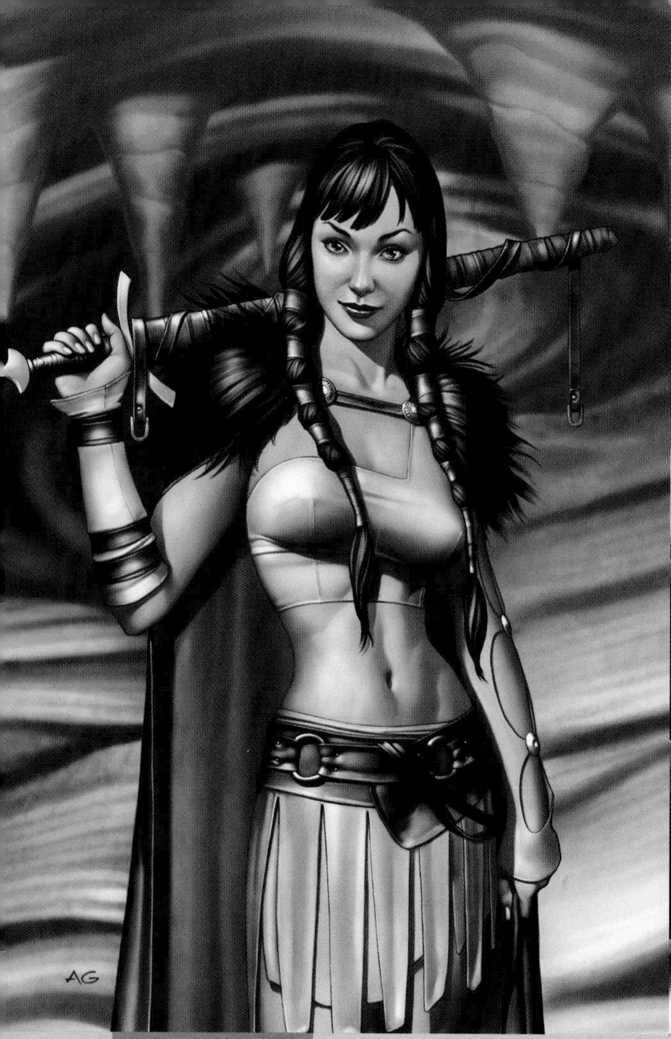
AG
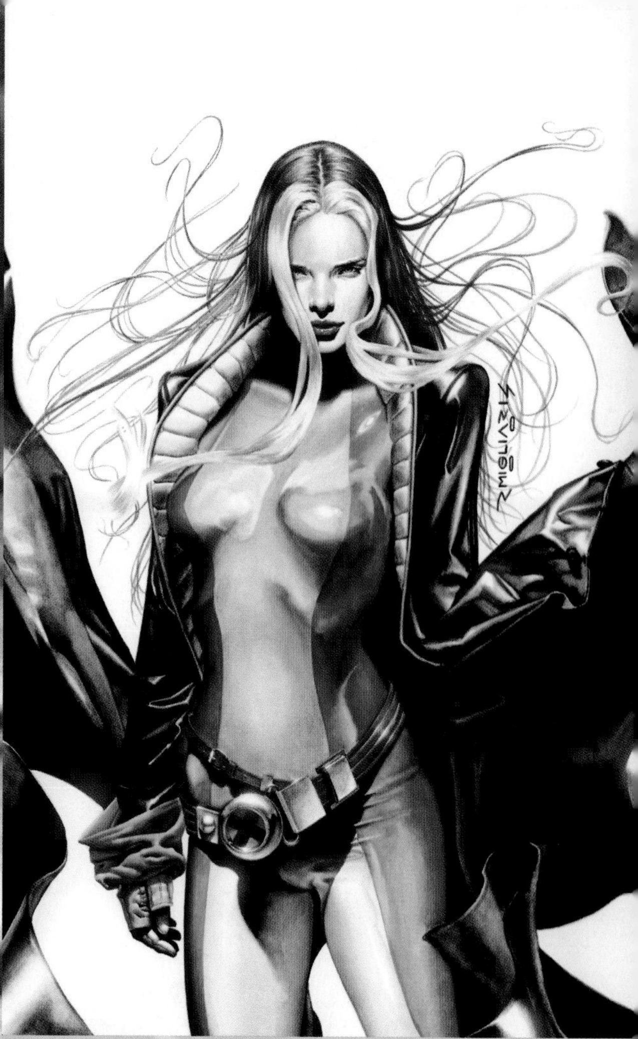
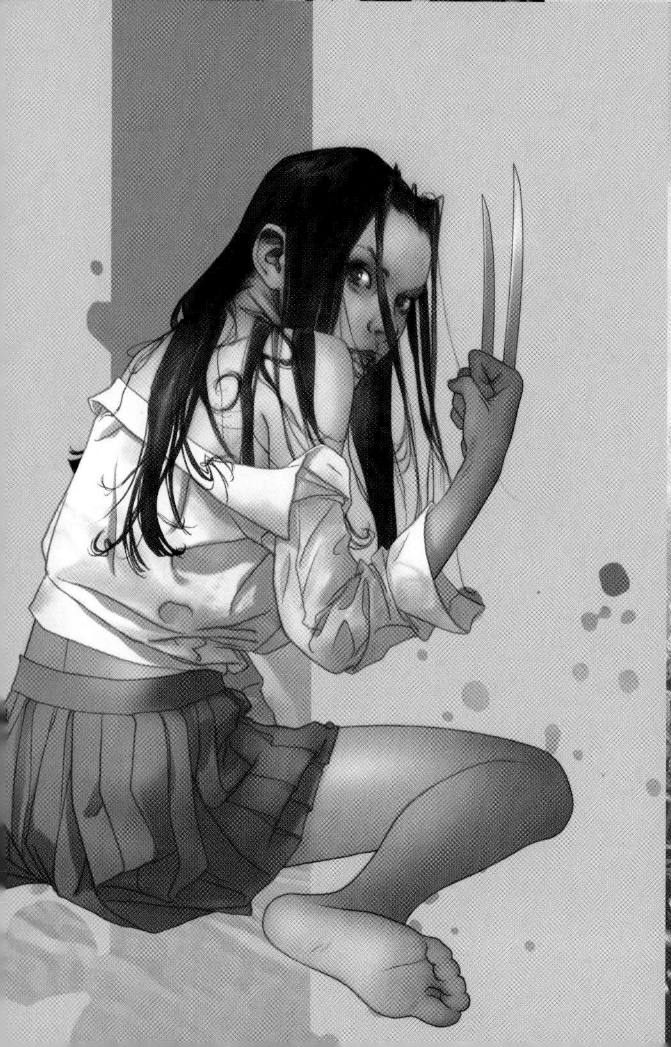
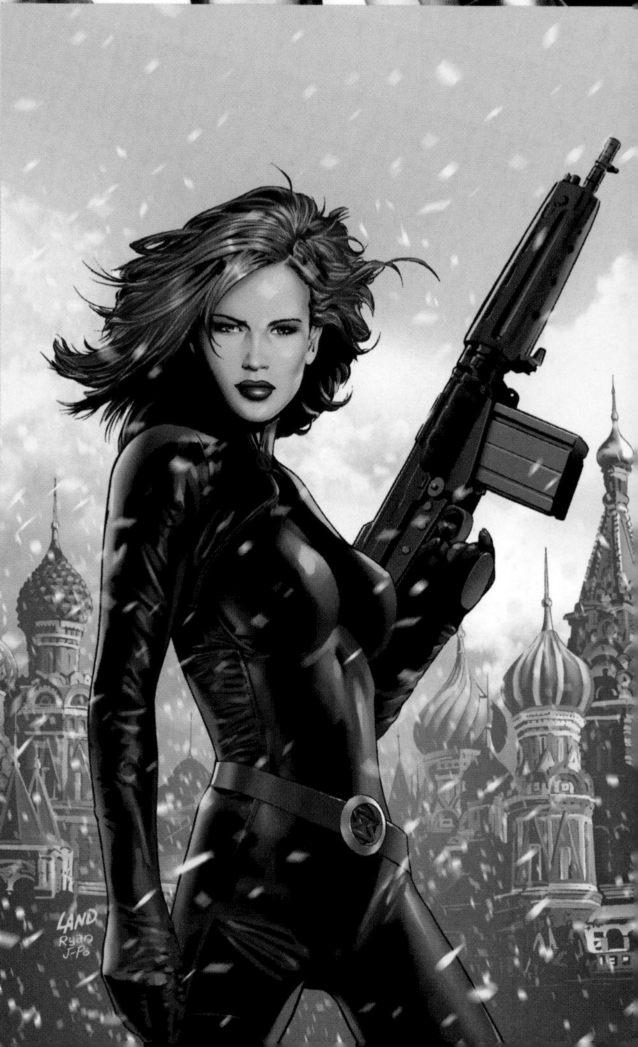
LAND
Ryan
J-Po

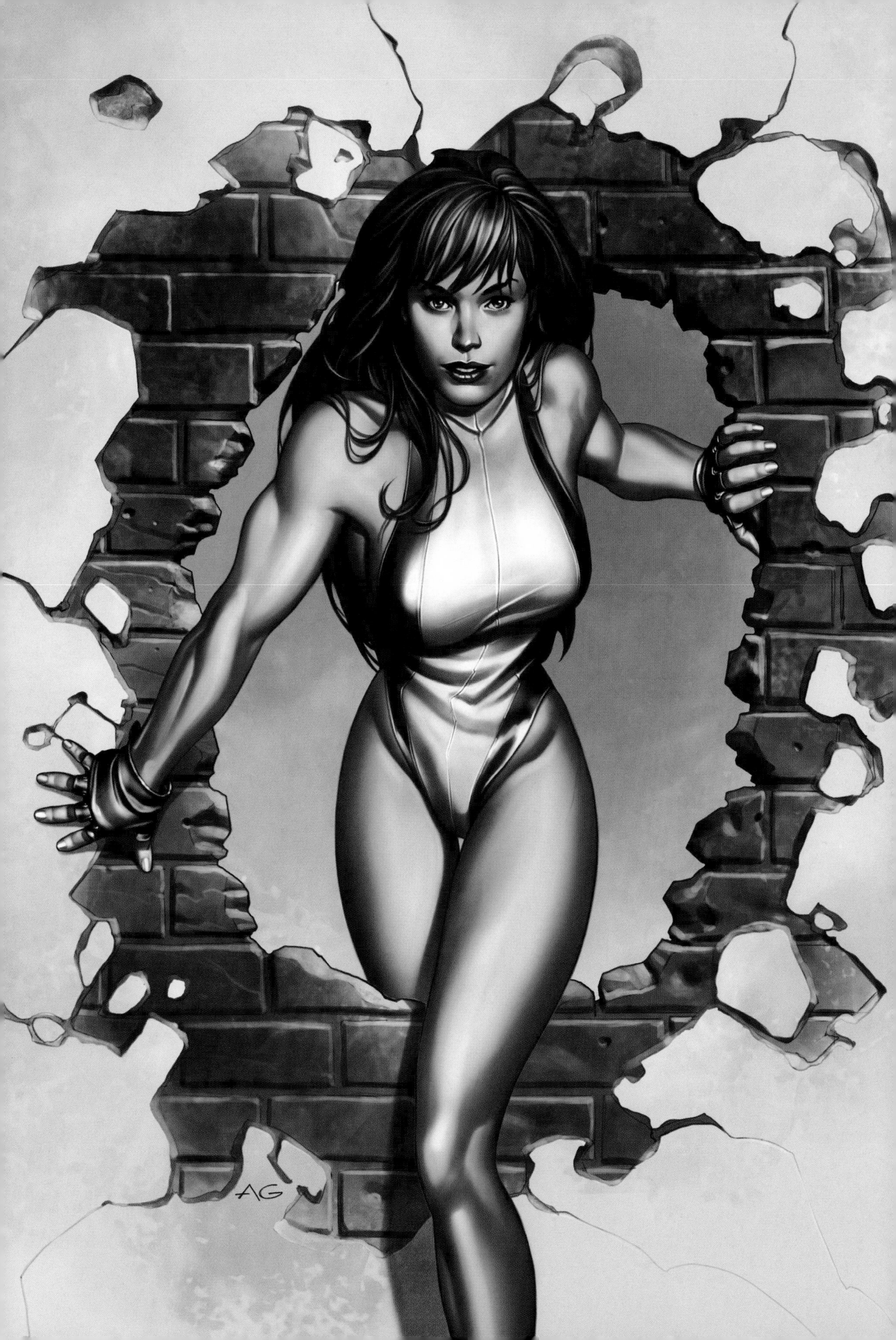
AG

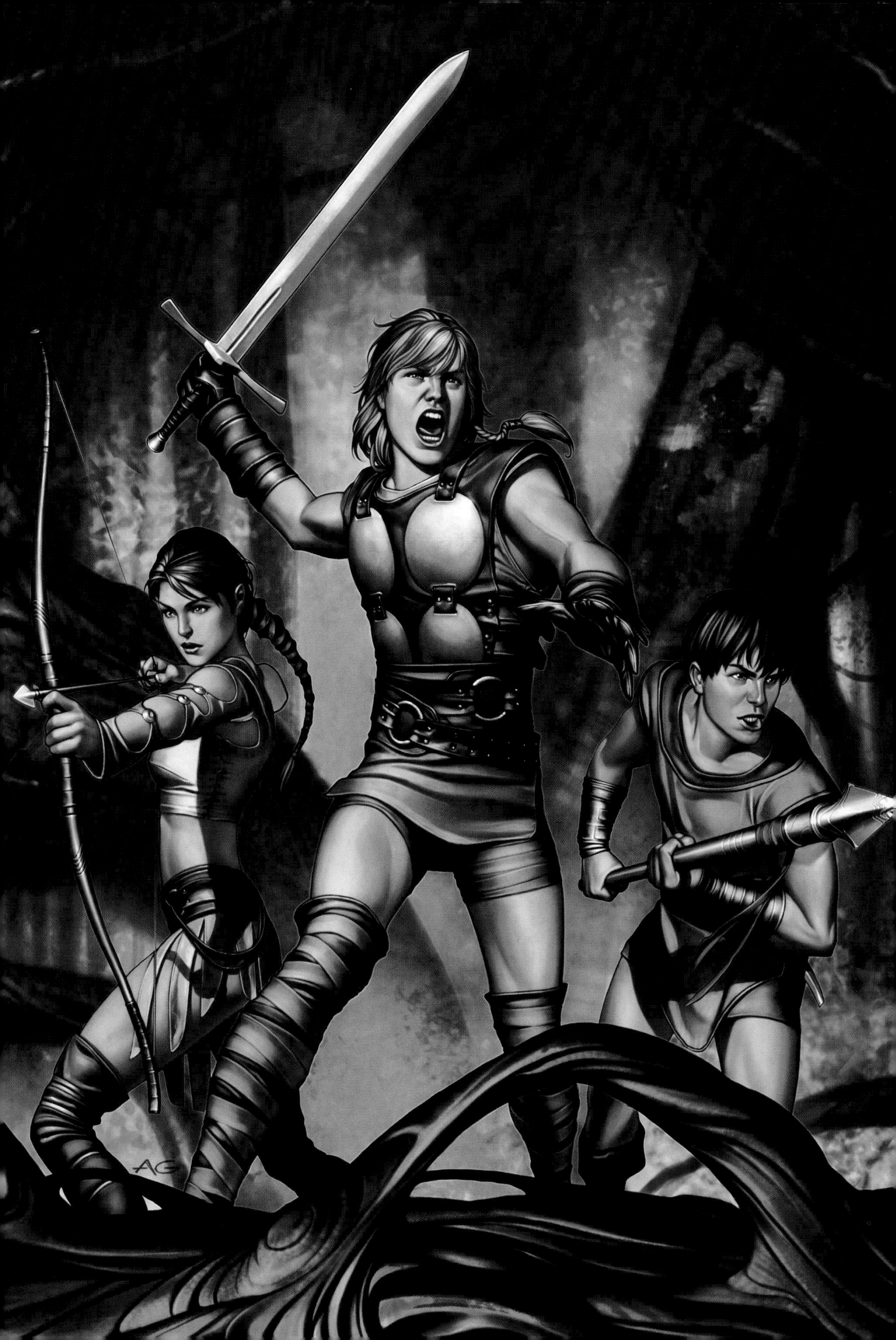

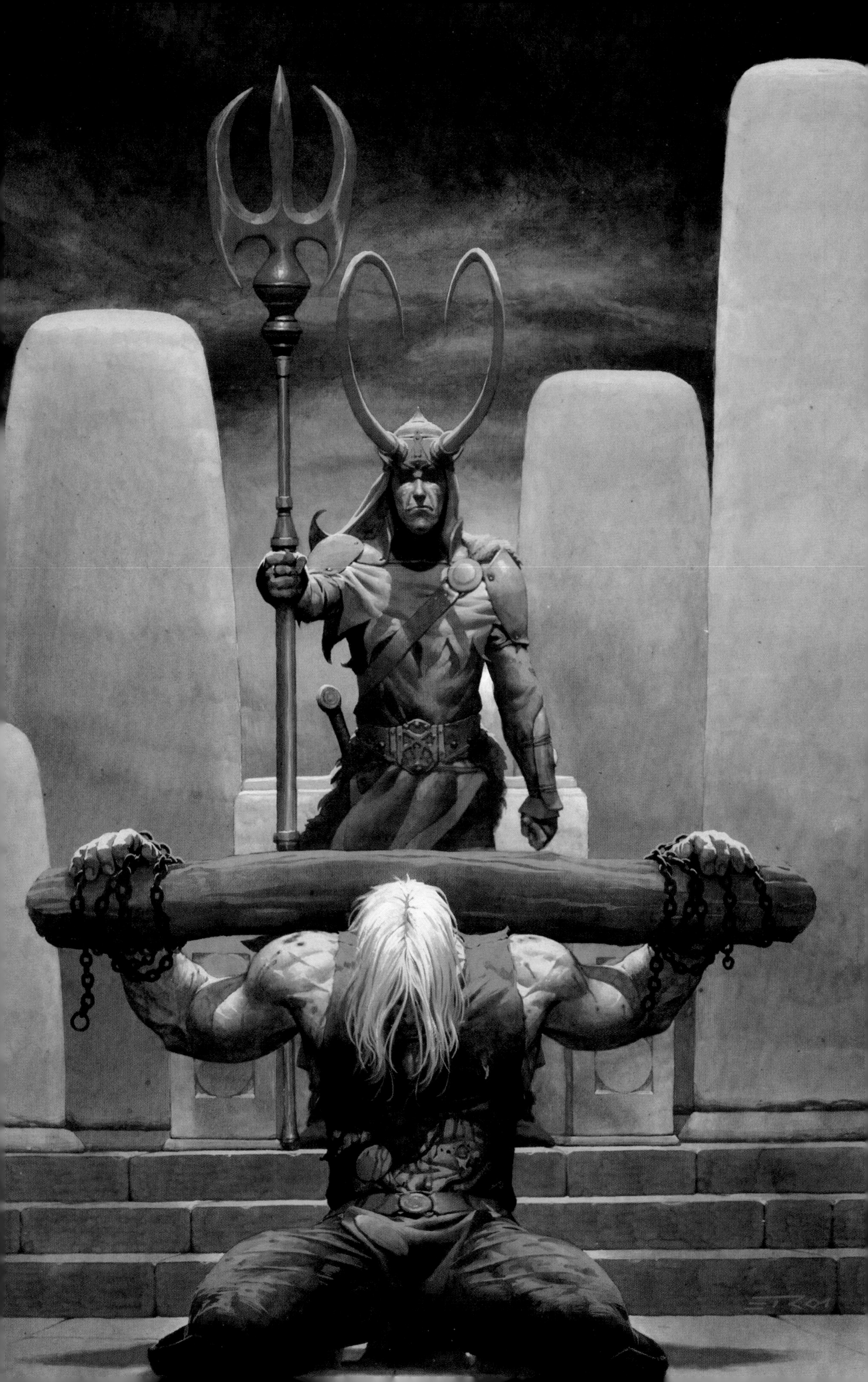

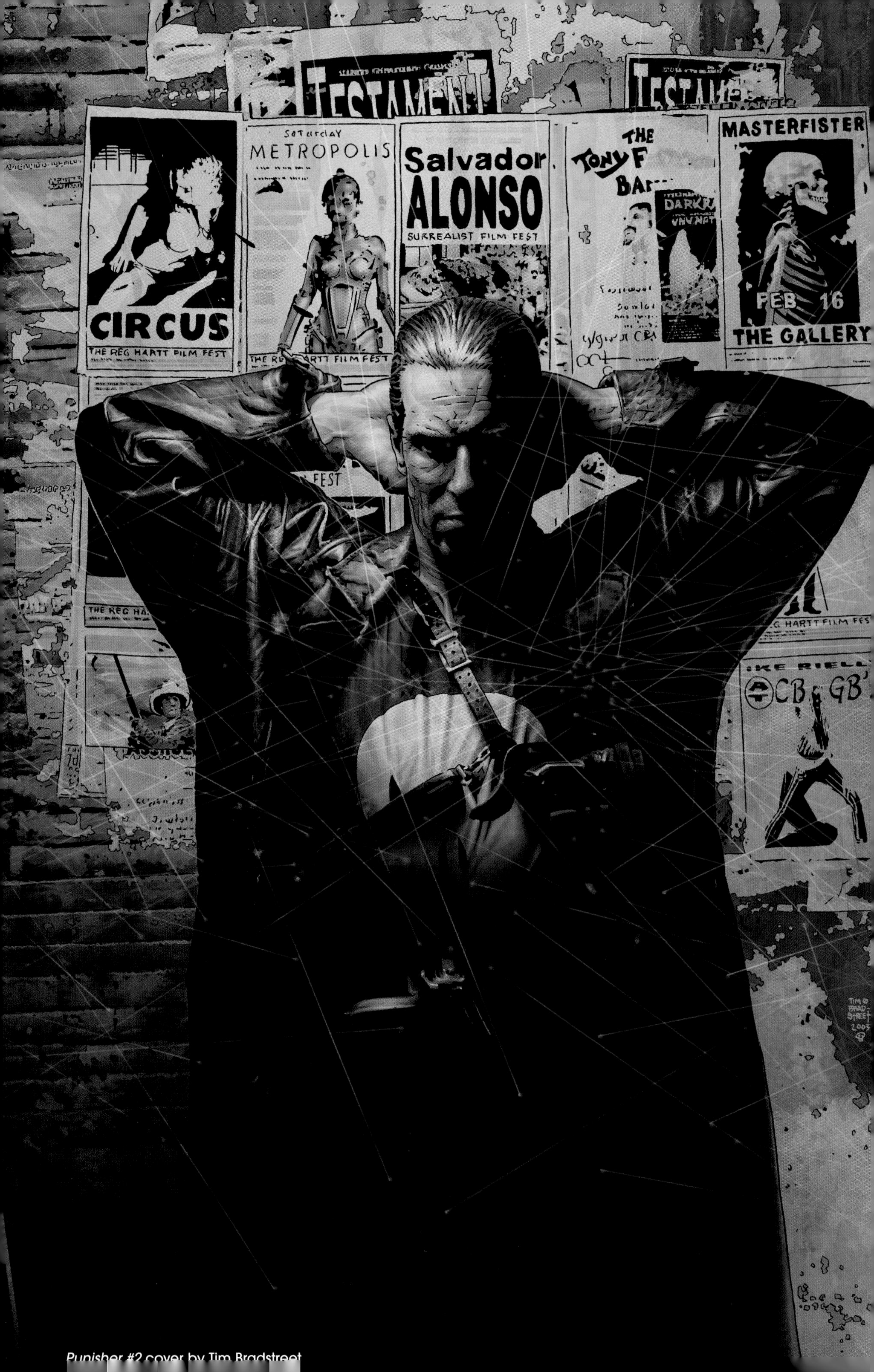
TESTAMENT
Saturday
METROPOLIS
Salvador
ALONSO
SURREALIST FILM FEST
MASTERFISTER
FEB 16
THE GALLERY
CIRCUS
THE REG HARTT FILM FEST
THE REG HARTT FILM FEST
TIM BRADSTREET 2003

*Punisher #2 cover by Tim Bradstreet*